EXPLORING WILD SOUTH FLORIDA

The Exploring Wild Florida series covers the state in four volumes:

Exploring Wild Central Florida by Susan D. Jewell. From New Smyrna and Crystal River in the north to Hobe Sound and Punta Gorda in the south, including Lake Okeechobee.

Exploring Wild North Florida by Gil Nelson. From the Suwannee River to the Atlantic Shore, and south to include the Ocala National Forest.

Exploring Wild Northwest Florida by Gil Nelson. The Florida panhandle, from the Perdido River in the west to the Suwannee River in the east.

Exploring Wild South Florida by Susan D. Jewell. The southern tip of the Florida peninsula, from Hobe Sound and Punta Gorda south to include the Keys and the Dry Tortugas.

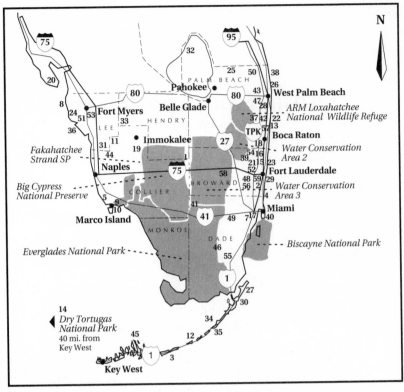

Key to Natural and Semi-Natural Areas on Map
1. Ah-tha-thi-ki Museum
2. Arch Creek Park
3. Bahia Honda State Park
4. Bill Baggs Cape Florida State Recreation Area
5. Briggs Nature Center and Rookery Bay
7. Castellow Hammock Nature Center
8. Cayo Costa State Park
9. Collier-Seminole State Park
10. Corkscrew Marsh
11. Corkscrew Swamp Sanctuary
12. Crane Point Hammock
13. Deerfield Island Park
14. Dry Tortugas National Park
15. Dupuis Reserve State Forest
16. Easterlin Park
17. Fairchild Tropical Garden
18. Fern Forest Nature Center
19. Florida Panther National Wildlife Refuge
20. Gasparilla Island State Recreation Area
21. Greynolds Park
22. Gumbo Limbo Nature Center
23. Hugh Taylor Birch State Recreation Area
24. J.N. Ding Darling National Wildlife Refuge
25. J.W. Corbett Wildlife Management Area
    (and Hungryland Slough)
26. John D. MacArthur Beach State Park
27. John Pennekamp Coral Reef State Park
28. John Prince Park
29. John U. Lloyd State Recreation Area
30. Key Largo Hammock Botanical State Park

31. Koreshan State Historic Site
32. Lake Okeechobee Hoover Dike Trail
33. Lake Trafford Park
34. Lignumvitae Key State Botanical Site
35. Long Key State Park
36. Lovers Key State Park
37. Loxahatchee Preserve Nature Center
38. Marinelife Center of Juno Beach and
    Loggerhead Park
39. Markham Park
40. Matheson Hammock Park
41. Miccosukee Indian Village
42. Morikami Museum and Gardens
43. Mounts Botanical Garden
44. Naples Nature Center
45. National Key Deer Refuge
46. Navy Wells Pineland Preserve
47. Okeeheelee Park and Nature Center
48. Oleta River State Recreation Area
49. Redland Fruit & Spice Park
50. Riverbend Park
51. Sanibel-Captiva Conservation Foundation
52. Secret Woods Nature Center
53. Six Mile Cypress Slough Preserve
54. South County Regional Park
55. Southern Glades Wildlife & Environmental Area
56. T.Y. (Topeekeegee Yugnee) Park
57. Tradewinds Park (and Butterfly World)
58. Tree Tops Park
59. West Lake (and Ann Kolb Nature Center)

Note: Carl E. Johnson Park (#6 in earlier editions) has been incorporated into Lovers Key State Recreation Area.

THIRD EDITION

EXPLORING WILD SOUTH FLORIDA

**A GUIDE TO FINDING THE NATURAL
AREAS AND WILDLIFE OF THE SOUTHERN
PENINSULA AND THE FLORIDA KEYS**

SUSAN D. JEWELL
with drawings by Manabu Saito

PINEAPPLE PRESS
Sarasota, Florida

In memory of Marjory Stoneman Douglas
1890–1998
and
Larry Lipsky, wildlife photographer and friend
1954–1999

Copyright © 2002 by Susan D. Jewell

Inquiries should be addressed to:
Pineapple Press, Inc.
PO Box 3889
Sarasota, FL 34230
www.pineapplepress.com

Library of Congress Cataloging-in-Publication Data

Jewell, Susan D. (Susan Diane)
    Exploring wild south Florida : a guide to finding the natural areas and wildlife of the Everglades and Florida Keys / Susan D. Jewell ; with drawings by Manabu Saito. — 3rd ed.
        p.   cm.
    Includes bibliographical references and index.
    ISBN 1-56164-125-1 (alk. paper)
    1. Natural history—Florida—Everglades—Guidebooks.   2. Natural history—Florida—Florida Keys—Guidebooks.   3. Natural areas—Florida—Everglades—Guidebooks.   4. Natural areas—Florida—Florida Keys—Guidebooks.   5. Everglades (Fla.)—Guidebooks.
6. Florida Keys (Fla.)—Guidebooks.   I. Title.
QH105.F6J49   1997
508.759′39—dc21   96-54879
                                                          CIP

Third Edition
10 9 8 7 6 5 4 3 2 1

Design by Octavo
Composition by Ramonda Talkie
Printed in the United States of America

CONTENTS

VII: NATURAL AREAS: COUNTY, CITY, AND PRIVATE 211

FOREWORD

South Florida is a very new land in every sense of the word. It emerged from the sea only recently as geologic time is reckoned. In the early years of the nineteenth century, most of its residents were still Native Americans. The movers and shakers of modern development were slow to discover the potentials of south Florida, and the pace of growth did not really pick up until the 1920s. But it has been accelerating ever since! In the rush to build south Florida, patches here and there were overlooked. It is these relatively untouched fragments of Florida that Ms. Jewell wants her readers to explore.

While south Florida offers a fascinating mix of things tropical and temperate, it is more akin to the Caribbean than to the North American continent and presents unique opportunities to visitors who are interested in the unusual habitats and species to be found here. The diversity of life approaches that of the true tropics—more species of trees and shrubs are found on North Largo Key than in all of the northeastern United States!

South Florida is an area of startling contrasts—from the quiet depths of Corkscrew Swamp and the tropical hardwood forests of the Keys to the thriving, bustling atmosphere of Miami. As Ms. Jewell states, appreciating the landscapes of south Florida takes some adjustment on the part of the observer. You won't find the grandeur of towering trees and spectacular mountains that draw visitors to our older, western parks. But south Florida is a land of great beauty—the quiet, subtle beauty of wide vistas of sky, grassy plains, and shallow, colorful seas balanced with a counterpoint of shady hammocks of tropical vegetation.

Exploring Wild South Florida offers a great deal more than the usual guidebook. It presents the reader with a synopsis of the human and natural history of the area combined with "all the visitor needs to know" to learn about, interpret, and enjoy the complex natural systems of south Florida. It is hoped that this awareness will encourage a greater interest in preserving the unaltered bits and pieces of south Florida so that future generations may continue to enjoy them.

Alexander Sprunt IV
Tavernier, Florida

ACKNOWLEDGMENTS

Numerous people contributed their knowledge and expertise for the benefit of this book. I would like to thank the following people for their help: Paul Allen, Steve Alvarez, Kristie Anders, Jon Andrew, Lisa Andrews, Oron (Sonny) Bass, Gary Bremen, Lois Chapman, Dan Cotter, John Curnett, Fred Davis, Robert Ducham, Charles DuToit, Michael Duever, Michael Eng, Ted Fleming, Lynne Frazer, Frank Fusiak, Richard Haley, Roger Hammer, Wallace Hibbard, Lou Hinds, Dawn Jennings, Archie Jones, Jim Krakowski, James Laray, Andrew Mackie, Joyce Mills, Burkett Neely, Jr., Mike Owen, Laura Richards, Jay Robinson, Jr., James Sanders, Camille Sewell, Rob Shanks, Alexander (Sandy) Sprunt IV, Barry Stieglitz, Janet Tachi, Tony Terry, Stephen Tiger, Pat Wells, Wesley Wilson, and Andy Zavenelli.

I am especially indebted to John Ogden of the South Florida Water Management District for numerous helpful suggestions on the text and continuous encouragement. Also, I thank the late Bill Robertson and Bill and Sue Smith for tackling the mountainous task of creating a south Florida bird list.

As always, I'm grateful to my family, whose moral support never waivers, no matter how wild my schemes may be. I also wish to acknowledge Pineapple Press for their patience and concern for me while I dug myself out of Hurricane Andrew's wake. I'm indebted to Tony Gola for accompanying me on many of my explorations and assisting my work in many ways.

INTRODUCTION

Fantastic! If you're reading this book, you must be seriously considering a trip to explore the less beaten paths of south Florida. What an exciting place you've chosen to spend your free time. You will be rewarded with endless expanses of wilderness, lush tropical vegetation, and wild animals not found anywhere else in the United States.

But if you're anticipating the equivalent grandeur of the lofty Rocky Mountains, the towering redwoods, the bizarrely shaped pinnacles of southwestern rock formations, the colorful desert wildflowers in spring, or the crashing ocean waves on our northern coasts, you must redirect your expectations. South Florida has just as many natural wonders as other regions, *but they are subtle*. They don't shout at you. They whisper. They entice you to take a closer look, to listen a little harder, to wait just a little longer.

To many people, the subconscious definition of "scenic" is a break from monotony: more topographic relief for the eye, more colors, more shapes and objects to keep the eye and brain occupied. That's why many people don't think of the Everglades region as scenic. The vast flat expanses of mangroves or sawgrass afford little change and are often silent and monochrome. By this definition, the Keys seem slightly more scenic: the colorful exotic flowers, the bright blue and green waters, the rustling palm fronds in the breeze, and the islands dotting the bay all keep the mind busy interpreting them. Now take a closer look!

A flock of roseate spoonbills sifts through the water, straining for small shrimp or fish. A zebra butterfly dances vivaciously through the air, then alights on a leaf to rest. A rainbow tapes the sky together as a thunderstorm threatens to rip it open. Underwater, a bevy of dazzling parrotfish pokes around the purple sea fans, rasping the nourishing algae from a star coral. This is the south Florida you won't want to miss!

Wilderness is a concept conceived by the white man. The Native Americans did not have a word for wilderness—wilderness was the normal world. There aren't many truly wild places left in south Florida. Even places that appear to be untouched have been indirectly altered, such as Everglades National Park and A.R.M. Loxahatchee National Wildlife Refuge, whose upstream waters have been tampered with outside their boundaries. What are referred to as natural areas in the pages that follow have not escaped the human touch.

I
AN OVERVIEW

HOW TO USE THIS BOOK

Geographically, this book concentrates on Broward, Collier, Hendry, Lee, Miami-Dade, Monroe, and Palm Beach counties, the southernmost counties in Florida. Visitors who use Miami as a central location will find that most of the places described below can be explored in a day trip. Not all parks and natural areas in the seven counties were included.

If this is your first trip to south Florida, you'll probably want to stick to the "major" attractions, such as the Anhinga Trail at Everglades National Park, Corkscrew Swamp, J.N. "Ding" Darling National Wildlife Refuge, and Pennekamp Coral Reef State Park. If you've already been to those places or have more time, you'll be looking for new sights. Included are a variety of places from tame to wild (barely venturing from the road to canoeing 50 miles from civilization). Some will require less than a half day to explore and some will warrant several days. There should be something for everyone who wants to get outside and learn about the natural world of south Florida. This book will help the first-timer, the repeat adventurer, the high school or college ecology class, and the foreign visitor to find the most interesting natural areas to explore. And you folks who live here year-round, have you explored your own "backyard"? Whether you're a nature photographer, an amateur naturalist, or just tired of the city, you can discover a retreat with this book.

No conscientious naturalist would divulge specific locations of rare plants and animals to the general public. While most readers would respect the regulations protecting our natural resources, an unscrupulous collector may not. Therefore, only general locations will be given.

1

This book is not intended as a field guide to plants and animals, and no attempt is made to be all-inclusive. Some species of special interest are discussed and illustrated, such as poisonous plants and endangered wildlife.

Distances and measurements are given in miles, feet, and acres. Temperatures are given in degrees Fahrenheit (°F). Here are some conversions that foreign travelers may find helpful:

1 mile	= 1.6 kilometers	1 kilometer	= 0.62 miles
1 foot	= 0.3 meters	1 meter	= 3.3 feet
1 acre	= 0.4 hectares	1 hectare	= 2.47 acres
1 pound	= 0.45 kilograms	1 kilogram	= 2.2 pounds
(°F-32) 5/9	= °C	(9/5 °C) + 32	= °F

Information on pet regulations in the parks is included for a very important reason: Florida can get very hot even in the winter. There is a Florida statute that prohibits leaving pets in unattended vehicles because they can suffer greatly or even die from the heat. Since many parks don't allow pets (except guide dogs), and pets usually cannot be left unattended at a park or motel, your visit may be greatly restricted if you bring Fido with you. If possible, leave your pets at home with a friend or relative.

PLANNING YOUR TRIP

Getting to South Florida

Public transportation to Miami is very convenient. The arrival point by air is most frequently Miami International Airport, a 45-minute drive from Homestead. Other major airports are Ft. Lauderdale International and Palm Beach International. Occasionally people fly to Marathon or Key West if they plan to tour the Keys. However, this usually requires a connecting flight from a mainland airport, which is costly and time-consuming. Buses and trains also serve the east coast. Major highways connect greater Miami from all directions, allowing a person to drive easily from elsewhere in Florida. To visit the natural areas on the Gulf Coast, you can also fly to Fort Myers or Naples.

Public transportation to and within the Keys is poor. There are no trains, and bus service is minimal. It is usually necessary to rent a car. The major car rental agencies can be found in the Miami area; smaller independent agencies are scattered throughout the Keys.

South Florida Weather

There is continual controversy over whether south Florida should be classified as tropical or subtropical. The problem is that there are several definitions for both. If only the latitudes between the Tropic of Cancer and the Tropic of Capricorn are considered tropical, then south Florida is not tropical. If the definition is an area that has historically remained frost-free, then the part of the Keys south of Key Largo would qualify. If the definition is an area where tropical plants grow, then many parts of south Florida would qualify. South Florida is at least subtropical.

Regardless of official definitions, south Florida *feels* tropical. Its southern latitude and maritime surroundings result in high year-round temperatures and humidities. Table 1 shows representative air temperatures for several locations in this area.

The warmest month is usually August and the coldest month is January. Notice how much warmer the average temperature is in the Keys (Tavernier and Key West) than on the mainland. The three-digit temperatures that wilt other parts of the country don't occur here. The moderating influences of the Atlantic Ocean, the Gulf of Mexico, and Florida Bay are responsible for that. It doesn't seem to matter—the relative humidity makes it feel just as hot! Hence, there is the southern equivalent of the

TABLE 1. 30-year average air temperatures (°F) of selected locations in south Florida (1961–1990)(NOAA 1994).

Month	Ft. Myers	Miami	Key West	Tavernier	West Palm
Jan	63.8	67.2	69.9	69.4	65.1
Apr	73.1	75.2	77.0	76.1	73.4
Jul	82.8	82.6	84.4	84.1	82.2
Oct	77.2	78.3	80.0	79.5	77.8

wind-chill factor, called the "heat index." The National Weather Service defines the heat index as "the temperature that a human body would feel when humidity and air temperature are factored in"—and it's frequently above 100 in the summer, meaning the air *feels* like it's over 100°F.

While northern Florida has four relatively distinct seasons, southern Florida has only two. The latter's air temperature extremes range from the upper 20s to the upper 90s. A normal year would register from the lower 40s to the mid-90s. It is precipitation more than temperature, however, that gives south Florida its two seasons—wet and dry (some would claim the two seasons are "mosquito" and "nonmosquito"). The wet season extends from May to October, and the dry season is November to April. Table 2 shows the mean rainfalls for the 1961–1990 period.

The rainfall begins to increase in late May or June and then decline in November, with peaks in June and September. The precipitation from May to August frequently falls in short, intense daily rainstorms. A visitor to south Florida during those months can expect rain (usually in the form of a thunderstorm) for 10–30 minutes almost every day. The clouds form from convection—the sun's rays evaporating water in the Everglades and ocean. The precipitation in September and October tends to fall less frequently but in larger amounts per event. This is because tropical storms are more frequent then and often drop many inches of rain in one event.

The most reliably good weather (less chance of thunderstorms, tropical storms, cold fronts, intense heat, or mosqui-

TABLE 2. 30-year average rainfall (inches) of selected locations in south Florida (1961–1990) (NOAA 1994).

Month	Ft. Myers	Miami	Key West	Tavernier	West Palm
Jan	1.84	2.01	2.01	2.12	2.80
Apr	1.06	2.85	1.75	2.00	2.91
Jul	8.26	5.70	3.63	3.63	6.14
Oct	2.94	5.74	4.42	5.80	6.60
TOTAL ANNUAL	53.37	55.91	39.59	41.12	60.75

toes) is in March and April. The weather is truly delightful. In fact, it's often so dry that some species of trees lose their leaves regularly every April, and great piles of crunchy leaves can be raked from beneath barren trees. A New England "fall" is in the autumn, while south Florida's "fall" is in the spring.

The months of November and December are also good times to visit for several reasons. The rainy season has ended, but the vegetation is still lush. The weather is cooler and less humid. There is only a small chance of a cold front strong enough to discourage you from exploring. As a bonus, the lodging rates are usually the lowest until mid-December.

WHEN YOU ARRIVE

Driving in Miami

Driving around the greater Miami area (which includes Homestead and Florida City) can be simplified if you know a few tips about the layout of the roads. There are four quadrants, like Washington, D.C.: Northwest, Northeast, Southwest, and Southeast. Roads are numbered beginning with the lowest in downtown Miami and ascending outward. Thus, there is a NW 60th Street, a SW 60th Street, and so on. "Streets" are oriented east-west, and "Avenues" are oriented north-south. Many of these larger roads are blocked occasionally by the network of canals that laces the city. The "Avenues" ending in the number "2" or "7" (such as 72nd Avenue or 107th Avenue) are most likely to have bridges over the canals and continue straight through. The smaller "Courts" (north-south) and "Terraces" (east-west) are rarely more than a few blocks long.

Homestead and Florida City have dual street numbering systems, just to confuse visitors! The numbering system from Miami continues as far south as Florida City: the "Street" numbers will be in the 200–300s and the "Avenue" numbers will be in the 100–200s. Interspersed are Homestead's and Florida City's own numbering systems, which have the same pattern as Miami's, originating in the centers of the respective towns.

If you're looking for a specific address, the building's street number will give you a clue. Most addresses have long numbers that indicate their block. For example, 24850 SW 187th Avenue would be between 248th Street and 249th Street in southwest Miami.

If you're the type that gets lost easily, head for the Keys. It's almost impossible to get lost—there's only one main road! That road is US 1, also called the Overseas Highway. Beginning at the southern end of Florida City, the road is marked with small green "Mile Marker" signs placed at one-mile intervals. The numbers descend from about 126 in Florida City to 0 in Key West. Thus, you can always tell how far you are from Key West. Addresses in the Keys are given by Mile Marker numbers or fractions thereof, such as MM 102.5. Occasionally you'll hear the added qualifier of "bayside" (the place you're looking for is on the side of the road toward Florida Bay) or "oceanside" (on the side toward the Atlantic Ocean). From almost anywhere in the Keys, you can easily tell which side is which.

Two roads bisect the Everglades east to west. They are locally known as Tamiami Trail and Alligator Alley. Tamiami Trail is actually US 41 and runs between Miami and Naples. It was completed in 1928 after 13 years of construction. Alligator Alley runs from just west of Fort Lauderdale to Naples and is part of Interstate 75. Since most of the locals (and most maps) use the colloquial names of Tamiami Trail and Alligator Alley, they will be used hereafter.

What to Wear

The weather information above should give you an idea of the type of clothing you'll need. Most of the year, shorts or lightweight pants are comfortable. Any time you plan to go on a trail, it's better to wear lightweight long-sleeved shirts and long pants to prevent mosquito, chigger, poisonwood, and sunburn problems. Clothing should be loose so that it doesn't stick to you from the humidity.

It's amazing how cold it can feel during a winter cold front, when the temperature is in the 40s or 50s (°F), the wind is blowing, and it's damp. At these times (usually from late December to early March), it's good to have several lightweight layers of sweaters and jackets.

Sunglasses and a sun hat are necessary most of the year. Comfortable walking shoes or jogging shoes will be suitable for the trails, especially if you don't mind getting them wet.

Restaurants are very casual in south Florida, particularly in the Keys. Even in restaurants that serve gourmet food, most people wear casual clothing. Shorts are not uncommon in restaurants.

Fishing Licenses

A state saltwater license is required for Florida residents and nonresidents, with the following exceptions: 1) an individual under 16 years of age, 2) an individual fishing from a charter boat that has a vessel saltwater fishing license, 3) any Florida resident 65 years of age or older, and 4) any Florida resident fishing in saltwater from land or from a structure fixed to the land. Residents may obtain a 1- or 5-year license, and nonresidents may obtain 3-day, 7-day, or 1-year licenses. Freshwater fishing licenses are also required. Licenses may be obtained from county tax collectors' offices or from bait and tackle shops. Be forewarned that some freshwater fish (for example, largemouth bass, gar, bowfin, warmouth, yellow catfish, and oscar) in most of the Everglades are contaminated with mercury. Limited consumption of these species caught in A.R.M. Loxahatchee National Wildlife Refuge and part of Everglades National Park is recommended, and no consumption is recommended for most of the rest of Everglades National Park and Water Conservation Areas 2 and 3.

The State Park System

The many state parks (including recreation areas, preserves, and reserves) are managed to maintain the lands as they were when the first Europeans arrived. The historic sites preserve the cultural heritage. Entrance fees are charged at most sites. If you plan to explore a number of parks, or live near a park that you visit frequently, you should consider buying an annual individual or family pass.

The parks are open from 8 AM to sunset every day of the year including holidays (a few open earlier). The gate may close at an odd time, such as 7:22 PM. Parks with campgrounds generally allow check-ins after sunset. Primitive campsites have no facilities, and campers must pack out their trash. Pets are permitted only in designated areas and must be kept on a 6-foot (maximum) hand-held leash. Pets are not allowed in swimming, beach, or concession areas and some campgrounds. Guide dogs for the disabled are welcomed in all areas. Dogs in campgrounds will incur an extra fee per night.

The National Wildlife Refuge and National Park System

The National Wildlife Refuge (NWR) system is composed of over 530 refuges and management areas across the country. Many were established to protect habitat for migratory birds, such as waterfowl. The first refuge, Pelican Island in central Florida, was created to protect a colony of nesting water birds. Many refuges have been established to protect habitat for a single endangered species, such as Crocodile Lake National Wildlife Refuge for crocodiles, Florida Panther National Wildlife Refuge for panthers, National Key Deer Refuge, and so on.

The refuges were created solely for protecting natural resources. Only compatible activities are permitted, which may or may not include visitors. This is why few public amenities are offered. Some are unstaffed, such as Crocodile Lake and Ten Thousand Islands. Many have multifaceted educational facilities, such as Loxahatchee and "Ding" Darling. Some have concessions that rent canoes or offer guided tours (such as "Ding" Darling). None of the south Florida refuges permits camping. When you visit a refuge, come prepared with drinking water and anything else you may need. Pets may or may not be permitted (see a specific park's entry in this book or call the refuge to confirm).

Unlike the refuges, the national park system was established to protect our natural resources while providing a way for people to enjoy them. Thus, they usually have more tourist facilities than the refuges.

Most national parks and refuges are U.S. fee areas; the remainder do not charge entrance fees. Daily entrance fees are available, of course, but purchasers of a "Golden Eagle" pass ($65) are allowed free admission to almost any U.S. fee area for one year from the date of purchase. This includes all national parks, monuments, seashores, historic sites, and national wildlife refuges in the United States. A pass to just the national park service units is $50. Handicapped individuals may obtain a free "Golden Access" pass (good for lifetime free admission to any U.S. fee area). Senior citizens may obtain a "Golden Age" pass for a $10 one-time fee, good for lifetime free admission to any U.S. fee area. All passes may be obtained at any U.S. fee area. Purchasers of a federal Duck Stamp (available at most post offices and refuges for $15) are allowed free admission to all national wildlife refuges. Duck stamps are good for one year from July 1 to June 30, and nonhunters may purchase one. The funds from the stamps are used to buy habitat for more refuges.

Conservation Tips

Good conservationists bring their creed with them wherever they go. Because of the tremendous volume of tourists coming to south Florida every year, the natural resources are being stressed to the limits. You can help to make sure that your visit here has a minimal environmental impact by observing a few suggestions:

1. *Conserve water.* Except during periods of heavy rainfall, south Florida often has a critical water shortage. This shortage usually occurs during the dry season, which coincides with the winter tourist season. During droughts, a county may impose water restrictions. Historically (and ridiculously) these have come when there was already a

water shortage—not earlier, when it could have prevented one. Restrictions can include a requirement by restaurants that waiters serve water only on request. You should refuse water at restaurants unless you plan to drink it. Don't criticize the restaurant for poor service if water is not automatically provided.

Other restrictions may include watering lawns and washing cars. Keep your showers short and use your ingenuity to think of other ways you can save water. The lack of water is bad enough, but a compounding problem is that it drives engineers and city planners to find new ways to retrieve water (like drilling a new well), usually at a cost to the environment.

2. *Drive carefully to avoid hitting wildlife.* Watch for snakes warming themselves on roads in the winter as the air cools in late afternoon or escaping high water after heavy rains (especially on the main Everglades National Park road to Flamingo). Drive slower than the speed limit in Key deer areas (such as Big Pine Key), crocodile areas (such as the stretch of US 1 from the mainland to the Key Largo), and panther areas (such as Tamiami Trail). Headlights, particularly high beams, temporarily blind animals and cause them to freeze in their tracks; keep this in mind when driving in rural areas at night.

If you are motor boating, watch the water ahead of you for ripples that might indicate a manatee is surfacing. If you are near a manatee, cut your motor to neutral until the manatee has moved away. Observe posted signs warning of manatee areas.

3. *Be a responsible angler.* Anglers should not leave monofilament line in the water or on land; a state law makes this illegal. Everyone should collect line they find littering the water—many animals have been slowly strangled by discarded fishing lines. Don't go fishing just for sport. Fishing just for human enjoyment is pure harassment of the fish. The fish do not play games for fun with fishermen—they fight for their lives. Fish that are to be released should be

handled carefully with wet hands and placed promptly and gently underwater.

4. *Protect coral reefs.* If you snorkel or dive, don't touch the corals. Simply touching a live coral can cause the sensitive polyps to die. Don't stand on the bottom or kick up silt. Collecting of coral (even if it's dead) is illegal in Florida. Collecting of tropical fish for aquaria usually causes them to die prematurely. Do not feed the fish on the reef because it changes their natural diets and habits.

5. *Don't collect souvenirs from the wild.* All national and state parks prohibit the collection of plants, animals, rocks, and so on. This is a good policy to follow everywhere. Take photographs instead.

6. *Don't feed wild animals.* Key deer, alligators, raccoons, and other wildlife learn to associate food with humans. This has caused many Key deer to wander into busy roads and get killed. It has caused some attacks on humans by alligators looking for handouts. The gator usually gets shot as punishment.

7. *Recycle your containers.* Recycling bins (made from recycled plastic) are located in Everglades National Park. The state parks have bins for aluminum and other recyclable materials. If you keep a lookout while you're driving outside of the parks, you may see a shopping center parking lot with trucks or bins for recycling aluminum, glass, plastic, and newspaper.

8. *Leave endangered and threatened species alone.* It is illegal to touch or disturb a listed species. This includes manatees, Key deer and sea turtles.

Local Precautions

There are probably no more hazards in south Florida than anywhere else in the country . . . just some different ones. You have chosen an adventurous and occasionally risky hobby. Everyone should have a safe and enjoyable trip. However, every person is different and has varying reactions to adverse conditions. While park rangers and other staff are well-trained, they cannot predict the weather, wildlife-people interactions, and the experience level of each person they advise. You must rely on your own common sense and recognition of your experience level to have a safe trip.

Your trip to Florida should be perfectly delightful, without any of the misfortunes mentioned below. The chance of a safe trip is increased if you are aware of the following.

Weather
Thunderstorms

The thunderstorm season begins around May and lasts until October, the duration of the wet season. The most active months are June to September. Within these months, a thunderstorm is possible almost daily. In extreme southern Florida, daily thunderstorms occur on an average of 70–80 days per year. Thunderstorms may occur at any other time of the year. They are caused by heat rising from the warming land, creating unstable air above. A cumulonimbus cloud (or "thunderhead") indicates a potential thunderstorm.

The major hazard of these storms is the lightning they produce. In Florida, a single day of intense thunderstorms can cause 10,000 lightning strikes. Next to being under the center of a thunderstorm, the most dangerous place is near the leading edge. Don't assume you are safe if the storm hasn't quite hit. And don't underestimate lightning. It causes about 10 deaths and 25 injuries a year in Florida, or about 10 percent of lightning-caused deaths in the United States.

If you are on the water when a thunderstorm approaches, try to get to land, where you are not as exposed. Do not get into the water, since water conducts electricity. Don't stand under the tallest object around. Drop anything metal you are carrying (sorry, that includes binocs and cameras). If you find yourself in the midst of lightning strikes with no shelter, as on an open boat, kneel down on your hands and knees, away from the motor, antennas, and console. The hands and knees posture makes a "path of least resistance" for the electricity to follow and gives you a better chance of survival than by sitting or lying down.

Other hazards from thunderstorms include high winds and

hail. High winds are almost always associated with thunderstorms, while hail is infrequent. High winds can be a problem for canoeists, who should always be vigilant for thunderstorm development.

Hurricanes

Southern Florida has the highest probability of any region in the country of getting struck by a hurricane. The National Weather Service considers June 1 to November 30 as the official hurricane season. There have been hurricanes or tropical storms in the Atlantic Ocean during every month of the year except April. The height of the "tropical activity" (tropical waves, depressions, storms, and hurricanes) is mid-August to mid-October. Therefore, you can minimize the possibility of encountering a tropical storm or hurricane by avoiding these months for your trip.

Hurricanes play an important ecological role. During late summer, when the temperature of tropical waters can rise too high for marine organisms to survive, hurricanes disperse the heat. That is why higher ocean temperatures increase the chance of a hurricane forming.

Don't count on the local municipal emergency shelters being able to accommodate tourists during a storm. Especially in the Keys, the shelters cannot even support all the residents. If you travel to south Florida during the hurricane season, it is possible you will be mandated to evacuate to higher ground. There are only two roads off the Florida Keys that everyone must use, and there is little controversy that they are inadequate to handle a major evacuation. Campers in Flamingo are also vulnerable and may be evacuated by rangers before campers in any other area are. Before heading south during hurricane season, check the National Weather Service (see "Other Sources of Information") for tropical weather activity.

Tornadoes and Waterspouts

Tornadoes are common in Florida. March, April, and May are the busy months for tornadic activity. Tornadoes are not as common in the southern tip of the peninsula as in the central and northern parts. South Florida also has the aquatic version of the tornado—the waterspout. A waterspout is a tornado that forms over a large body of water, such as the ocean. Most often, a waterspout is short-lived, relatively weak, and never reaches land. The funnel may never even touch the surface of the water. Such a waterspout is not hazardous, but if you see a funnel cloud of either type, seek shelter in a sturdy building.

Poisonous Plants

The initial panic an amateur botanist feels when seeing south Florida plants for the first time is that so many of them look alike. The generic morphology (form) of a tropical leaf is a shiny surface with smooth edges and a pointed tip. This facilitates water dripping off the leaf in such a humid, rainy environment. The myriad of look-alike plants presents a problem to the careful naturalist who won't touch any plant that he or she can't identify. Some plants in this region have parts that are caustic if ingested or touched by a sensitive person. Only three are likely to give the average person a rash if merely touched, and those three are described below. Two of those (manchineel and poisonwood) fall into the category of having a tropical-looking leaf, and they are considered tropical trees.

The three described below are not the only poisonous plants in the area. To be safe from an irritating rash or worse, always identify a plant before touching it. If you find you have brushed against one of the three species mentioned, wash your skin with plenty of sudsy cold water as soon as possible.

Manchineel

The most infamous of our native poisonous plants is manchineel in the spurge family. This small tree (up to 30 feet) has shiny alternate leaves 2–4 inches long, with faintly round-toothed margins and pointed tips. Manchineels are known for their caustic sap, very irritating if it contacts human skin or internal tissues, and the fatally poisonous (if ingested) fruit, which looks like a small green apple (1–1.5 in. long). Manchineels can be found locally in the Keys, around Whitewater Bay, and on Cape Sable (particularly in the buttonwood hammocks along the coast), but it is unlikely that you will encounter one. Public pressure to remove these "undesirable" trees has caused most of them near houses, trails, or roads to be destroyed. The tree is also very sensitive to frost. It is on the state's protected list and is classified as endangered.

Poisonwood

The second of the three poisonous plants is another tree, known as poisonwood or Florida poisontree. It is in the poison-ivy family and shares the characteristic caustic sap. Touching the leaves yields a blistering rash similar to poison-ivy. Poisonwood has alternate compound leaves with five shiny leaflets that are smooth-edged and pointy-tipped. Unlike manchineel, there is a good chance that you will encounter a poisonwood tree in extreme south Florida. It grows in wet and dry habitats, near roadsides and in unspoiled wilderness, in hammocks, in

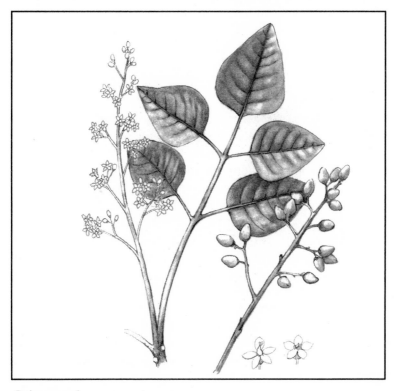

Poisonwood

pinelands, and in coastal regions—in other words, just about anywhere. But it is becoming increasingly scarce, suffering the same fate as the manchineel. Because of its irritating sap, many homeowners obliterate this tree from their yards. This causes problems for wildlife, since the fruits are a valuable food. The state-threatened white-crowned pigeon, a tropical fruit-eating bird found in the Keys, is especially dependent on poisonwood fruits. Biologists from the National Audubon Society's Research Department in Tavernier, who recognized the value of poison-wood to the pigeons, have been trying to educate the public to save poisonwood trees.

Poison ivy

The third poisonous plant is the familiar three-leaved poison-ivy. Since this plant is so common elsewhere in the country, it's not necessary to describe it here, but you should expect it just about anywhere around south Florida, including the Keys.

Vertebrate Animals
Snakes

There are four kinds of venomous snakes in south Florida: the eastern diamondback rattler, the dusky pygmy rattler, the Florida cottonmouth (also known as the water moccasin), and the eastern coral snake. Encounters with these snakes are rare. The nonvenomous Florida water snake is often mistaken for the less common cottonmouth, and the nonvenomous scarlet snake and scarlet kingsnake can be confused with the coral snake. Coral snakes are primarily nocturnal and burrow under loose litter, so it is not likely you will encounter one by accident. If you see a brightly colored snake whose identity you are unsure of, recall the adage "Red touch yellow kills a fellow" to remind you that if the red and yellow bands are touching each other, you are looking at a venomous snake.

Pygmy rattlesnakes are the most likely venomous snakes you will see. They often warm themselves on paved roads. They are usually less than two feet long, with a dusty appearance and round, dark blotches. Their rattles are so tiny they often go unnoticed.

Sharks

Sharks are common in the warm Florida waters. The majority are small, nonaggressive, and nonthreatening to humans. In the very few attacks that have occurred, the sharks were not intentionally attacking humans. Swimmers in shallow murky water are at risk because the sharks can smell something swimming nearby, but they can't see what it is. Spear-fishermen have had fish they just caught snatched from their hands. One diver lost her hand this way. Some sharks eat lobsters, so sport lobsterers also should be cautious.

To decrease your chances of getting bitten by a shark, avoid standing or swimming in shallow, murky water and don't hold fish or lobsters in your hand underwater. This is also a good reason for divers and snorkelers to refrain from attracting reef fish by feeding them.

Alligators

Although they appear lethargic and slow-moving, these giant reptiles can react with blinding speed when provoked. Normally, alligators that have never seen a human are no threat to people. The problem arises when a gator that lives near houses or a park becomes accustomed to people feeding it. Thereafter, that gator recognizes humans as a source of food. Since an alligator has little intelligence, it can't distinguish that the food does not include the whole package! A state regulation prohibits people from feeding gators. It is extremely important to observe this regulation for everyone's safety.

In the wild, female gators are very protective of their young. Since they may guard them for over a year, no time of year is without defensive females. Therefore, if you are walking in an area where there are gators, look and listen carefully, and be ready to back off if you hear the babies' squeaky whimpering defense calls.

Insects

Most people deal with insects by applying repellents. While this works, repellents are not without hazards sometimes worse than the original problem. The active ingredient in most repellents, called DEET (N,N-diethyl-m-toluamide), has been linked to seizures and several deaths in the United States (MMWR 1989). It is absorbed through the skin and into the circulatory system. About 10–15 percent of the amount applied to the skin passes into the urine. Insect repellents with DEET can eat through vinyl and plastic. Watchbands and car seats can be damaged if your DEET-covered skin contacts them. Here is a summary of some precautions to take when using repellents (MMWR 1989):

- wear long sleeves and pants and apply repellent only to exposed skin or to clothing
- use low concentrations of DEET
- never apply repellent to wounds
- apply once every 4–8 hours; over-application will not improve effectiveness
- wash skin after returning indoors

Certain people, such as children, are more sensitive to repellent than others. Be courteous by not spraying repellent near other people. Never spray it indoors—some people don't dare venture outside without first saturating their skin and clothes, leaving others inside to breathe the DEET.

Mosquitoes

From June to November, coinciding with the wet months, the mosquitoes can be unbelievable. It's been suggested (tongue in cheek?) that Everglades National Park should be closed for the summer because of mosquitoes, analogous to northern parks closing for the winter due to heavy snow. Too many foreigners have had miserable trips to the southern Everglades because they didn't know about the mosquitoes.

Now that you have been sufficiently warned of the worst, you'll be happy to know that many months of the year can be devoid of mosquitoes. The months of December to May usually are dry enough to prevent mosquitoes from hatching, and cold fronts kill the adults.

Mosquitoes need water to hatch their eggs. The eggs hatch 5–10 days after flooding by rains or high tides. Standing water, such as accumulates in old tires, flower pots, and gutters, is perfect for the proliferation of mosquitoes. Therefore, many residents contribute to their own mosquito problems by allowing mosquito breeding places in their yards.

You are more likely to encounter mosquitoes in the coastal mangrove areas and hammocks than in the freshwater marshes. The common saltmarsh mosquito shuns strong sunlight, so you are better off in the open than in the shade and better off in the daytime than at night.

The female mosquito needs the protein from blood to form her eggs, thus it is only the female that bites. The males feed on nectar; they do for marsh flowers what bees do for meadow flowers—they pollinate them. We need mosquitoes.

County mosquito control commissions spray insecticides daily in developed areas during the peak of the mosquito season. The aerial spray (Dibrom) contains diesel to help it settle to the ground. Dibrom and the ground-sprayed Baytex and malathion are killers of butterflies and bees.

Scorpions

The scorpions in Florida are not the same as the ones found in the southwestern United States. Ours are not fatally venomous, but their stings can make a person ill. Scorpions are found throughout south Florida, including the Keys, but you will not be likely to see one unless you are searching for it. Scorpions prefer to hide under wood (such as fallen trees or lumber) rather than rocks. If you turn over a piece of wood, do not use your bare hands—use a walking staff or tripod leg instead. Always put the wood back exactly as you found it, so unseen creatures are not left homeless.

Fire ants

People can ignore swarms of mosquitoes, listlessly swat at horseflies, and calmly step around rattlesnakes. But have you ever seen a human do anything other than frantically explode at the attack of fire ants? The ants in question are the red imported fire ants (*Solenopsis invicta*), which were accidentally introduced into Alabama from Brazil in the 1920s. Since then, they have spread throughout the southeastern United States, eventually reaching south Florida in the early 1970s.

Fire ants are red and less than an eighth of an inch long. They are not often seen unless their mound is stepped on. Fire ants have one of the quickest reaction times to nest agitation of any ant, and it's usually too quick for the agitator. They leave itchy, raised pustules that persist for weeks. The nest mounds are piles of dirt about 6–12 inches high and can most often be found in disturbed areas, like the side of a road.

Other insects

No-see-ums or "sand-gnats" (*Culicoides furens*) are minuscule insects which take painful bites that leave welts. No-see-ums are so small and quick that most people don't even see what bit them, hence the colloquial name. They appear at dawn and dusk, usually near mangroves and salt water, and stay for a brief but nasty hour. Because of these tiny insects, camping tents must have the fine-meshed no-see-um-proof netting, not just mosquito netting.

Deerflies (*Tabanus* spp.), which look like giant house flies, are large and slow enough so that it's hard to miss them even before they bite. This is lucky, because their bites take more than their fair share. They are active in open sunlight, usually in the summer.

Chiggers are almost microscopic orange larval mites (not true insects) that burrow under the skin, causing itchy welts that can last for weeks. The best prevention for chiggers is wearing long pants tucked into your socks, not sitting on rocks or logs, and showering immediately after hiking.

Miscellaneous
Humidity

Photographers beware! The south Florida humidity and salt spray can wreak havoc on your delicate equipment. Binoculars and spotting scopes are often victims, too. Wipe moisture and salt spray off the exterior surfaces frequently. Carry a heavy plastic bag with you in case of a sudden downpour. Additionally, there is the intense heat to contend with. Keep your equipment and film in the shade or in a cooler.

Sunburn

Locals can usually tell who the tourists are—they have the peeling sunburns or the dark tans. People who have lived a long time in Florida have learned how harmful the sun's rays can be. They protect their skin and consequently look pale compared to visitors. Skin cancer is prevalent in the South and getting more common every year as the protective ozone layer in the atmosphere is depleted. No time of the year is safe. In winter, although the Earth's axis is tilted away from the sun, the Earth is closer to the sun, so the rays are very strong. In summer, the Earth is farther from the sun but the rays are more direct. If you are swimming, boating, or just wading through water, you'll get a double whammy, because the rays will reflect off the water. Use sunblock, or wear a hat and long sleeves to keep the sun off your skin. Prolonged exposure to strong ultra-violet (UV) rays can damage the retinas of your eyes, so wear glasses that block UV rays.

Crime

Regrettably, the greater Miami-Ft. Lauderdale area has attained a high crime rate, some of which is aimed at tourists. Thieves watch people for signs of vulnerability, such as being lost or in unfamiliar surroundings. Crime is not common in most of the places mentioned in this book, but disguising yourself as a local and using common sense will go a long way toward deterring it.

A BRIEF HUMAN HISTORY

The first Europeans to gaze upon the shores of Florida were the Spanish explorers, lead by Juan Ponce de León in 1513. Ponce de León, who was seeking riches and natives to capture as slaves, bestowed the name "Florida" and claimed the area for Spain.

The native Tequesta inhabited southeast Florida and the Calusa inhabited southwest Florida until they were eradicated by Europeans or fled to West Indian islands. The Seminoles and Miccosukees, the two Native American tribes currently in southern Florida, were not original inhabitants. These two tribes were descended from Creeks who settled here after being chased from their ancestral lands in present-day north Florida, Georgia, and Alabama by intolerant Europeans. Both tribes preferred to live quietly without interference from Europeans. They retreated farther and farther south until they ended up in the Everglades, a vast wetland scorned by the Europeans. Still, the federal government, supported by wealthy white landowners eager to acquire more land, wanted all the native people expelled. The Indian Removal Act of 1830 forced the southeastern Indians, including the Seminoles, to march on foot over 800 miles to a reservation in what is now Oklahoma. The forced exodus is known today as the "Trail of Tears," because so many died of hunger, exhaustion, cold, heat, and disease. Some Seminoles resisted the removal, including the Seminole leader Osceola. Osceola led his people in this struggle against the federal government, which became known as the Second Seminole War (1835–42). The Seminoles never surrendered, but the war wound down after the federal government lost 1,500 men and $30 million.

The Seminoles and the Miccosukees are recognized as separate tribes by the federal government. The Seminoles' Big Cypress Reservation (one of five reservations in Florida) is in Hendry County, near the northern side of Big Cypress National Preserve. Most Miccosukees live on several reservations in south Florida. Both tribes try to keep their cultures flourishing by hunting and selling crafts.

Spain and Britain alternated ownership of the Florida peninsula until 1821, when Florida was ceded to the United States.

John James Audubon, the famous artist and naturalist, first visited the Florida Keys in 1832 and lived in a house on Whitehead Street in Key West for a few months. The house has been preserved as a museum and is open to the public.

Until the late 1800s, few Americans lived in south Florida. Much of the area was marsh and swamp. Only a narrow strip of coastal ridge from Miami northward was dry enough for development. There were few roads—most people traveled by boat.

In the late 1800s, Miami became a boomtown for several reasons. The area grew into a popular winter vacation spot for wealthy people from northern states. The Florida Keys were attractive to farmers for the year-round growing season. The fashion industry in New York, London, and Paris dictated that egret plumes were a must for stylish women's hats, and milliners looked to the Everglades as the source of plumes.

By the early 1900s, large-scale developers had devised schemes to drain the Everglades and provide more land for development. It was a multipronged assault on the irreplaceable wetland: they dug canals from Lake Okeechobee to divert water to the ocean, built levees to keep water out of developed areas, and planted thirsty exotic trees to drink up water. The methods worked over much of the Everglades. Little did they realize their near-sighted actions would ruin a perfect system created by nature.

Another self-appointed savior was Henry Flagler, who dreamed of creating a quick passage for travel from the mainland to Havana. His idea was to extend the Florida East Coast Railroad from Miami to Key West, where a ferry would deliver the passengers across the short watery stretch to Havana. Flagler was an old man with plenty of money to finance the construction and a desire to do something sensational with his last years.

Originally, Flagler planned the route to go overland from Miami to Cape Sable and then mostly over water across Florida Bay to Key West. His engineers tried for two years to find a route through the Everglades to Cape Sable. But the land was too mucky to support a railroad. Then Flagler sent his engineers to test the Florida Keys. They reported that the route was possible, so Flagler approved it.

Spend a minute now contemplating what the Everglades would be like today if Flagler had succeeded in his initial route. The railroad tracks would cut across what is now Everglades National Park. Houses, hotels, stores, roads, and farms would probably line the entire route, and more of the Everglades would have been drained to prevent flooding. Flamingo would be a bustling port like Key West. The Everglades would not exist as we know it today, even in its current sorry state. It's a small consolation that the Everglades was spared at the expense of the Keys.

The railroad construction was begun in 1904 and completed in Key West in 1912. Since Key West was the most populated town in Florida at the turn of the century, there was not enough land for the terminal station. So 134 acres were created by pumping mud and marl from the Gulf of Mexico.

The engineers originally wanted to connect all the Keys with ramparts (causeways), with no more than six miles of bridges. But the local people protested, claiming it would prevent the flow of seawater between the islands during storms and cause the water to flood over the islands instead. They were proven right during the 1909 and 1935 hurricanes, and that is why there are so many bridges on the Overseas Highway. The longest one, the Seven-Mile Bridge in Marathon, is the longest bridge of its kind in the world.

The big hurricane of 1935 was the last curtain for the railroad. So much was destroyed that the cost to rebuild was too great. The railroad had already been losing money, and it had facilitated a loss of population in the Keys (the impoverished locals had a way to leave, and many never returned). In 1938, the railroad bed was converted into a road, which is still the only road that goes to Key West. Portions of the old track are still visible along the middle and lower Keys.

A QUICK LOOK AROUND THE MAINLAND

The two outstanding topographic features of southern Florida are the amount of surface water and the flatness of the terrain. Combined, they make the tip of the peninsula look like a giant,

The walking dredge, displayed at Collier-Seminole SP, changed the way water flows across South Florida.

shallow lake at certain times of the year. Actually, it's a giant, shallow, and very slowly moving *river*. Marjory Stoneman Douglas recognized this and coined the name "River of Grass" for the Everglades in the 1940s. Historically, the Everglades began at the southern end of Lake Okeechobee, where the water overflowed the banks and gradually drifted south to Florida Bay and the Gulf of Mexico. The topographical gradient is so small—only one or two inches per mile—that early white settlers didn't even know the water flowed.

West of the Everglades basin is Big Cypress Swamp, one of the largest remaining wilderness areas in Florida. It has a slightly higher elevation than the Everglades basin. Although it contains marshes, it is predominantly forested with cypress and pines. It is underlain by the fossiliferous Tamiami limestone. The hydroperiod (the amount of time the area is covered by water) is shorter than in the Everglades, leaving marl instead of peat for the soil. Old growth pine stands contain small populations of the endangered red-cockaded woodpecker. Because of limited accessibility in the Big Cypress, less exploration has been done here than in the Everglades, and less is known about the flora and fauna.

A rock ridge composed of limestone outcroppings extends from Miami southwest to Long Pine Key in Everglades National Park. This region of higher elevation between the coast and the interior marshes was preferred for development and farms because of the lack of flooding. The highest elevations in Homestead are about 13 feet above sea level and in Miami about 23 feet above sea level. The latter can clearly be seen by driving along South Bayshore Drive in the Silver Bluff area of Miami (between Coconut Grove and the Rickenbacker Causeway). The old shoreline, which abutted the limestone bluffs, can be seen in the yards of the houses on the west side of the road.

The Atlantic coastal ridge, which punctuates Palm Beach, Broward, and Miami-Dade counties, prevents most of the Everglades water from flowing east into the Atlantic. A few rivers, such as the Hillsboro, Miami-Dade, and New Rivers, historically penetrated the ridge and allowed some water to pass. But the remaining water backs up against the western side of the ridge. Formerly, the water pressure pushed through the limestone in some places, creating high volume springs that emerged east of the ridge (for example, in Miami Springs). The decrease in water level over the past 80 years has caused the springs to cease flowing. The rivers are now entirely channelized.

The huge pool of water that collects west of the ridge—the real Everglades—not only flows southward but also downward. By percolating through the porous limestone, it recharges the underlying Biscayne Aquifer. Most of south Florida's residents, farmers, and industries depend on this aquifer, and therefore the Everglades, for their water.

The colonization by Europeans caused some development to begin in south Florida, but it wasn't until the 1900s that serious environmental degradation began. Huge dredges dug canals to drain the water from the Everglades, creating more farmland. The fill from the canals was used to build levees for flood protection and roads. The series of canals, levees, and pumping stations that now criss-cross the southern Florida peninsula have changed the face of the Everglades. In some places the water no longer flows. In others, the hydroperiod has decreased so much by draining that the peat is exposed and fires ravage the fertile soil. Complications too numerous to elaborate on here have arisen because of the juxtaposition of a sensitive wetland with a burgeoning metropolis.

In the 1970s, an insidious enemy began to reveal itself. Observant land managers in the Everglades noticed dense stands of cattails growing where formerly sawgrass grew. The problem was traced to excess nutrients (primarily phosphorus) in agricultural runoff, exacerbated by the artificial manipulation of water flow. The canals were carrying the phosphorus far downstream from the farms into the Everglades. This "overfertilized" the natural system, which was adapted to very small amounts of nutrients. Plants started growing too tall and too dense. The wrong plants, such as cattails, started taking over the sawgrass. This is just one of the easy ways of seeing the problem, although much more is not readily visible.

In 1988, U.S. Attorney Dexter Lehtinen filed a suit against the State on behalf of A.R.M. Loxahatchee National Wildlife Refuge and Everglades National Park to protect them from this polluted water. In 1991, the State conceded that it had not enforced its water quality standards for the Everglades. Since then, A.R.M. Loxahatchee NWR, Everglades National Park, the South Florida Water Management District, Florida Department of Environment Protection, U.S. Environmental Protection Agency, U.S. Army Corps of Engineers, the agricultural community, and others have begun a major cleanup of the water.

The water quality improvements are just part of the massive ecosystem restoration that's occurring from Kissimmee River to Florida Bay. Other aspects include restoration of the quantity, pattern, and timing of the water flow as well as exotic plant control, land acquisition for habitat protection, dechannelization of the Kissimmee River, and endangered species recovery. For more information, see www.sfrestore.org.

A QUICK LOOK
AROUND THE FLORIDA KEYS

The word "key" as it relates geographically to south Florida originated from the Spanish word *cayo* for "little island" or "island reef." It is used for all small marine islands in south Florida. When capitalized, it refers specifically to the group of islands that make up the chain from Key Largo to Key West. The dozens of islands that shape this archipelago stretch about 125 miles from Key Largo to Key West. Actually, that is what is linked by road and 42 bridges, but there are undeveloped and unconnected islands on both ends.

The islands are made of several forms of limestone. Exposed very recently geologically, these 5,000-year-old islands are barely separate from the sea. They rise an average of 2–4 feet above sea level, with the highest islands (Key Largo, Plantation Key, Windley Key, Lignumvitae, and Big Pine) rising only to 18 feet. Actually, the landfills create the highest land now in the Keys.

From Soldier Key in the north to part of Big Pine Key in the south, the substrate rock is Key Largo limestone, an old coral reef. Fossilized remnants of coral skeletons can be easily seen on surface rocks in many places on the Upper Keys. Look for a place, even a parking lot on US 1 in Key Largo, that has rocks on the ground and you will probably see striations from former coral colonies. The more serious geology students will want to visit Windley Key Quarry (see "Lignumvitae Key") to get the real picture.

From Big Pine south to Key West, the rock is called Miami Oolite, named for the tiny calcareous spheres that look like eggs or ooids. Note on a map the difference in shape between the two groups of islands.

It is the difference in substrate between the Upper and Lower Keys that determines the availability of fresh water on the islands. In the Upper Keys, the Key Largo limestone is permeable and rain water quickly soaks through to mix with the brackish groundwater. There are few freshwater wells or ponds in the Upper Keys. In the Lower Keys, the dense Miami Oolite retains water which sits in pools or "lenses" above the denser salt water. The pinelands of the Lower Keys exist because of the availability of fresh water. Many mammals, reptiles, and amphibians not found in the Upper Keys can survive in the Lower Keys because of the fresh water. The Key deer and Key mud turtle are examples.

You may notice that it rains less in the Keys than on the mainland. Frequently in the summer you can drive from earth-shaking thunderstorms in Florida City south across the "18-Mile Stretch" (a colloquial name for the section of US 1 south of Florida City to the drawbridge at Jewfish Creek near Key Largo), and when you arrive in Key Largo the sun is shining. Because the air and ground are both drier, there are very few natural sources of fresh water on the Keys. The public water supply is piped from Navy Wells in Florida City to Key West, a distance of 135 miles. Virtually every person on the islands is dependent on this one aqueduct. The aqueduct is mostly buried, but you can see it where it crosses the bridges. Now you can understand why fresh water is expensive and precious in the Keys.

The vegetation of the Keys is distinctly West Indian. Since the Keys are islands, the most likely way for seeds to reach them would be by drifting on the ocean or the wind. Most of the West Indian plants are adapted to those forms of dispersal, but most of the mainland ones are not. Furthermore, the most likely species to survive would be ones adapted to island features, like salty air. The climate resembles that of the West Indies more than that of the mainland. One's overall impression of the Keys is that one is on a Caribbean island.

As a group, the most distinctive trees are the graceful palms. Some botanists would argue that palms aren't trees, since they are monocots and lack a true woody structure. But they are tree-like in form and function and are considered trees by most people. There are only eight species native to south Florida. The coconut palm, so common in this area, is not one of them. Many species of palms have been introduced and thrive in the mild climate.

The animal life, however, brings a northerner back to reality. You will recognize many species from the mainland of Florida: opossums, raccoons, rat snakes, green treefrogs, spadefoot toads, ospreys, and mockingbirds, to name a few. Aside from the birds and insects, which could fly to the islands from far away, other animals were restricted to shorter distances and perhaps less intentional methods of transportation. Mammals, except bats, either swam island-hopping fashion or drifted on flotsam. Some of them may have walked during extremely low tides and sea levels. Most reptiles probably also arrived this way. Small mammals, reptiles, amphibians, and flightless insects probably hitched rides on floating logs or were carried by hurricanes. More recently, humans have aided dispersal (intentionally and unintentionally) with roads, ships, and other methods. Through the pet trade, humans have brought species from all over the world that subsequently escaped and established themselves. The wildlife present now is a blend of three parts continental, two parts West Indian, and one part totally bizarre.

Key limes, a local specialty, are actually of Mexican origin. The lime trees were imported to the Keys by botanist Henry Perrine in the 1800s and have become commercially important. The small, round yellow fruits are used for the famous Key Lime Pie.

On a drive down the "18-Mile Stretch" from November to March you are likely to pass roseate spoonbills and other wading birds. Another road, called the Card Sound Road (SR 905A), leads from Florida City to North Key Largo. This was the original road and is less traveled and more picturesque than US 1. The southern end, near where Card Sound Road intersects with SR 905, may harbor a well-concealed crocodile in the shallow water around the mangroves (Crocodile Lake National Wildlife Refuge).

ECOLOGICAL EFFECTS OF HURRICANE ANDREW IN SOUTH FLORIDA

On August 24, 1992, one of the most powerful storms in United States history slammed into the southern tip of the Florida peninsula. Roaring in from the Atlantic Ocean at sustained wind speeds near 150 miles per hour and gusts over 175, Hurricane Andrew was the worst natural disaster ever to befall the country.

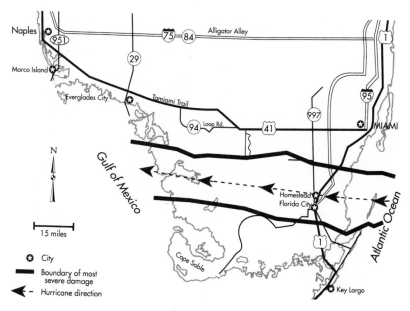

Hurricane Andrew's path as it traveled from east to west across south Florida, August 24, 1992. Dashed line shows center of storm. Boundary includes eye plus eye wall. Damage also occurred outside boundary. Hurricane track information is courtesy of South Florida Water Management District and National Weather Service.

That honor was acquired primarily by the size of the financial damage estimate and the number of people left homeless. But how did nature fare?

Recall that hurricanes are spawned as the waters in the ocean warm up during the northern hemisphere's summer (see "Hurricanes" under "Local Precautions" above). If the water becomes too warm, the ocean's creatures will become physically stressed or will die. To remove the tremendous amount of energy stored in the warm ocean, the heat must rise. As it rises, it creates a well-defined air mass that gathers strength when it passes over more warm water. The objective is to move the heat to somewhere else, such as the colder North Atlantic waters. Considering the primary ecological function of a hurricane, Andrew was a success.

If the air mass is strong, it may become defined into a circular

The gumbo limbo trees of Everglades National Parks's hammock at Royal Palm showed extraordinary resilience to Andrew's wind damage. This photo was taken exactly 4 years after Color Plate #17 in the center of this book.

wind pattern, with the strongest winds near the center. In the center itself, called the eye, there is no wind, and the barometric pressure is extremely low. At the edge of the eye, the wind begins abruptly at the "eye wall." The wall is a sheer vertical face of wind rising like a hollow column tens of thousands of feet above the ocean. It is along this wall that the strongest winds are sustained. In the northern hemisphere, the wind always travels counter-clockwise around the eye.

As Andrew approached the Florida coast, it was traveling due west. It made landfall in Homestead, about 25 miles south of Miami (see map). The winds in the first half of the storm, therefore, came from the north. After the eye passed by, the winds shifted 180° and came from the south.

The high winds pushed a wall of water, called a storm surge, across the ocean. Storm surges often cause more damage than the winds in a hurricane, but that was not true of Andrew. The highest surge was 16.9 feet near Perrine and smaller surges extended for a relatively short distance north to Miami Beach and south to North Key Largo. Perhaps because the storm sprinted past so quickly (its forward speed was about twice that of most hurricanes), it did not linger long enough to pound the coast. Furthermore, the natural barriers presented by the coral reefs and mangrove shores performed their functions as nature intended.

As the storm moved across the land, it did not waver in direction or intensity. It left a swath about 25 miles wide across the southern Everglades. Its path of destruction began around Elliott Key in Biscayne National Park and Homestead Air Force Base in the east, then continued west through Homestead and surrounding towns, and through the main entrance of Everglades National Park. In the park, it struck Chekika, Royal Palm, Long Pine Key, Pinelands, Pa-hay-okee, and Shark Valley visitor access areas.

Effects on Terrestrial Habitats

In a totally natural environment, a hurricane accomplishes some beneficial functions in the areas it strikes. These include sweeping accumulated leaf litter from the ground to allow seedlings to sprout, dumping needed rain before the start of the dry season, and flushing the estuaries that have become choked with vegetation. The native vegetation has adapted to hurricanes. For example, some have flexible trunks and some can releaf quickly. When unnatural factors are added, a hurricane can become an ecological disaster. That is what happened with Andrew.

Much of the mangroves that once existed along the coast south of Miami had been destroyed by development years before. Those trees would have absorbed the shock of the storm surge and prevented coastal erosion. Of the mangroves that were left, the worst damage was to the western shore of Biscayne Bay, where 85–90% were destroyed.

The hardwood hammocks were also severely damaged. Many trees were windthrown (blown over), many were snapped off at the trunk, and all were denuded 5 or 10 feet above the ground. The trees that were left standing were reduced to only the thickest branches. Many of the native trees, such as gumbo-limbo, will survive if not further assaulted by freezes or droughts in the near future. For many years to come, the skeletons of the windthrown trees will be visible in Everglades and Biscayne National Parks, Castellow Hammock, and Matheson Hammock.

The pinelands initially survived slightly better, although the optimism was short-lived. While many trees were snapped in two or windthrown, about 20–50% of them remained intact with only the loss of needles. The slash pines seemed an example of a native tree that had adapted to hurricanes. Months later, the surviving trees began to succumb. Soon they died over most of the area. The only stand that may survive on its own is in Everglades National Park. The theory is that preexisting stresses, such as a long-term lowering of the water table, did not manifest themselves until the hurricane. If the taproots could no longer reach the water table, the trees would have been living from rainfall to rainfall. When the needles and branches blew off, the stress could have been too much. The weakened trees succumbed to a pine bark beetle (*Ips* sp.). Worried that the few remaining pinelands would be lost forever, the Florida Department of Forestry collected pine cones and grew seedlings for reforestation. Unfortunately, some of the pinelands in southern Dade are too rocky to plant seedlings.

The ecological problems created by humans and merely assisted by Andrew may be south Florida's worst enemy. Hazardous wastes in the form of paints, solvents, cleaners, batteries, and pesticides were scattered on the ground and in canals after the storm swept them out of garages and porches. Fuel tanks leaked. In the aftermath, some people used the storm as an excuse to dump toxics anywhere. They laughed at "No Littering" laws (the signs themselves had become litter). Debris became a major problem. So, in a humanitarian move, the Secretary of the Department of Environmental Regulation (now the Department of Environmental Protection) issued an emergency order to ease restrictions on waste disposal and open burning of debris. Open fires, as many as 80 with permits, burned into October. Severe smog resulted in respiratory problems for the residents. Air quality standards over Everglades National Park were undoubtedly violated. Furthermore, the scores of backyard swimming pools and hot tubs that had filled with debris became giant stagnant cesspools, perfect for the proliferation of mosquitoes. The mosquito control folks called in the big guns—the insecticide bombing planes. Even the military got into the aerial spraying business. The few butterflies that had quietly slipped back in a few days after the storm vanished after the spraying. Another alleged health threat involved rats, which feasted on the piles of garbage.

Perhaps the greatest fear that environmentalists have for the future as a result of Andrew is the uncontrollable spread of exotic plants. Prior to the storm, melaleuca and Brazilian pepper were already threatening the floral integrity of the Everglades. Those two species, which thrive after disturbance, may have received the added boost they needed to outcompete the native plants beyond our ability to recover them. Just as menacing are the climbing vines that were becoming a nuisance before the storm. These plants responded to the sudden opening of the canopy with explosive growth. Furthermore, their seeds and pieces of reproductively viable stems were blown west into pristine areas.

Effects on Wildlife

At the end of August, there is typically a lull in wildlife activities in south Florida. That timing, plus the lack of flooding, saved much of the wildlife from harm. For example, wading birds had finished nesting, so presumably no nests were destroyed. Bald eagle nesting generally commences in mid-October and had not yet begun. True, some nests from previous years (which the faithful eagles reuse) were destroyed, but the birds could build new ones. Most snail kites were farther north, out of the path of the storm. Red-cockaded woodpeckers in Big Cypress, already an isolated colony, probably lost vital nesting trees.

All 23 radio-collared Florida panthers survived and had normal movement patterns after the storm. White-tailed deer fawns were already 5–6 months old and self-sufficient.

A small and insignificant number of alligator eggs may have been destroyed. Crocodiles had already hatched, and most of their nests were outside the severely impacted area. Sea turtle nests in Biscayne National Park and some on Cape Sable in Everglades National Park were destroyed, but the majority of sea turtle nests were located in counties farther north of the impacted area. Some sand deposited on Cape Sable may help future turtle nesting.

Two invertebrate species may have suffered delayed mortality due to the defoliation of the host trees. Tree snails lost the shade cover that keeps them sheltered from the intense sunlight. The adult Schaus' swallowtail butterflies were not emerged on their breeding area on Elliott Key and North Key Largo at the time of the storm, but the pupae were present. The effect of salt spray and lack of shade was probably serious. Many were probably killed, although they survived on Elliott Key. This swallowtail existed only on Elliott Key and a few other islands in Biscayne National Park at the time of the hurricane. What saved the species from possible extinction is the efforts of University of Florida's Dr. Thomas Emmel, who collected eggs before the storm and successfully released adults when the vegetation returned. The fate of the butterfly is a good example of how quickly a species can become extinct. Biologists fear letting a species become too few or restricted geographically, because one catastrophe can erase it forever.

A major problem, the introduction of exotic animals to the wild, may not manifest itself for years. The hurricane's winds ripped open the cages of thousands of non-native animals that were in zoos, tourist attractions, and private homes. Dozens of state wildlife officers from all over Florida were immediately sent to the ravaged area to capture the animals. Some escapees were dangerous, but most were helpless. Some will never be caught and will adapt and reproduce, creating unknown ecological repercussions.

Effects on Marine Waters

The coral reefs suffered damage to 60-foot depths in the worst areas, such as Triumph Reef near Elliott Key. Large brain and star corals broke off and rolled like bowling balls. In the shallow reefs, soft corals ripped from the bottom and staghorn and elkhorn branches snapped off. All were covered with a layer of silt. The worst damage seemed to be at the artificial reefs, where ships had been sunk to provide a substrate for coral to anchor to. Since the wrecks themselves were not anchored, they crashed around the ocean bottom, scraping all delicate sea life in their paths.

Other marine problems included increased turbidity for many days after the storm, leakage from the oil and gas tanks of sunken boats, and coastline erosion.

There was little disturbance to the seagrass beds in Florida Bay. Local environmentalists lamented that the hurricane did not flush out Florida Bay with fresh water as needed. That would have been one positive aspect of hosting a major hurricane. It would have ripped out the dying seagrass and created room for healthier recolonizing grasses.

Scientists will be assessing the effects of Hurricane Andrew on south Florida for many years. There will be visible signs of the hurricane for 50 years, such as windthrown trees and snapped off trunks. You can assess the effects in your own way when you visit the impacted areas.

II
HABITATS

CORAL REEF

Coral reefs are extremely valuable and complex marine eco-systems existing only in the warmer oceans of the world. They buffer the adjacent shorelines from storm waves, giving stability to the soil and vegetation, and they concentrate highly produc-tive and diverse marine life.

The only coral reefs in the continental United States are off the south Florida coast. Although occasional corals may be found north to about latitude 30°, reef development reaches its peak in the Florida Keys archipelago, where the warm Florida Current flows. Corals flourish on the eastern sides of continents, because the water is usually warmer from ocean currents. Clear water, with salinities about 35 parts per thousand, temperatures between 68–86°F, and a good food supply are the controlling environmental factors. Water clarity is essential because an inte-gral part of the reef-building coral organism is the one-celled alga known as zooxanthella, which requires sunlight to be able to photosynthesize. Thus, the clearer the water, the deeper the corals can live.

Corals are animals belonging to a group known as the coelen-terates, along with jellyfish, anemones, and hydroids; they are radially symmetrical. They have two life stages: asexual sessile polyps and sexual free-swimming medusae. The stony corals that form the backbone of the coral reef have hard, calcareous skeletons of calcium carbonate secreted by the soft polyp. Each polyp looks like a small sea anemone, with its base attached to a little limy cup that it hides in during the day. Unless you go snor-keling or diving at night, all you'll see is the rocklike limestone skeleton.

Elkhorn coral   [Larry Lipsky]

The coral reefs gained notoriety with the early European explorers and traders (particularly the Spaniards visiting Mexico) because of the danger of wrecking on the shallow "rocks." Many lives and cargoes were lost. Some early Keys residents supported themselves by salvaging shipments of gold, silver, and other valuables. Today, treasure hunters spend fortunes and lifetimes searching for the leftovers. While this may seem harmless enough, rarely can they sift and rake through the sediment without agitating and destroying the sea bottom life.

The Florida Keys reefs are the number one diving destination in the world. Not even the Great Barrier Reef in Australia garners as many underwater explorers. The Florida reefs are home to about 400–500 species of fish and numerous invertebrates, many of them extremely colorful, and all worth at least a glass-bottom boat or snorkel trip. Along with the benign-sounding names of angelfish, trumpetfish, butterflyfish, and rock beauties, a few names conjure up apprehension: barracuda, moray eel, southern stingray, and tiger shark.

Barracudas always look as if they are about to strike, but in reality they must swim with their mouths open to breathe. Barracudas have rarely been reported to attack humans, and incidents usually occurred when the water was murky or the person was wearing something shiny. Moray eels are dangerous only if you stick your hand in their hiding holes or crevices. Stingrays are a problem only if you step on them, so watch where you walk in shallow water. They camouflage beautifully, so you must be observant. And sharks are also very maligned. The rare shark attacks generally occur in murky water, when the victim is wearing contrasting tones, when there is blood or chum present, or when the victim is splashing around. In general, with a little common sense, the reef is a safe and enjoyable place to be.

On the other side of the coin, are the reefs safe from humans? Divers and snorkelers often don't realize how easily they can kill coral. Touching the surface of a coral head can injure the protective mucous membrane. Because water clarity is so essential, kicking up silt is also extremely destructive to coral. In heavily used areas, whole patches of coral have been killed, often by people trying to be considerate but bumping or kicking them by accident.

All corals, soft and hard, are protected by law from collecting. The coral souvenirs found in the local gift shops are imported from other countries, such as the Philippines.

You can see the coral reefs by visiting Biscayne National Park, Dry Tortugas National Park, Bahia Honda State Park, and John Pennekamp Coral Reef State Park.

MANGROVE

Four tree species in Florida are collectively considered mangroves: red mangrove, black mangrove, white mangrove, and buttonwood. Only red mangrove, however, is in the mangrove family (Rhizophoraceae). All four share the common traits of being very tolerant of salinity and water level changes. Thus they thrive in tidal zones and represent the transition between the sawgrass marshes and the ocean. Black and white mangroves

Pneumatophores of black mangrove   [Larry Lipsky]

have mechanisms to excrete salt (you can see the salt glands at the base of each white mangrove leaf), while red mangroves don't allow salt to enter their tissues. Thus, they do not need salt water and can thrive in freshwater habitats, though they are rarely found there because they are outcompeted by freshwater-adapted trees.

Red, black, and white mangroves have seeds, called propagules, that begin germination while still on the tree. Mangrove propagules and roots can anchor well only on low-energy shorelines—that is, shorelines with such shallow slopes that the waves and tides are barely noticeable. Much of Florida, especially the southwest coast, is like that. Another environmental requirement is a warm climate. Together, these reasons make south Florida home to the most extensive mangrove swamps in the United States.

Mangrove systems are vital as rich nursery grounds for fish and invertebrates, such as snook, tarpon, mullet, mangrove snapper, spiny lobster, pink shrimp, oyster, and blue crab. Many birds nest on mangrove trees, such as wood storks, roseate spoonbills, brown pelicans, and white-crowned pigeons.

Red mangrove trees are easily recognized by their prop roots which resemble a spider's legs. Black mangroves (and occasionally white mangroves) have pencil-like root appendages, called pneumatophores, that grow under the tree like new shoots of asparagus. Buttonwoods have no distinguishing root structures.

Mangrove trees are protected from human destruction by Florida law because of their vital roles as nursery grounds and shoreline stabilizers. Good places to see mangroves are Everglades National Park, Biscayne National Park, John Pennekamp Coral Reef State Park, Rookery Bay, Long Key State Recreation Area, J.N. "Ding" Darling National Wildlife Refuge, Collier-Seminole State Park, John U. Lloyd State Recreation Area, and MacArthur Beach State Park.

CYPRESS

Scattered throughout the freshwater wetlands of southern Florida (particularly in Big Cypress National Preserve, Corkscrew Swamp Sanctuary, Fakahatchee Strand State Preserve, A.R.M. Loxahatchee National Wildlife Refuge, and Everglades National Park) are vast stands of conifers known locally as cypress, although they are not true cypress but bald-cypress. The name "Big Bald-Cypress National Preserve" just wouldn't have the same ring. Although they are conifers, cypress shed their needles around November each year (hence look bald) and sprout new ones in February or March. Taxonomists argue whether the pond-cypress is a separate species or a variety of bald-cypress. They grow side-by-side at the Administrative Office of A.R.M. Loxahatchee NWR.

Cypress grow best with their roots in water and are the most flood-tolerant freshwater trees in Florida. Two of their most recognizable characteristics, the swelling buttresses and spindly "knees," are adaptations to their watery environment. The knees are projections of the roots that emerge from the water, probably to assist with respiration when the oxygen levels surrounding the roots are low. Although the seeds need to soak in water, they won't germinate under water.

Cypress dome

Cypress in south Florida are often found growing in one of two types of arrangements: domes and strands. Cypress domes are small, circular concentrations of cypress trees in a pond-like situation. The tallest trees are in the center where the water and soil are deepest, and the shortest trees are around the edges, giving a dome-like silhouette. This may be seen along the road to Flamingo. Cypress strands are long and narrow, sometimes many miles in length. Their alignment generally indicates the direction of water flow during high-water periods. Fakahatchee Strand is an excellent example. Another excellent example is the strand that formerly stretched 70 miles from Lake Okeechobee to Ft. Lauderdale. The largest intact remaining section is at A.R.M. Loxahatchee NWR and the current terminus is at Fern Forest Nature Center in Pompano Beach.

Vast cypress swamps across the southeastern United States were logged for their rot-resistant lumber. Cypress lumbering is still big business in some areas. Whole trees are killed to make wood chips for home gardens. The largest and oldest trees left are in Corkscrew Swamp, fortunately protected in perpetuity by the National Audubon Society. Some animals that use cypress habitats are swallow-tailed kites, turkeys, deer, otters, panthers, and bobcats.

PINELAND

Much of central and northern Florida is covered by pine flatwoods, but the pinelands of extreme south Florida are different. They are associated with the south Florida rocklands and are restricted to outcroppings of limestone. These limestone ridges have the highest elevations in the area.

Three main areas have pine rocklands: the Miami Ridge (from Miami to Long Pine Key in Everglades National Park), the lower Florida Keys, and Big Cypress Swamp. The Miami Ridge, composed of Miami limestone, is the largest outcropping. The Lower Keys (from Big Pine to Key West) are also on Miami limestone. In Big Cypress, the older Tamiami limestone is exposed. The bedrock in these pinelands is often exposed, and the soils are very shallow. Numerous pits, pinnacles, and solution holes are formed when the acidic leaf litter, mixing with rain water, dissolves the limestone. This is a very characteristic feature. The early settlers had to plant their crops in the solution holes, the only places with deep enough soil.

Pine flatwoods are found from Palm Beach County northward and occur on level, often low-lying and poorly drained, terrain. The main overstory species comprising the south Florida flatwoods is slash pine. The canopy is rather open, with a well-developed low shrub layer and an often sparse herbaceous layer. The plants are fire-adapted and able to withstand months of drought in the dry season and months of inundation in the wet season. Typical shrubs found in the flatwoods are staggerbush, wax myrtle, and saw palmetto. Some reptiles that are common in pine flatwoods are the pine woods treefrog, pine woods snake, eastern diamondback rattlesnake, eastern glass lizard, and Florida box turtle. Typical mammals are fox squirrels, eastern moles, black bears, gray foxes, and bobcats. Brown-headed nuthatches, red-cockaded woodpeckers, Bachman's sparrows, and pine warblers typify the bird life. Pine flatwoods can be

Slash pines

found at Corbett Wildlife Management Area, Dupuis Reserve State Forest, and Corkscrew Marsh.

Essential to the continual regeneration and success of the slash pines is fire. Without the lightning-caused fires that swept through the pines over the centuries, the pinelands would have reverted to hardwoods. Much of the original pinelands have been lost that way, since we newcomers have suppressed fires. The suppression has been direct in many cases and indirect in many others. The networks of roads, canals, and farms throughout the area have served as effective firebreaks. Natural resource managers in parks containing pinelands (such as Everglades and Big Cypress) practice prescribed burning, however, to keep the pines regenerating.

The understory vegetation of the pinelands must have fire-resistant roots or seeds to be able to regenerate quickly after fire. Saw palmetto, velvetseed, willow bustic, tetrazygia, varnish leaf, and myrsine are common. Coontie formerly was more common. Much of the vegetation is West Indian. Pinelands can be seen in Everglades National Park, Big Cypress National Preserve, Navy Wells Pineland Preserve, and National Key Deer Refuge.

Another major destroyer of pinelands has been lumbering. Unfortunately for the local variety of slash pine found, its wood is virtually insect- and rot-resistant, making it a blessed building material in south Florida. So much of early Miami and Homestead depended on this tree for construction that it is known locally as "Dade County pine."

SAWGRASS MARSH

The Everglades is a vast freshwater marsh generally known as a sawgrass marsh. Some of it is characterized by deep organic soils (peat) and hydroperiods of over nine months. Where hydroperiods are slightly shorter, marl substrates may form instead of peat. Sawgrass is the most common plant, but many other plants grow also. The name sawgrass is both accurate and misleading. The blades do indeed have saw-like edges, but the plant is a sedge, not a grass. Sawgrass may grow ten feet tall.

Mixed in with the sawgrass are spike rush, bladderwort, pickerel-weed, muhly grass, and many other wetland plants. Another species, the cattail, is becoming a scourge in the sawgrass marshes. Thriving on the added nutrients released upstream by the agricultural practices around Lake Okeechobee, the cattails are outcompeting the sawgrasses. This is devastating to the natural community because cattails deplete dissolved oxygen and can form such dense stands that wildlife movement and usage is impaired. A major conservation effort is underway to change farming practices to reduce the added nutrient load to the Everglades.

Sawgrass marshes can be seen in Everglades National Park,

Sawgrass marsh with basking alligator   [Larry Lipsky]

Big Cypress National Preserve, A.R.M. Loxahatchee NWR, Southern Glades Wildlife and Environmental Area, the Water Conservation Areas, and Fakahatchee Strand State Preserve.

HAMMOCK

Hammocks are "islands" of trees generally growing on higher elevations than the surrounding landscape or on lower elevations in pines where greater moisture reduces fire threats. They have evolved from lack of fire exposure and are the upland climax community. They grow on rich organic soils and are generally densely canopied and diverse in flora. Hammocks occur as bay heads, rock reefs, or tropical hardwood hammocks.

Bayheads, small clumps of hardwoods in the freshwater marshes, consist of such trees as redbay, sweet bay, wax myrtle, and coco-plum. Bayheads are found in the sloughs of Everglades National Park, A.R.M. Loxahatchee NWR, and Big Cypress National Preserve. From the air, their characteristic teardrop shape is apparent. The teardrop forms when water flowing down

Hardwood hammock   [Larry Lipsky]

the slough washes detritus from the upstream end and deposits it at the downstream end.

Rock reefs are ridges of limestone that create higher elevations that allow hardwood trees to flourish. From a bird's-eye view, a rock reef looks like a giant snake of trees crawling through the marsh. Rock Reef Pass in Everglades National Park is a good example.

Tropical hardwood hammocks, which exist from Miami south to the Keys, are dense stands of primarily West Indian trees. They are the only tropical hardwood forests in the continental United States and are probably the most endangered habitat in the country. Their demise began in the 1500s when early Spaniards began leveling the giant mahogany trees for shipment back to Europe. West Indian mahoganies, native to south Florida, have valuable wood. They are now on the state's endangered plants list. The current land-grab and development boom in this resort area is destroying what's left of this geographically limited habitat. Conservation groups must work very hard to save the remaining tropical hardwood hammocks. Everglades National

Park, Castellow Hammock, Crane Point Hammock, Matheson Hammock, Biscayne National Park, Key Largo Hammocks, and Lignumvitae Key all have tropical hardwood hammocks.

LAKE AND RIVER

One lacustrine feature is outstanding in the region—it is Lake Okeechobee, so large it is identifiable from space. Lake Okeechobee was formed in a depression in the bedrock. The lake is fed primarily by rainfall and inflowing rivers like the Kissimmee and Fisheating Creek. It has no natural outflowing rivers. Before the Hoover Dike and outflow canals were built, the water would slowly spill over the natural bank at the south end and flow imperceptibly through the Everglades. The lake is so shallow that the average maximum depth is less than 16 feet. Historically, it had a broad littoral zone in the northwest section—a zone with water only a few inches to 2 feet deep, where aquatic plants flourished and much of the animal life was concentrated. The artificial manipulation of water levels by humans, aided by pumping structures and a massive dike built around the entire lake, has destroyed much of this rich nursery, where many species of fish reproduce. The man-made connections from the lake to the Gulf Coast via the Caloosahatchee River and the St. Lucie Canal have greatly altered the lake's ecological components. Fishermen lament that the sport and commercial fisheries have suffered substantially from these alterations. The South Florida Water Management District, the U.S. Army Corps of Engineers, and numerous other agencies are working to restore the ecological functions of the lake, but it is a monumental project.

The rivers of south Florida are generally sluggish, due to the shallow grade. Whitewater exists only where a rock breaks the surface and causes a ripple. This feature made many rivers ideal for travel in the early days of Florida's history. The color of the water is usually brownish, caused by tannins from oaks and other leaves. The major rivers of south Florida are the Caloosahatchee, Loxahatchee, and Fisheating Creek. The 75-mile-long

The Loxahatchee River in Jonathan Dickinson State Park is one of Florida's only two designated National Wild and Scenic Rivers.

Caloosahatchee was named for the Calusa Indians that once cherished it as their larder and highway. It was channelized and connected to Lake Okeechobee by the famous swamp-drainer Hamilton Disston in the 1800s. Loxahatchee River and Fisheating Creek have been left nearly undeveloped and natural. During many months of the year, manatees feed in the rivers, sometimes swimming many miles inland.

ESTUARY

Where the rivers meet the oceans is a nebulous area of half land, half water. This is where the estuaries lie—those rich nurseries where many species of fish, crustaceans, and mollusks start their lives. Wading birds, dolphins, sea turtles, and small sharks are attracted to the bonanza of prey that thrive in the brackish water. Oysters, conchs, blue crabs, shrimp, mullet, and snook are some of the prey that humans are attracted to. The high productivity of commercially valuable fish and shellfish cannot be disputed or ignored. The estuaries include salt marshes, lagoons, seagrasses, and mangroves.

Salt marshes are one of the most highly productive habitats in the world. They are periodically flooded, treeless coastal areas that depend on the tides to wash in nutrients and flush out detritus regularly. They act as filters by keeping pollution from upland development from entering the estuaries. They stabilize the shore so that sediment isn't continually eroding. Cordgrass, saltwort, and glasswort are three plant species common to Florida salt marshes.

A lagoon is a confined body of water located near the ocean but with few openings to it. Water doesn't flush well from it and may remain for months or years, until an extremely high tide occurs.

Seagrasses are flowering plants that grow completely submerged and are rooted to the bottom. They provide the forage for such grazing animals as manatees, sea turtles, and some ducks. Turtle grass and widgeon grass are two examples. Many small fish, seahorses, crabs, and shrimp forage in the dense cover of seagrasses. Large seagrass beds may be seen in Florida Bay and Biscayne Bay.

This estuary in Naples shows the mangrove mixing zone where the fresh and salt water meet. A narrow strip of beach is evident in the upper left.

Some of the larger estuaries in south Florida are in Florida Bay, Whitewater Bay, and the rest of western Everglades National Park; Matlacha Pass, Estero Bay, Rookery Bay, and Biscayne Bay. They are exciting places to canoe because of the variety and abundance of wildlife, although novice canoeists should not attempt such trips due to the winds, tides, and risk of getting lost.

BEACH AND DUNE

Along the seaward sides of the barrier islands and the coasts without barrier islands, the beaches and dunes lie restlessly. They shift with the winds, the tides, and the currents. One storm alone can remove 6 to 8 feet of sand from a beach. When left unaltered by humans, however, beaches and dunes have a way of equilibrating—that is, where the sand is removed from one place, it is deposited somewhere else. The salt-tolerant dune plants (such as sea oats, sea purslane, and bay-cedar) are the

The low dune (left) at MacArthur Beach State Park protects the inland hammocks from storm tides. The beach is perfect for sea turtles to lay their eggs.

sole stabilizers. This is why it is so important for them to be left undisturbed. Sea oats, which can have 5-foot-deep roots and rhizomes that ably bind the sand, are protected by state law. Nesting sea turtles and oldfield beach mice depend on the sandy beaches and dunes.

Beaches and dunes can be seen at MacArthur Beach State Park, Hugh Taylor Birch State Recreation Area, John U. Lloyd Beach State Recreation Area, Bill Baggs Cape Florida State Recreation Area, Cayo Costa State Park, and Lovers Key State Park.

III
A PEEK AT THE
SPECIAL WILDLIFE

TREE SNAILS

Bejeweling our south Florida tropical hardwood hammocks are the colorful tree snails (*Liguus fasciatus*). There are 58 named color forms of *L. fasciatus*, some of which have vanished forever. These native snails, about two inches long, were once found from Collier and Broward counties southward to and including the Florida Keys.

General habitat destruction has eliminated many hammocks and the tree snails that depend on them. Development has destroyed hammocks outside park boundaries. In undeveloped areas, hammocks have burned because poor water management practices artificially simulate droughts that cause hotter and more widespread fires than the hammocks can withstand.

Tree snails grow during the wet season, mainly from May to September, adding more spirals of color. They feed on fungi, lichens, and mold growing on the bark of wild-tamarind, Jamaica dogwood, and other smooth-barked trees. Their role in the ecosystem is to clean mold and algae from trees. Courtship and mating occur from late June to September, and since tree snails are hermaphroditic (individuals possess both male and female sex organs), they need only find another tree snail to reproduce. Eggs are laid in the leaf mould in early fall and hatch at the beginning of the next rainy season.

During the dry winter months, the snails aestivate to protect their bodies from moisture loss by sealing themselves tightly to a tree. Removing a snail at this time will break the protective seal

Tree snail

and may cause the snail to die. Unless you see a tree snail actively crawling around, *do not touch it.* Occasionally a warm winter rain will reactivate a snail temporarily.

SPINY LOBSTERS

Unlike their northern cousins, spiny lobsters (*Panulirus argus*) have no pincers. Spiny lobsters are just as tasty, but the meat lies mainly in the tails. The name comes from the spines on the antennas and carapace.

Harvesting by commercial and sport lobsterers is permitted. The harvesting season runs from early August to March 30, when any person possessing a Florida saltwater fishing license and a lobster stamp may collect lobsters. Sport lobsters can use nooses, nets, or other noninjurious devices except traps. Traps are used only by commercial lobsters and may be seen during the off-season (April-July) stacked along the roadside in the Keys. Since egg-bearing and undersized lobsters must be released, such injurious methods of capture as spearing are not permitted.

Lobsters may be caught by snorkeling or scuba diving. While most people are ecologically conscientious when they capture lobsters, some are careless or destructive. During the day, these nocturnal creatures hide under ledges with their sensory feelers exposed. At the first sign of trouble, a lobster will withdraw as completely as possible into the rocks, making it difficult to extricate it. Impatient humans have torn the rocks open to free a lobster. Sometimes the rocks destroyed are actually living coral. People have even poured bleach into the rocks to drive lobsters out. Repeated poking and prodding at a group of lobsters may drive them out of hiding to walk across exposed sea bottom to find a safer place. This harassment makes them easy prey for sharks and other large predators.

The most conscientious way to capture a lobster is to: 1) learn to judge the relative size of a lobster by its antenna length, so you leave undersized ones alone; 2) try only two or three times to catch a lobster (after that, your chances of success decrease and you will be only be harassing it); and 3) leave the area if you see that the lobsters are becoming agitated and may try to flee for other cover. Check for egg clusters on the abdomens and immediately release any egg-bearing females.

Until 1992, the last full weekend in July every year was the opening weekend of the state's sport lobstering season. The mania that surrounded it was phenomenal. It is probably safe to say that it was traditionally the busiest weekend of the year in the Keys. Local merchants planned for it months in advance. Diving equipment and motel rooms were all taken. Travel on US 1 slowed to a crawl. In 1992, the state changed the season to begin in midweek, hoping to avoid the insanity of that intense two-day harvest. But the federal season (in waters three miles or more offshore) still begins that last weekend, so the situation is not much improved.

CONCHS

If you want to sound like a local, make sure to pronounce this "conks," ignoring the "h." You'll hear the word frequently, especially in the Keys. Queen conchs (*Strombus gigas*) are large marine snails, sometimes weighing as much as five pounds, found in shallow seagrass beds and sandy bottoms from southern Florida to the West Indies.

For centuries before Europeans arrived, conchs were harvested for food by the native people. The shells were used for tools, bowls, and ornaments. With the influx of white people to the southern end of the peninsula, conch harvesting reached exorbitant levels. Conchs were a staple diet for the early settlers to the Keys. In fact, a person who was born and raised in the Keys is often referred to as a "conch."

Queen conchs were also collected as souvenirs for tourists. Since 1985, conchs have been completely protected in Florida, because the conch population had reached critically low numbers. They are still harvested in the Bahamas and West Indies, which is the current source of conchs sold in Florida.

Conchs are considered a delicacy by some people. Others feel that their reputation is undeserved. True, it is a local specialty, but that is not equivalent to a delicacy. Conch meat is tough and rather bland. It has to be pounded into oblivion (or "cracked" as the locals call it) and spiced to the hilt to be tender and tasty enough to qualify as a delicacy. Cracked conch (pounded and breaded), conch fritters, and conch chowder (usually spicy) are the three most frequent conch items on local menus.

FLORIDA PANTHERS

While settlers from the 1600s to 1900s were systematically destroying the wilderness haunts of the panthers and hunting them almost to extinction (they were hunted for bounty until 1950), a small population survived in the untamed Everglades and Big Cypress. The Florida panther (*Puma concolor coryi*) is a subspecies of the mountain lion (or cougar), which once roamed almost every habitat from the Atlantic to the Pacific oceans. In 1958 the panther became protected in Florida, and in 1967 the U.S. Fish and Wildlife Service listed it as endangered. Today, only 60–70 panthers roam Florida, most from Lake Okeechobee south to Long Pine Key. The number is only slowly increasing in spite of intensive cooperative efforts by the U.S. Fish and Wildlife Service, Florida Fish and Wildlife Conservation Commission (FFWCC), the National Park Service at Everglades National Park and Big Cypress National Preserve, and other agencies. Radio-tagged panthers are being tracked by National Park Service staff in Big Cypress and Everglades National Park and by the FFWCC elsewhere. A captive breeding program has been established by the agencies listed above and is being conducted by zoos in Florida.

Known mortality is due primarily to collisions with automobiles and malnutrition. Of 65 panther deaths investigated from 1978 to 1997, 25 were the result of motor vehicle hits. Most occurred on Alligator Alley and Tamiami Trail, which is the reason the nighttime speed limit on those roads was 10 mph less than the daytime limit. It was also the "driving force" for designing wildlife underpasses as part of the conversion of Alligator Alley into I-75. Since the underpasses and the accompanying chain link fences that line both sides of the Interstate and State Road 2A were completed in 1991 and 1995, respectively, no panthers were killed on either road. Evidence from video cameras and tracks shows that panthers, deer, and other wild animals are using the underpasses.

A decrease in the number of white-tailed deer (the preferred diet) has caused the panthers to feed on smaller prey (such as raccoons and young alligators) in some areas. Panthers may survive on small prey items, but they are not likely to reproduce. Studies have shown that a female panther needs large prey items like deer to reproduce and raise her cubs. Another problem is arising with the switch from large to small prey. The fresh waters of the Everglades are contaminated with mercury, which becomes concentrated in predators of aquatic animals, such as raccoons, otters, and gators. Panthers that feed on such animals will acquire contamination themselves. In the Shark Slough drainage area of Everglades National Park, mercury levels of necropsied panthers have been at the toxic level and are responsible for at least one death.

Florida panthers resemble western mountain lions with a few minor differences. Panthers are more red than the tawny mountain lions, have a "cowlick" in the middle of their backs, and have a sharp bend in the distal end of their tails. They also are slightly smaller, with females weighing about 50–100 lbs. and males 100–140 lbs. Other subspecies introduced or escaped into Florida have intergraded with the native cats, so some individuals do not carry the above traits.

DOLPHINS

Anyone who spends a little time in a canoe or motorboat in the warm shallow waters of Florida Bay, Whitewater Bay, Biscayne Bay, or the Gulf Coast is likely to catch a glimpse of these beautiful creatures. Many people are treated to an even grander spectacle when the dolphins approach their boat. Such dolphins are either engrossed in feeding or are curious about the boat. Dolphins will occasionally drive fish into the shallow water around the tiny mangrove islands in Florida Bay, trapping the fish for easy feeding.

The Atlantic bottle-nosed dolphin is the most likely species of cetacean to be seen in these waters. This is the dolphin made famous by the television show "Flipper" that was filmed partly in the Keys. They are extremely intelligent animals; some scientists believe they are even more intelligent than humans.

Don't be alarmed if you find yourself staring at a menu in a seafood restaurant in south Florida and see "dolphin" as the catch of the day. That dolphin is a common fish harvested locally for human consumption. The bottle-nosed dolphin is a mammal that enjoys protection from intentional commercial harvesting. Many people also know it as a porpoise, although it is not a true porpoise.

Dolphins are common in Florida Bay and the Ten Thousand Islands year-round. Canoeists often see them. If you camp on a beach, such as at Cape Sable, Flamingo's walk-in sites, or the island campsites, you may hear a dolphin spouting at night when it surfaces to breathe.

MANATEES

One of the most treasured experiences a naturalist can have in Florida is to see a manatee. You could go to the Seaquarium in Miami or the Epcot Center in Orlando if you want to guarantee a close-up view, or you can take your chances and patience to the shallow south Florida coast and try to see one in the wild.

Manatees may be visible in south Florida any month of the year. The colder the winter, the more likely it is to find them around. They are sensitive to cold water, and a prolonged cold spell may drive them down from farther north in Florida.

Manatees are also known as "sea cows" because they are giant marine mammals that graze on underwater vegetation. They are even more harmless than cattle, because they have no hooves or horns to inflict injury. In fact, manatees are so defenseless and nonaggressive that they fall easy prey to humans. They lack defensive mechanisms because, as adults, they have no natural predators; most of the large sharks remain off-shore in deeper water than the manatees.

The greatest danger to manatees in the last hundred years is from humans. The early settlers in the Keys depended on manatees for fresh meat, since there was little land for raising cattle. A waterway through a patch of mangroves near Plantation Key is known as "Cowpens Cut," because (before refrigeration became a part of Keys life) the local people would trap manatees in the waterway by blocking the ends. The manatees would survive in this cow pen until their captors needed fresh meat.

Manatees are protected from hunting now, but they face more modern dangers. One is from motorboats. Since manatees are mammals and must breathe air, they forage in shallow water where they can surface easily. This puts them squarely in the path of motorboats, whose deadly propellers and hulls killed 83 in 1999 and 78 in 2000. In 2000, 94 manatees died from human-related causes (34% of the deaths), including getting crushed in water-control structures. Some comfort may be garnered from the record number of manatees (3,276) counted in January 2001, although excellent survey weather combined with a cold winter that concentrated the manatees contributed to the high count. State and federal conservation agencies are working on laws to add more slow-speed zones and manatee sanctuaries.

Finding a manatee will be a real challenge. Most manatees in Everglades National Park dwell along the mangrove-lined rivers and creeks between Flamingo and Everglades City. Thus, canoeing the Wilderness Waterway may provide some encounters. Try asking the rangers at Everglades or Biscayne National Parks if any have been seen recently. Occasionally manatees loll around the Flamingo Marina. Manatees utilize the Intracoastal Waterway from Miami-Dade County north. They also frequent the canals in the Keys where the residents treat them to fresh water from garden hoses. Because we humans have restricted the flow of fresh water coming down from the Everglades into Florida Bay and have destroyed the natural springs that once poured fresh water into nearshore seawater, manatees can sometimes be stressed for fresh drinking water. Although it is very tempting to attract a manatee by feeding or watering it, *it is illegal* and should not be done. Feeding and watering causes them to lose fear of humans and linger around canals and docks. This places them dangerously close to boats. Another place to look is the Florida Power and Light plant in Riviera Beach (561-552-8440). In the winter, FPL allows visitors to view their warm water discharge area where 75–100 manatees may be seen; call for an appointment.

If you are fortunate enough to encounter manatees while you are canoeing, don't panic. They are very docile and will swim sluggishly around you. If you make a sudden move that startles them, you'll be amazed at the energy they will display when they turn tail and flee. It is legal to swim with these gentle giants as long as you do not alter their behavior; for example, you can't cause them to swim in a direction other than that in which they were headed. If you find an injured or dead manatee, call the Florida Marine Patrol at 1-800-DIAL-FMP.

ALLIGATORS AND CROCODILES

Few creatures in North America evoke as much fear and curiosity as the two largest native reptiles, the American alligator and the American crocodile. So much myth and mystery surrounds them.

Alligators are found from North Carolina to Florida and west across the Gulf states to Texas. They number in the millions. Alligators prefer fresh water, although occasionally they'll be found swimming in salt water around the Ten Thousand Islands, Flamingo, and so on. Crocodiles, which number 600–1,000 and are endangered, have a limited U.S. range of southern Florida. Never venturing far from the sea, they prefer salt water but will occasionally wander into fresh water.

Differences in appearance are subtle. An alligator's skin color is black (although it often appears and is depicted as green), while a crocodile's is gray. A gator has a wide snout, while a croc has a narrow one with the large fourth tooth from the lower jaw protruding when the mouth is closed.

Neither species is especially dangerous to humans. The local crocs are not the same species as the so-called man-eaters of Australia, Africa, and India. Our crocs and gators are generally nonaggressive to humans (see "Alligators" under "Local Precautions").

Alligators disperse during the wet season and may be difficult to locate. During the dry season, they are easily seen at the Anhinga Trail, Eco Pond, and Shark Valley Tram Road in Everglades National Park as well as A.R.M. Loxahatchee National Wildlife Refuge, Big Cypress Bend, and Corkscrew Swamp Sanctuary. Crocodiles are quite rare and always difficult to find. Your best, but not necessarily reliable, bet is to drive down Card Sound

Road (the road from Florida City to North Key Largo) and stop just before the intersection with SR 905. There is a group of mangrove ponds known as the Crocodile Lakes which is part of the Crocodile Lake National Wildlife Refuge (no visitor services, contact National Key Deer Refuge for information). Look from the road with binoculars for a croc's head, preferably on a sunny day when the reptiles are basking. Also try the Buttonwood Canal by the Flamingo Marina or West Lake in Everglades National Park. One occasionally is seen at "Ding" Darling NWR's Wildlife Drive.

GOPHER TORTOISES

The gopher tortoise is the only species of land tortoise in the eastern United States. It is found throughout the drier parts of Florida and is known as a "keystone species" because so many other types of animals depend on tortoise burrows for survival. More than 100 species of vertebrates and invertebrates, including indigo snakes, gopher frogs, Florida mice, burrowing owls, lizards, and many insects, regularly retreat to the burrows or at least seek refuge during fires. As many as 250 more species have been found to use the burrows at least occasionally.

A tortoise digs its burrow with its shovel-like front feet. The burrow may be 10 feet deep and as much as 40 feet long. It provides cooling shade during the heat of the day and insulating warmth during cold fronts. The soil must be well-drained and loose, which is just the type of substrate that developers seek. This competition for scrub habitats has caused the tortoise to lose substantial habitat, such as the coastal ridges along the Atlantic seaboard. A distinguishing feature of the tortoise burrow is that the entrance is oblong, unlike the round armadillo and pocket gopher burrows. This accommodates the tortoise's shell, which is wider than it is high. A large sandy mound a foot or more in diameter next to the hole (called the "apron") makes it easy to spot gopher tortoise burrows.

An additional assault on gopher tortoises is a respiratory disease that can be passed from one tortoise to another. It may have been spread by the release of tortoises at Sanibel Island. The relocation of gopher tortoises from areas slated for development was a standard mitigation method until this disease was discovered. It is a clear example of what wildlife biologists have been trying to convince people of for years—that releasing an animal anywhere besides its own territory can have serious repercussions. Relocations of most species of animals by the U.S. Fish and Wildlife Service and state agencies are usually preceded by quarantines and veterinary examinations.

Gopher tortoises and their burrows may be seen at MacArthur Beach State Park, on Sanibel Island, and on Cape Sable. Anywhere you see prickly-pear cactus growing, you may see a gopher tortoise, since that's a favored food. Another favored food is gopher apple. Gopher tortoises are listed as a "Species of Special Concern" by the state.

SEA TURTLES

Florida is well-known to tourists for its thousand miles of white, sandy beaches with warm waters and gentle tides that make them perfect for sunbathing and swimming. For these same reasons, sea turtles also think Florida beaches are the greatest and flock by the tens of thousands to lay their eggs here every summer. The densities of nests along Florida's eastern coast are among the highest in the world. Sea turtles spend most of the year at sea or feeding along a coast. When the nesting urge overtakes the females, they head for their own birth place, even if it's thousands of miles away. No one knows for sure how they navigate, but it is probably a combination of methods which include using the sun, landmarks on the ocean floor, currents, and scents. If they do use olfactory cues to guide them to ancestral beaches, imagine how confused they are when we dump our sewage into the water.

Sea turtles have suffered directly from drowning in shrimp nets. The nets are dragged along the ocean floor, scooping up the scavenging shrimp. When a turtle gets caught, it drowns because it can't escape to the surface to breathe. Special devices that attach to shrimp nets and allow turtles to escape (called Turtle Excluder Devices or "TEDs"), are now mandatory for most shrimp boats. Plastic bags are another nemesis of those sea turtles which prey on jellyfish. Floating plastic bags so resemble jellyfish to the nearsighted turtles that they eat them and die from blocked digestive systems.

Causes of reduced nesting include the presence of garbage on the beach, which interferes with the turtles crawling on the sand and digging their nests. Another major culprit is fishing line, which entangles the turtles. The roots of the exotic tree Australian-pine prevent turtles from digging their nests. Hatching turtles become disoriented from artificial light cast onto the beach at night by adjacent hotels, condominiums, and parking lots. Since the hatchlings are drawn towards the lightest horizon, normally the ocean which reflects the stars and moon, the lights turn them inland where they die or are killed by cars, raccoons, snakes, opossums, and so on. Laws now prohibit such lighting in some places, but more towns need to abide.

Four species of sea turtles found in Florida are federally endangered and one is threatened. The latter is the most common nesting species, the loggerhead, which may weigh up to 350 pounds (although historically they reached 1,000 pounds). The reddish-brown carapace color is the easiest way to distinguish the species. Loggerheads lay their eggs from May through August on both the Atlantic and Gulf coasts.

Green turtles nest from June to September and only on the Atlantic coast. They are common in the Caribbean, where they were hunted for food for centuries. They have a green carapace and can weigh up to 450 pounds. Leatherback turtles are the largest of all living turtles; they can grow to 1,200 pounds. Their carapaces don't have scutes (thus no hard shell) but are covered instead by dark, leathery-looking skin. Although they are not hunted for their meat, their eggs are sought for food. The Atlantic hawksbill rarely nests in Florida but may be seen in Florida waters. The Atlantic ridley does not nest in Florida but feeds offshore.

The following places have sea turtle nesting beaches: Atlantic coast—MacArthur Beach State Park and other public beaches along Palm Beach and Broward County coasts; Gulf coast—Sanibel Island, sandy beaches from Ten Thousand Islands to Cape Sable, and Cayo Costa State Park.

RAPTORS

Many of the local raptors are familiar to people from other parts of North America because the birds have migrated from those parts. Red-shouldered hawks, kestrels, and ospreys are three examples. Our resident red-shouldered hawks, however, differ slightly in appearance by having pale gray heads.

Many raptors pass by the region as they migrate farther south to Central and South America. The peninsula of Cape Florida and the string of Florida Keys create the typical bottleneck that concentrates raptors before setting off across the Straits of Florida. Reluctant to leave the thermals, resting places, and prey that the land provides, the migrating raptors often linger around Cape Florida State Recreation Area and Boot Key in Marathon during September and October. A few species of special interest and where to find them are highlighted here.

Snail kites are medium-sized hawks that require shallow fresh water where their staple food, the apple snail (*Pomacea paludosa*), dwells on sawgrass, spike rush, and other aquatic plant stems. The kites are present in south Florida throughout the year, although they may concentrate at Lake Okeechobee and the Kissimmee region during periods of extended drought in the Everglades. It may take several years of suitable water levels after a marsh dries out to restore the snail populations and attract the kites again. A 2000 statewide survey revealed an estimated 2,800 kites, higher than any previous year. This is partly because biologists using radio transmitters on some kites have followed the birds to roosts they may not have otherwise found. The snail kite has been listed as an endangered species since 1967. The primary problem facing snail kites is the loss of habitat, both by development of wetlands and artificial manipulation of the remaining wetlands. Another problem is the presence of exotic plants such as water lettuce and water hyacinth. These cover the water and prevent the kites from seeing their prey, the snails. Look for the kites along the Tamiami Trail, especially near the Miccosukee restaurant by the Shark Valley entrance to Everglades National Park and along the Shark Valley Tram Road. They may occasionally be seen at the Headquarters area of A.R.M. Loxahatchee NWR. Also check the Solid Waste Authority's mitigation area in West Palm Beach at dawn or dusk: go west on 45th Street from I-95, passing the Turnpike and Haverhill Road, to Jog Road. Look around here or north on Jog. Before the plant was built, a roost of 372 kites was found in a drought year on the intended site. Modifications were made to the construction plans, and the roost area was left intact. Kites still roost there year-round (mostly June-October), though in smaller numbers. They also nest here in the summer.

Swallow-tailed kites are fairly common between March and August over pinelands and cypress and mangrove swamps. They may be seen gliding gracefully over the treetops, ready to seize a lizard or snake from a branch. Look for them around the pinelands of Everglades National Park.

Peregrine falcons may be seen in winter from the Observation Deck at Flamingo hunting over the mud flats or around concentrations of shorebirds on Cape Sable. Peregrines, merlins, and kestrels are often seen on Cape Florida and in the Keys during October.

Burrowing owls prefer open, well-drained short grass fields, including fallow farm land, college campuses, and airports. A drive along an inland road, such as SR 80, may produce the owls if you watch for levees or small mounds of dirt on which they like to stand. Burrowing owls may be seen at Kendall-Tamiami, Homestead General, Opalocka, and Marathon airports. For safety reasons, however, people are not allowed to walk around most parts of the airports. Therefore, get permission from the airport manager before walking off any road or parking lot. A safer way to see burrowing owls is to go to Sombrero Beach in Marathon (if southbound, turn left at K-mart, across from Crane Point Hammock Museum at MM 50). The owls nest at the park from February to August. Observe the ropes around the burrows; you can see into the nests from the ropes. The owls also nest at the Florida Atlantic University Campus in Boca Raton.

Ospreys have fortunately recovered since their perilous decline from the pesticide DDT in the 1950s and 1960s. They may be seen anywhere along the coast, Florida Bay, canals, lakes, and ponds. They often build their sturdy large stick nests atop utility poles; nests can be seen along US 1 in the Keys and US A1A on the east coast, although the nests are active only from December to May.

Bald eagles also have recovered since suffering the same fate as the ospreys and brown pelicans in the 1950s. In fact, their status was downgraded from endangered to threatened by the U.S. Fish and Wildlife Service in 1994. Bald eagles can be seen year-round near large bodies of water where they hunt for fish or steal prey from ospreys. Eagles nest on the larger islands in Florida Bay and the coastal prairies of Everglades National Park. Bald eagles may be seen around Mahogany Hammock because they roost near there (see Mahogany Hammock under "Everglades National Park") and Lake Okeechobee (a pair has been nesting along the Hoover Dike about two miles east of the Miami Canal in South Bay).

Short-tailed hawks are Florida specialty, although nowhere common. They are usually found in central Florida in the summer and south of Lake Okeechobee in the winter. Both light and dark color phases may occasionally be seen soaring in thermals with vultures, and they may be found in pinelands or grasslands, such as the various stops along the road to Flamingo.4

Crested caracaras are vulturelike members of the falcon family, with a range in the southeastern United States that is restricted to central Florida (they are also found in Texas and Mexico). Specifically, most are found north and west of Lake Okeechobee; they may occasionally be seen southwest of the lake. Caracaras prefer open grassland where they feed on carrion, especially if cabbage palms are present for them to nest on. There are only about 400 caracaras left in Florida because of habitat loss—citrus groves are taking over. As you drive along such roads as SR 80 or US 27, watch the utility poles and fence posts for a perching bird.

WADING BIRDS

One of the great attractions the Everglades holds for many people is the promise of seeing large flocks of graceful and colorful egrets, ibises, herons, spoonbills, and storks painting the sky at dusk. The protection of such flocks was one reason part of the region was set aside as a national park.

Prior to human intervention, approximately 100,000 pairs of wading birds nested in the southern Everglades. Now it may be only 10,000 pairs in a good year, a reduction of 90%. Part of the decrease was caused by the practice, in the late 1800s and early 1900s, of killing the birds during the breeding season to collect plumes for sale to the fashion moguls. Some species recovered, but some (like the reddish egret) have maintained low populations. The rest of the decrease has been attributed to water management practices that altered the quality, quantity, and timing of water that flowed through the Everglades. Those practices still continue and still affect wading birds.

Enough wading birds remain in the Everglades to make a thrilling sight. Species you are most likely to see are great blue heron, great white heron, great egret, snowy egret, little blue heron, tricolored heron, green heron, black-crowned night-heron, white ibis, roseate spoonbill, and wood stork. A small group of flamingos occasionally feeds in the mud flats off Snake Bight and Sandy Key in northwest Florida Bay, but this is the northern edge of their range and their occurrences here are sporadic. Debate exists over the origin of the flamingos in Everglades National Park; they may be escapees from a tourist attraction or wanderers from Cuba or the Bahamas.

One of the hardest-hit species is the white ibis, the most numerous wading bird in the state. Populations have plummeted so sharply from loss of habitat that the species was listed by the state in 1994 as a "species of special concern." This is an example of a wildlife agency trying to prevent a currently populous species from becoming endangered, when it is clear from the signs that it will. Remember the passenger pigeon, which numbered in the billions about a hundred years ago and is now extinct? It could happen again with the white ibis.

Another suffering species is the wood stork, which seems to be gradually pulling out of its population slump. Loss of wetlands contributed to its decline. Historically, the stronghold for wood stork nesting was south Florida. In the 1980s and 1990s, a new trend began emerging. Storks were shifting their nesting sites farther and farther north. Currently, central Florida holds the greatest concentration of stork colonies. The place to see wood storks in south Florida is Corkscrew Swamp Sanctuary.

Add the snowy egret to the list of declining populations—it never quite recovered from the slaughter for its plumes in the early 1900s. Snowy egrets do not seem as resilient as tricolored and little blue herons, with which they share feeding and nesting habitats.

Roseate spoonbills nest primarily in Florida Bay. After the nesting season, they disperse northward along the coasts (May through August). Then they may seen at MacArthur Beach State Park, "Ding" Darling National Wildlife Refuge, Flamingo, and other coastal areas.

The best time to see wading birds is from November to June, when the decreasing water levels concentrate the birds around their aquatic prey, and winter migrants are also present. The best places to look in Everglades National Park are the mud flats at Flamingo, Eco Pond at dawn or dusk, the Anhinga Trail, and the Shark Valley Tram Road. Also check the Ten Thousand Islands at Everglades City, the "18-Mile Stretch" of US 1 between MM 108 and MM 111, "Ding" Darling NWR, and A.R.M. Loxahatchee NWR. Wood storks usually nest at Corkscrew Swamp Sanctuary from January to June. Even if local foraging or water conditions prevent nesting, they should still be in the area.

RED-COCKADED WOODPECKERS

Known in birding lingo as "RCWs," red-cockaded woodpeckers were once characteristic of mature, open pine forests of the southeastern United States. They are dependent on extensive stands of old pines for foraging, 75- to 95-year-old pines for nesting cavities, a relatively dense population to accommodate their complex social structure, and fire to control understory growth. Due to commercial logging, RCWs were added to the federal endangered species list in 1970, but the species continues to decline. One reason is that timber companies prefer to harvest their stands in less time than it takes for the pines to mature. Another is that the RCWs' favorite tree, the longleaf pine, is not easily cultivated and is usually substituted with slash pines when stands are replanted.

RCWs depend on the presence of the red heart fungus (*Phellinus pini*), which is a heart rot found in older trees that makes the heartwood softer. These woodpeckers are unique because they excavate living trees for nesting cavities, as opposed to using dead trees as other woodpeckers do. It may take years to excavate enough for a nest, but the nest may be used for more than 50 years by succeeding generations.

Both sexes have white cheek patches and barred patterns on their backs. Males have a small red spot (cockade) on each side of head, displayed only during courtship and threatening behaviors. RCWs still persist in the slash pines of Big Cypress National Preserve and Corbett Wildlife Management Area.

FLORIDA SCRUB JAYS

Many of the wildlife species that inhabit the scrub of Florida are also found in the desert areas of the western United States, but not in the states in between. The scrub jay is one of them. Climatic changes caused the split that isolated the Florida jays, now considered a separate species from the scrub jays in the southwestern U.S. Although the two populations of jays look nearly identical (the Florida ones have a lighter forehead), the behaviors differ markedly. The threatened Florida birds have evolved a complex social structure with nest helpers, possibly because the amount of scrub habitat is so limited (even without development). With most other animal species that have territories, the young must leave their parents' territory and seek their own. These scrub jays, however, would die if they had to leave, because there is nowhere for them to go that isn't already taken by another jay. Thus, they stay with their parents and siblings, helping to raise more young by bringing them food and watching for predators. When death causes a territory to become available, one of the sons (evidence suggests the eldest) takes over. This results in a higher survival rate for the whole family.

Florida scrub jays prefer oak habitats along ridges (such as the Atlantic Coastal Ridge) where Chapman's oak, sand live oak, and myrtle oak provide their staple food, the acorn. The jays line their nests exclusively with the threadlike fibers from the leaf blades of the scrub palmetto. Territories cover about 20 acres each. Scrub jays may be found along the Atlantic Coastal Ridge in Palm Beach County.

IV
THE UNWANTED PESTS

For several reasons, Florida is host to scores of plant and animal species that are not native to the area. Some of these live nearly innocuous lives, but the majority interfere with the natural ecological balance. A few are extreme pests that must be eliminated or we may face ecological disaster.

EXOTIC ANIMALS

One reason for the high concentration of exotic animals in Florida is that the mild climate allows many people to keep exotic pets outdoors year-round. Occasionally these escape or are released illegally when the owners tire of caring for them. Another reason is that Miami is a major U.S. port of entry. Animals intended for the pet trade occasionally escape while docked or are released by the shippers if the animals were illegally obtained and the authorities are closing in. Many of these animals can survive and even reproduce around the suburbs. Florida has the highest number of exotic fish species in the lower 48 states, partly because the numerous wetlands contain warm water year-round and the canal network makes a convenient vehicle for widespread dispersal. Fish from the aquarium trade have spread this way. Adding to the problem is that, occasionally, even the state wildlife agency has intentionally introduced exotic fish to promote sport fishing and birds (such as the white-winged dove beginning in 1975, which had not bred in Florida prior to introduction) to promote sport hunting.

Parrots, snakes, and lizards are three types of animals that seem to adapt to the Florida suburbs with ease. Great flocks of monk parrots, budgerigars, and canary-winged parakeets (some of which destroy fruit crops) can be found in the skies and trees of southern Florida. Also established are muscovy ducks and spot-breasted orioles. Established lizards include brown anoles, Mediterranean geckos, and Indopacific geckos. Other exotic herps found in the area include giant (marine) toads, Brahminy blind snakes, and assorted boas and pythons.

Muscovy ducks have become a nuisance around ponds near development. These ducks, native to Central and South America, are the only species of duck in the world besides mallards to be domesticated. Their black or white (or both) plumages and red warty faces are familiar around artificial ponds, which are abundant in south Florida. In this flat, low-lying terrain, builders must first dredge an area to provide the fill they need to build upon. This creates a depression that soon fills with water. As the new homeowners gaze across the barren pond, they yearn for something living to entertain them. They obtain one of the few animals that can survive in this artificial habitat—domesticated ducks. The muscovies and domesticated mallards do just fine, reproducing exponentially until the pond and all the surrounding lawns are filled with their droppings. Then neighbor confronts neighbor, tempers flare, and soon there are lawsuits over getting rid of the ducks!

Two introduced mammals that have become nuisances are the armadillo and feral hog. In 1943, a man brought a female nine-banded armadillo and six young from his native state of Texas to Wakulla, Florida. These spread, and probably others were introduced as well. Eventually, all the drier parts of Florida (except the Keys) became home to this prehistoric-looking animal. Although inoffensive, the omnivorous armadillos are considered a nuisance species. Their primary food is insects and other invertebrates, but they will consume fruits and berries, seeds, mushrooms, and eggs. The eggs may be those of game birds, freshwater turtles, sea turtles, lizards, snakes, salamanders, or other animals that lay eggs on the ground. Their method of foraging by rooting around in the leaf litter destroys the integrity of that forest stratum. Armadillos do not appear to have good defenses against fires and often perish in them. However, they have few other enemies, since their armored skin protects them.

Feral hogs (a.k.a. wild hogs and feral pigs) have been established in the southeastern United States for 400 hundred years—so long that many people assume they are native. As descendants of the barnyard pigs that the Spanish explorers brought, they have thrived on the mast crops, ground-dwelling animals, and whatever other foods they can dig up. It is never difficult to tell when pigs have been around—the ground looks like a rototiller played hop-scotch in the woods. These telltale "rootings" may be all you see of these nocturnal animals. Feral hogs will eat almost anything edible they encounter: eggs, snakes, and lizards, possibly including indigo snakes and other listed species. Some state parks have policies to eradicate the pigs from their lands. They cannot be trapped and released elsewhere without similar consequences. The carcasses are donated to state institutions for food. However, the pigs reproduce too fast for eradication efforts to keep pace. They will remain a pest for a long time to come. The only benefit that can be argued in their favor is that they are good prey for panthers. You can find feral hogs by walking at night wherever you see signs of recent rooting (such as Dupuis Reserve State Forest and Corbett Wildlife Management Area). Listen for gruntings and look with a flashlight, but keep your distance, for they are not domesticated anymore.

EXOTIC PLANTS

No animal has created as much turmoil as have some of the invasive, non-native plants in south Florida. More than a few biologists feel that they could be the ultimate destroyer of valuable habitat. Some of the plants were introduced from tropical and subtropical areas around the world and are cultivated in south Florida gardens. A number of plants were introduced for functions that were desirable at the time, such as coastal windbreaks and "swamp straws" (because they drink more than their share of water from the ground). These plants have now been classified as pests.

Some exotic plants are more destructive than others. It is important to distinguish between "noninvasive" (which do not seem to be pests yet) and "invasive" plants (which are pests). A noninvasive plant will not reproduce or spread on its own—it needs horticultural help from humans. Many ornamental trees are noninvasive outside their home ranges. An invasive plant, however, can spread entirely on its own, either reproductively (through seeds or spores) or vegetatively (by runners or budding). The main reason the invasive plants spread so rapidly is that they have no natural enemies here as they do in their places of origin.

A word of caution is in order to those readers who feel safer now about planting noninvasive exotics in their yards. Biologists are finding that some exotic plants that were originally noninvasive have gradually adapted to local conditions and become invasive! Thus, the only truly safe plants for your garden are the native ones.

The U.S. Fish and Wildlife Service, National Park Service, U.S. Department of Agriculture, and state and county agencies have exotic plant removal programs aimed at invasive exotic species; millions of dollars are spent annually. Programs include finding biological controls (such as insects, bacteria, or fungi) that will attack only the intended plant and not our native ones. It's a never-ending battle to eliminate plants that spread faster than they can be removed.

Three exotic plants have made the local conservationists' "most wanted to kill" list for decades. They are melaleuca, Brazilian pepper, and Australian-pine. Several more are gaining momentum.

Melaleuca

Melaleuca (also called punk tree or cajeput) was introduced to Miami in 1906 during the early swamp-draining era. Seeds of this tree were broadcast-spread by air over the Everglades in the 1930s to facilitate draining the marsh. A striking tree with papery white bark, melaleuca uses several times more water than our native vegetation does. A large stand of melaleucas steals water from and crowds out native plants, thereby out-competing them. The phenomenal growth and reproductive rates, coupled with the variety of habitats it can grow in and the difficulty in killing it, make melaleuca one of the most formidable environmental enemies south Florida faces today. Currently, there are no known methods of large-scale eradication of these "swamp straws," except for pesticides. A biological control may be the best solution. Fortunately, melaleuca was added to the Federal Noxious Weed List in 1992, the first "weed" to be added in over 12 years. Henceforth, transportation of the plant into the U.S. and between states requires a permit from the U.S. Department of Agriculture and other restrictions to prevent its spread. Stands of melaleuca can be seen along the Turnpike in Broward County, along Krome Avenue between Homestead and the Tamiami Trail, and along the Tamiami Trail west of Krome.

Brazilian pepper

Brazilian pepper is a fast-growing, quick-spreading small tree that arrived from Brazil around 1941. Its clusters of bright red berries ripen around Christmas, and some people collect the branches (and encourage their growth) for Christmas wreaths. However, since Brazilian pepper is related to poison ivy (same family), touching it causes dermatitis for some people. The berries provide food for raccoons, robins, and other animals, but this benefit does not outweigh the detrimental properties. It grows as an extraordinarily dense understory tree, impenetrable by all but the smallest animals. Brazilian pepper is now one of the most common plants along the roads of south Florida, where it is also known as Florida holly. Once Brazilian pepper becomes established, it is virtually impossible to eradicate, since it is resistant to fires, floods, and droughts. Approximately one million acres of Florida are infested with it.

Australian-pine

Australian-pine, also known as Casuarina, is from Australia but is not a true pine. In fact, it's not even a conifer. Its wispy needles and small conelike fruits are reminiscent of pine trees. Australian-pines were introduced as soil retainers and windbreaks along the coast and canals. They outcompete native trees, but their weak branches make nesting risky for large birds, such as swallow-tailed kites, which prefer the native pines. The roots of Australian-pine growing along the beaches interfere with sea turtle and crocodile nesting. As windbreaks, they turned out to be worse than worthless when it really mattered. When Hurricane Andrew struck, the same Australian-pines that were planted along canals as windbreaks snapped in pieces and piled in the canals in a tangled mass. Hundreds of miles of canals were clogged. The resulting intensive and expensive debris removal prompted the South Florida Water Management District to cut the standing trees along the canals outside Andrew's path to prevent wind damage in the future. The Florida Department of Transportation spent $7 million removing Australian-pines from roadsides. Some local town ordinances now require homeowners to fell their Australian-pines.

Aquatic plants

Exotic aquatic plants have plagued Florida for decades by clogging waterways, interfering with fish reproduction, and reducing the dissolved oxygen. The latter effect has caused numerous fish kills. Three such plants are water hyacinth (from Venezuela), hydrilla (introduced from Sri Lanka for the aquarium trade), and water lettuce. All spread uncontrollably when dumped into canals. Water hyacinth was spread from *one plant*, by a woman who brought it back from an exposition in New Orleans. She thought it would look pretty in her backyard fish pond by the St. Johns River. Some waterways have been rendered useless to wildlife and humans by these plants forming a solid mat on the surface, which blocks access to the water and prevents sunlight from penetrating to the native submersed plants. Hydrilla, which spreads only vegetatively in Florida, covers more than 65,000 acres, or about half of the state's public waterways. Boaters inadvertently spread these plants when the plants hitch rides on their boats or on their trailers, which then travel to uninfested waters.

Climbing vines

Another group of plants, known as the climbing vines, is rapidly becoming the newest scourge in Florida. Most of these invasive plants were introduced as house or garden plants, and they thrive in the warm humid climate. Two of the many compounding effects of Hurricane Andrew were to waft seeds and plant parts west into pristine hammocks where they could become established and to open the canopy in the already affected areas so that the vines could "explode." Some climbing vines have indeterminate growth, which means that they can keep growing as long as they have nutrients and proper weather. In comparison, determinate growers never grow more than a certain genetically determined height. Thus, a climbing vine can grow up a tree trunk to the upper branches, resulting in a forest of blanketed trees killed by vines that shaded the sunlight from their leaves. Examples of such vines are the air-potato and Old World climbing fern. Air-potato and other climbing vines may grow a foot a day. Air-potato is rampant in Broward's and Dade's county parks. Climbing fern is easily seen at Hungryland Slough.

Bromeliads grace every cypress tree along the boardwalk at A.R.M. Loxahatchee NWR.

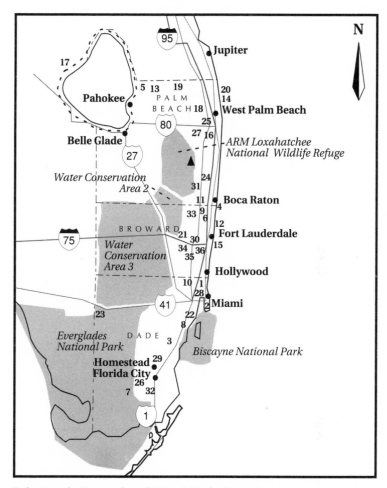

Palm Beach, Broward, and Miami-Dade Counties

1. Arch Creek Park
2. Bill Baggs Cape Florida State Recreation Area
3. Castellow Hammock Nature Center
4. Deerfield Island Park
5. Dupuis Reserve State Forest
6. Easterlin Park
7. Everglades National Park Visitor Center
8. Fairchild Tropical Garden
9. Fern Forest Nature Center
10. Greynolds Park
11. Gumbo Limbo Nature Center
12. Hugh Taylor Birch State Recreation Area
13. J.W. Corbett Wildlife Management Area and Hungryland Slough
14. John D. MacArthur Beach State Park
15. John U. Lloyd State Recreation Area
16. John Prince Park
17. Lake Okeechobee Hoover Dike Trail
18. Loxahatchee Preserve Nature Center
19. Loxahatchee River Canoe Trail
20. Marinelife Center of Juno Beach and Loggerhead Park
21. Markham Park
22. Matheson Hammock Park
23. Miccosukee Indian Village
24. Morikami Museum and Gardens
25. Mounts Botanical Garden
26. Navy Wells Pineland Preserve
27. Okeeheelee Park and Nature Center
28. Oleta River State Recreation Area
29. Redland Fruit & Spice Park
30. Secret Woods Nature Center
31. South County Regional Park
32. Southern Glades Wildlife & Environmental Area
33. Tradewinds Park (and Butterfly World)
34. Tree Tops Park
35. T.Y. (Topeekeegee Yugnee) Park
36. West Lake (and Ann Kolb Nature Center)
▲ Entrance and Visitor Center for Loxahatchee NWF

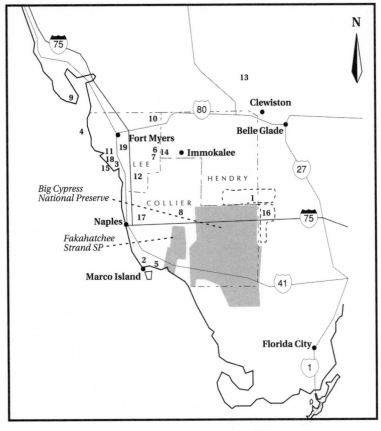

Lee, Hendry, Collier, and western Miami-Dade Counties

1. Ah-tha-thi-ki Museum at the Big Cypress Seminole Indian Reservation
2. Briggs Nature Center and Rookery Bay
4. Cayo Costa State Park
5. Collier-Seminole State Park
6. Corkscrew Marsh
7. Corkscrew Swamp Sanctuary
8. Florida Panther National Wildlife Refuge
9. Gasparilla Island State Recreation Area
10. Hickey's Creek Canoe Trail
11. J.N. "Ding" Darling National Wildlife Refuge

12. Koreshan State Historic Site
13. Lake Okeechobee Hoover Dike Trail
14. Lake Trafford Park
15. Lovers Key State Recreation Area
16. Miccosukee Indian Reservation
17. Naples Nature Center
18. Sanibel-Captiva Conservation Foundation
19. Six Mile Cypress Slough Preserve

Note: Carl E. Johnson Park (#3 in earlier editions) has been incorporated into Lovers Key State Recreation Area.

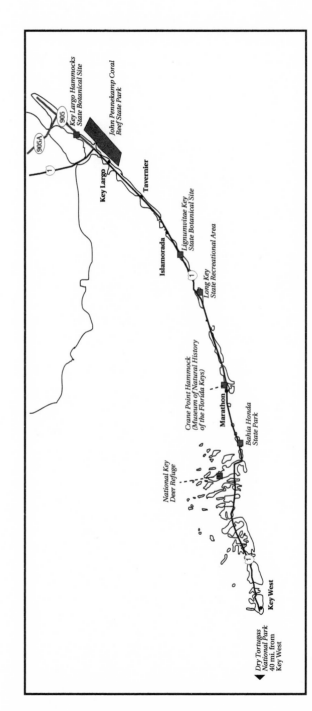

The Florida Keys (Monroe County)

V

NATURAL AREAS: FEDERAL LANDS

ARTHUR R. MARSHALL LOXAHATCHEE NATIONAL WILDLIFE REFUGE

The Everglades is a vast area. While it once covered almost 4,000 square miles, it now covers less than half of that. Part of what remains (221 square miles or 147,392 acres) is contained in A.R.M. Loxahatchee National Wildlife Refuge. The refuge contains the largest remaining undisturbed northern Everglades habitat. In fact, it was established in 1951 to protect this unique habitat, which is surprisingly different from the southern Everglades. The southern 'glades is fairly open, with relatively few scattered large tree islands and shallow peat. The refuge contains thousands of small tree islands and very deep peat—up to 12 feet thick. While the tree islands in the south are formed on the limestone bedrock that breaks the water's surface, tree islands in the refuge are formed from floating peat mats that eventually get rooted to the bottom.

The refuge, which includes Water Conservation Area 1, is located downstream of one of the country's most valuable agricultural areas. The agricultural runoff has caused water pollution, leading to a severe habitat imbalance in the part of the refuge that receives these excessive nutrients. As a result, the U.S. Department of Interior has undertaken a massive multifaceted program to clean the water before it enters the refuge and the rest of the Everglades.

Much of the refuge is off-limits to the general public. This prevents disturbance to the wildlife and the habitat. The primary visitor facilities (Visitor Center and trails) are at the

A baby alligator and a Florida redbelly turtle sun themselves in front of the Visitor Center at A.R.M. Loxahatchee NWR.

Headquarters Area. A 30,000-acre public use area at the refuge's southern entrance (Hillsboro Recreation Area) is also available for day use. This part of the shallow marsh requires a boat to access. It is used primarily by anglers year-round and waterfowl hunters from Thanksgiving to mid-January.

Loxahatchee is undeniably a wetland, but the levees and the boardwalk through the cypress swamp provide hikers a way to see some of the refuge while keeping their feet dry. Alligators, turtles, limpkins, anhingas, and purple gallinules are common residents. River otters and gray foxes are occasionally seen. Bobcats and deer roam the levees, especially at dusk. Wood storks and many other wading birds forage in the marsh all year. Black-necked stilts are easily seen in the summer, when they nest in the impoundments. Thousands of ducks spend the winter at the refuge, including fulvous whistling-ducks, mottled ducks, ring-necked ducks, and blue-winged teal. The refuge is designated as "Critical Habitat" for the endangered snail kites, which nest on the refuge in some years. Snail kites are most likely to be seen between March and May.

Location, Mailing Address and Phone

Main entrance (Headquarters Area): From I-95 (Exit 44) or Florida's Turnpike (Exit 86), take CR 804/Boynton Beach Boulevard west to US 441/SR 7. Turn left, go south 2 miles, and turn right at refuge sign (Lee Road). Hillsboro entrance: From Turnpike (Exit 71), go west to US 441/SR 7, turn right, go 2 miles to CR 827/Loxahatchee Road, turn left, and go 6 miles to end. Loxahatchee Road is 12 miles south of Lee Road via US 441/SR 7.

10216 Lee Road, Boynton Beach 33437; 561-734-8303 or 561-732-3684; e-mail r4rw_fl.lxh@fws.gov; http://loxahatchee.fws.gov/

Facilities and Activities

Self-guided nature trails, wildlife observation and photography, canoeing, boating (except airboats), bicycling, Visitor Center. Open daily, sunrise to sunset. Visitor Center hours vary (core hours 9 AM to 4 PM); closed Mondays and Tuesdays in summer. Canoe trail usually closed in summer. U.S fee area. Local canoe outfitter: Loxahatchee Canoeing, Inc.; 561-733-0192; www. canoetheeverglades.com

Nature Trails (Headquarters Area)

The profusion of bromeliads along the Cypress Swamp Boardwalk (0.4-mile loop, handicapped-accessible) is impressive. Every tree is festooned with plants—cardinal air plants, giant wildpines, needle-leaved wildpines, reflexed wildpines, and reddish wildpines to name some. A red lichen known as *baton rouge* (meaning "red stick", after the lichen-covered trunks) brightens the shady cypress swamp. Otters often play in front of visitors on the boardwalk. One year, an alligator made her nest next to the end of the boardwalk, in full view of visitors. Also that year, a great horned owl nested in a bromeliad directly over the boardwalk.

The Marsh Trail (0.8-mile loop, handicapped-accessible) circumnavigates a 31-acre impoundment. Wading birds, waterfowl, turtles, and alligators are frequently seen. An observation tower is located about halfway around. Other impoundments are easily accessible, allowing for several miles of hiking. In spring, nesting anhingas and great blue herons are occasionally seen from the levee. Allow at least an hour.

Some of the levee that surrounds Water Conservation Area 1 is accessible to pedestrians and bicyclists. A 12-mile section between the Headquarters and Hillsboro areas runs along a canal and provides views of the marsh.

The Visitor Center has a 50-seat auditorium where a variety of videos and slide shows are presented upon request. It contains exhibits of wildlife of the Everglades. The book store concentrates on local natural history.

Canoeing

The best way to see the refuge is via the canoe trail at the Headquarters Area. This 5.5-mile loop passes through wet prairies and deeper sloughs of northern Everglades habitat. In April and May, tricolored and little blue herons occasionally nest in the willows along the trail. Snail kites may infrequently be seen. Listen for the "click, click, click" of cricket frogs any time of day. Look for the clumps of pearl-like eggs of the apple snail on blades of sawgrass or pickerel-weed. The trail has a chemical toilet and picnic platform. Allow about one hour per mile, since submerged vegetation often slows paddling. Call ahead to see if the trail is open; it is often closed in summer when floating and submerged plants become too dense. No rentals available; no motors allowed.

Visitors may also canoe along the perimeter canal at the edge of the refuge. Long, straight distances can be paddled—it is 52 miles around! However, since camping is not permitted, only boats with motors can circumnavigate the entire distance. Canal canoeists must share the water with the occasional motor boat. Water lettuce and water hyacinth sometimes hinder paddling.

Bicycling

A 12-mile trail runs atop the unpaved L-40 Levee between Headquarters and Hillsboro. Mountain bikes are recommended.

Best Time of Year

November to April for observing birds and other wildlife, canoeing, and hiking. Canoe trail usually closed in summer; perimeter canal open all year. Mosquitoes rarely noticeable, except in summer twilight.

Pets

Not allowed.

BIG CYPRESS NATIONAL PRESERVE

Big Cypress is a national preserve, not a national park, and as such it has fewer restrictions than a national park. The preserve was established partly as a buffer to Everglades National Park and partly for its own ecological and recreational value. An immense international airport and satellite city were almost built here in the early 1970s to ease the burden on Miami International Airport. Environmentalists blocked the original plan but had to settle for a training airport north of Tamiami Trail, the Dade-Collier Training Airport (where commercial jet pilots practice take-offs and landings). Increased cypress logging, cattle ranching, and oil drilling added to the pressures.

The National Park Service was able to acquire 570,000 acres in 1974 but had to make concessions to landowners. These included allowing the existing hunting camps to be retained by the owners, allowing off-road vehicles (such as airboats and swamp buggies), hunting, and environmentally-safeguarded mining and oil-drilling. The Big Cypress National Preserve Addition Act, passed by Congress in 1988, added 146,000 acres in December 1996.

The name "Big Cypress" comes from the extent of the cypress strands, rather than the size of the trees. Most of the preserve consists of bald-cypress, and very little is old-growth. Most people see the preserve only from the pavement of Tamiami Trail or Alligator Alley, both of which bisect it. The Florida Trail (an unpaved hiking trail) has its southern terminus here. Pinelands and marshes comprise much of the remaining preserve.

Six species of endangered animals can be found within the preserve: wood stork, snail kite, red-cockaded woodpecker, Cape Sable seaside sparrow, West Indian manatee, and Florida panther. The preserve is the last stronghold in extreme south Florida for the red-cockaded woodpecker and the panther, both of which still breed here.

The southern end of the preserve (south of Tamiami Trail) experienced severe hurricane winds from Andrew. Damage to buildings (primarily ranger residences) was substantial. The Loop Road was closed for several weeks to clear fallen trees. The hammocks in the southwest were flattened. The park reopened quickly after the storm.

Location, Mailing Address and Phone

The Visitor Center is on Tamiami Trail (US 41), 37 miles west of Krome Ave. and 21 miles east of State Road 29. The Headquarters is on Tamiami Trail in Ochopee, 18 miles west of the Visitor Center. The eastern preserve boundary is 25 miles west of Krome Ave. on Tamiami Trail and the western boundary is just east of (and parallel to) State Road 29.

HCR 61, Box 11, Ochopee 34141; 239- 695-2000
Visitor Center 239-695-4111

Facilities and Activities

Visitor Center, hiking trails, camping. Because this is a national preserve, visitor facilities are intentionally minimized. No lodging or food facilities; nearest food service is at Ochopee (21 miles west). Visitor Center open daily 8:30 AM to 4:30 PM, except Christmas. No fee for admission or primitive campsites.

Visitor Center

At the Visitor Center, you can obtain backcountry information for camping (permits not required), permits for off-road vehicles (required), and hiking information.

Displays in the Visitor Center include tree snails and stuffed animals. A good selection of nature books and videos is sold. The 15-minute movie is shown on request in a small auditorium at the Center and explains the wet-dry season cycle in the Big Cypress area.

Camping

There are three primitive campgrounds along Tamiami Trail, maintained by the National Preserve. They have no hookups and no running water; there are chemical toilets in winter only. They are good for self-sufficient camper vehicles and tents and the maximum stay is 14 days. There are three primitive camp-grounds along the Loop Road. Dona Drive Campground on Tamiami Trail has potable water and a dump station (fee charged).

Tent camping is allowed on the Florida Trail. The safest way for you to ensure having a dry place to sleep is to carry a light-weight string hammock. The two primitive campsites desig-nated on the official map are on higher ground, but they have no shelter or cooking grill. Campfires are permitted with deadwood found on the ground. There is no guaranteed source of drinking water along the trail. You must bring your own potable water or methods to purify water.

Trails

The well-known Florida Trail begins or ends here, depending on your point of view. It stretches intermittently northward through the Florida peninsula and westward into the Panhandle. The section in Big Cypress (from Tamiami Trail to Alligator Alley) is about 28 miles long. Access from Alligator Alley is possible from a rest area and recreation access point. Access from the south end is at the Visitor Center.

From the Visitor Center, the trail leads north through cypress, pinelands, marshes, and hardwood hammocks. Even in the dry season, parts of the trail can be wet. Off-road vehicles are permitted to cross the trail but may not traverse it. Keep your eyes open for deer, feral hogs, bald eagles, swallow-tailed and snail kites, alligators, and possibly even a Florida panther. Two primitive campsites are available along the trail (see "Camping" above). A loop day- or overnight-hike of 13 miles or one of 26 miles can be done from the Visitor Center. Let a ranger know your intentions if you're leaving your car parked overnight.

Another section of the Florida Trail, eight miles long, is on the south side of Tamiami Trail and across from the Visitor Center in an area known as the Loop Road Unit. It is not well-marked on the roadside—look directly across from the eastern entrance to the Visitor Center parking lot to find this very narrow trail. This section is better for day hikes because off-road vehicles are not permitted anywhere in the Loop Road Unit. It's a beautiful section of trail, with bromeliad-festooned bald-cypress shading the way. The trail is wet until mid or late winter (south section year-round). Contact the Florida Trail Association (see "Other Sources of Information") for more information on the Big Cypress National Preserve section of the Florida Trail.

Loop Road

One way to see part of the Loop Road Unit is by driving the Loop Road. The Loop Road is a 26-mile stretch of narrow road between Forty-Mile Bend (near the Tamiami Ranger Station) and Monroe Station on the Tamiami Trail. The nine miles east of the Environmental Education Center is paved and is gentle on city cars. West of there, however, the road is pock-marked with potholes and occasional puddles, so expect to average about 15 mph. That means it may take over an hour to drive the unimproved section. Add a little extra time for stopping to view wildlife.

Although the Loop Road is entirely within preserve boundaries, it is a county road (the only Monroe County road on the mainland), and you will see homes of people that live along the road.

Aside from the homes, the road goes through some wild country, and you may see otters, bobcats, wild turkeys, snakes, wading birds, sandhill cranes, and rarely, a panther. Just west of Pinecrest is an environmental education center for Everglades National Park. Its main function is to teach local school children, so there is nothing of interest to the drop-in visitor.

The short Hammock Nature Trail (on the north side of the road, opposite the Education Center gate) leads to an old whiskey still and is open to visitors. The trail can be covered in a leisurely 15 minutes (not handicapped-accessible). Look for strap fern, white stopper, and gumbo-limbo.

This road is worth the trip if you have the time and a car that can take potholes. In the summer, the road may be flooded, so call ahead to the Visitor Center for the conditions. At any time of the day or night you'll probably see something interesting. If you go at night, make sure your car can make it out on its own.

Turner River Road

Several unpaved graded county roads in the preserve may be worth driving for wildlife viewing. One such road is the Turner River Road/CR 839, located 14.5 miles west of the Visitor Center and 4.1 miles east of Big Cypress Headquarters. It runs straight north for about 18 miles, and a borrow canal, which provided fill for the road, runs parallel the entire length. This road is not likely to flood but can get dusty or muddy. White ibises roost in the trees beside the canal. Panthers still roam this area, and the very lucky person may catch a glimpse of one.

Best Time of Year

Hiking the Florida Trail is better in the winter and spring (January–April). The summer rains usually flood the trail, and hiking is reduced to slogging through mosquitoes with nary a dry spot to pitch a tent. Driving the Loop Road is good year-round for seeing wildlife, but heavy rainfalls cause some flooding of the road in summer. Hunting seasons of different types (waterfowl, small game, turkey, archery) run from September to April. But the main big game season (deer and feral hog) occurs during the period from mid-November to January 1 and is not a good time to wander around the preserve. Many hunters park their cars along the Loop Road and set out from there. Call the Visitor Center in advance for local flooding conditions and hunting seasons. *If you hike during deer season, wear bright orange clothing.*

Pets

Allowed in campgrounds on a leash; not allowed in Visitor Center.

BISCAYNE NATIONAL PARK

This is truly one of the undiscovered gems of the National Park system! In 1968, President Lyndon Johnson turned the barrier islands into a national monument to protect them from inevitable development. After an enlargement in 1974, and another in 1980, it became a national park. Ironically, the coral reef, the northernmost in North America, was not the original concern. Now it is the main attraction. Farther down the Keys, the barrier islands (such as Key Largo, Plantation Key, and Upper Matecumbe) are developed and cause pollution problems to the adjacent reefs. Here, since the barrier islands are almost totally pristine, the coral is healthy and the water crystal clear. Compared with the Pennekamp Park area, there are fewer boaters.

Besides the 44 barrier islands and the reef, the park protects 14 continuous miles of mangrove shoreline, the longest uninterrupted stretch of mangroves along the eastern coast. But of the 181,500 acres the park encompasses, 95% is water. Newcomers to the park arrive at Convoy Point, the mainland "jumping off" point, take one look at the parking lot, the Visitor Center, the boat dock, and the store, and say "Is this it?" The answer is most emphatically "No!" But you have to find your way onto or into the water to see the best part. Fortunately, the National Park Service makes that easy. Take advantage of the opportunity to see this gorgeous reef by snorkeling or taking a glassbottom boat trip, and try a canoe trip along the mangrove shoreline. You may see manatees or dolphins or the colorful tropical fish. Biscayne Bay is a sanctuary for spiny lobsters where they are thoroughly protected.

The park hosts seven species of endangered animals. They are the American crocodile, hawksbill sea turtle, green sea turtle, leatherback sea turtle, wood stork, peregrine falcon, West Indian manatee, and Schaus' swallowtail butterfly.

Hurricane Andrew made landfall here. The entire park was directly in the path of the worst winds and storm surges. Damage to this park was extensive. All buildings (except the old stone ones on the islands) were damaged or destroyed. Most of the park's mangroves were damaged. There was damage on all reefs, but most was minor.

Location, Mailing Address and Phone

9700 SW 328th St./North Canal Dr., Homestead. Convoy Point is 9 miles east of Homestead. From the north, follow the signs from Florida's Turnpike or US 1. From the Keys, follow the signs on US 1, turning right onto SW 328th St.

For National Park Service information, write 9700 SW 328th St., Homestead 33033-5634. For concession information, write Biscayne Aqua Center, Inc., P.O. Box 1270, Homestead 33090-1270.

For Park Service information, call 305-230-PARK (230-7275). For concession information, call 305-230-1100.

Facilities and Activities

Snorkeling, diving, glassbottom boat, swimming, picnicking, canoeing, canoe rentals, hiking, camping, fishing, interpretive programs. Open 8:00 AM to 5:30 PM. No entrance fee; fees for concession tours and rentals.

Convoy Point Visitor Center

Hours are 8:30 AM to 5:00 PM. The large new visitor center, opened in early 1997 after delays by Hurricane Andrew, has innovative techniques for bringing the reef and the hammocks close up and inside for easier visitor viewing. Natural history books, including marine and seashore field guides, are for sale. A 12-minute video on Biscayne National Park ecosystems is shown on request in the auditorium. A slide program on the area's cultural history and closed-captioning are also available on request.

Elliott Key Ranger Station

The Ranger Station on Elliott Key has restrooms (handicapped accessible), picnic areas, and a few wall displays. There are no telephones on the island. In the winter (usually Christmas to Easter), it is staffed by an interpretive volunteer intermittently on weekends.

Canoeing and Kayaking

You can bring your own watercraft or rent one from the concession. You can paddle along the shore, around the mangroves, and to nearby islands by yourself. It's not recommended to go far from shore in a canoe. However, sea kayaks are frequently used to go the seven miles to Elliott Key. Be careful of the tides, since the currents can be very strong. Check with a ranger for the tide schedule and plan your trip so you paddle with the current. Also watch for strong winds and choppy waters that are frequent in the winter.

Boating

Visitors with their own motor boats will find much to see and do. Fishing for tarpon, grouper, snook, and so on is very popular, and it's easy to find snorkeling hot spots on your own. Mooring buoys are provided at several places around the reef; they are there to protect the coral, since it is illegal to anchor on coral. If no mooring buoys are available, you must anchor on sand. Due to the shallowness of Biscayne Bay and the reef, you should carry a NOAA nautical chart (#11451, "Miami to Marathon and Florida

Bay," available at Convoy Point) with you. The adjacent Homestead Bayfront Park (a county park) has a boat launch and gas dock; there are no such facilities in Biscayne National Park.

The harbor by the Ranger Station on Elliott Key has 66 slips. They are free and available on a first-come basis for day use or overnight. Docks are also available at Adams (day use only) and Boca Chita Keys.

Swimming

There are many places to swim, although the area you can get to without a boat (which is at Convoy Point) is small. The coral reef must be reached by boat. There are protected and shallow swimming areas at Elliott Key on the bayside. Seagrasses shelter the barracudas, grunts, and snappers that are commonly seen.

Fishing

Fishing in the park is entirely saltwater and is very popular with local people. Since most of the park is marine, there is ample room for everyone to fish. From Convoy Point, you can fish on the jetty opposite the marked channel and catch such fish as barracuda, grunt, mangrove snapper, and snook. There is no bait for sale at the park (available at the adjacent Homestead Bayfront Park).

Trails

If you can get to Elliott Key, allow time to hike around. A loop trail, about 1.5 miles round-trip, with a section of boardwalk on the ocean side, begins on the bayside near the Visitor Center. Interpretive signs tell the natural and human history of Elliott Key. The trail meanders through a West Indian hardwood hammock and mangroves. The mangrove land crabs (*Ucides cordatus*) scurry around by the dozens under the mangroves, above the tide line. The vivid purple and orange shells of these land crabs are a spectacular sight.

There is a much longer straight trail (an old road) running almost the entire length of the seven-mile island. From the Visitor Center, the trail goes for 2.5 miles north and 4.5 miles south.

Sea-grape

The habitat is tropical hammock, and many native hardwoods can be found.

There is also a half-mile loop trail on Adams Key. It doesn't have interpretive signs, but it penetrates a hardwood hammock (with seven-year-apple, white stopper, pigeon-plum, poison-wood, canker-tree) and openings (with buttonwood, bay-cedar, and sea ox-eye daisy). Adams Key is partially composed of fill pumped up from the ocean floor. That's why you'll see piles of clamshells on the island, resembling an Indian midden. Camping on Adams is reserved for school groups.

During the autumn and spring raptor, passerine, and shore-bird migrations, Elliott and Adams are resting and foraging places, thus also great for birding. Birding is good all winter. In fact, a LaSagra's Flycatcher has been seen on Elliot during several winters.

Biscayne National Park is one of the few remaining places left to see the Schaus' swallowtail butterfly (*Papilio aristodemus ponceanus*), listed as endangered since 1975 by the state and federal governments. The chief contributor to the species' demise is the long-term destruction of native hardwoods, like torchwood and wild-lime, on which it feeds. Since 1972, aerial spraying of pesticides targeted at mosquitoes is also contributing to the destruction. This beautiful butterfly, about 3.5 inches across, is black with yellow diagonal bands and black tails edged with yellow. The adults usually live only three or four days but may survive several weeks. Look for them from late April through mid-July. The islands in Biscayne National Park are one of the few places left to see this rare butterfly.

Mexican red-bellied squirrels (introduced) were occasionally seen foraging in the treetops of Elliott Key by hikers prior to Hurricane Andrew. These attractive squirrels are black with a rusty-colored belly. They somehow survived Hurricane Andrew.

The Jetty

Wayside exhibits line the 370-foot boardwalk and a half-mile breakwater jetty that tread the water from Convoy Point. Anglers often surf-cast from the non-channel side of the jetty, and the winter shore-birding can be great. White mangrove, sea-grape, sea purslane, and sea ox-eye daisy grab a tenuous roothold along the jetty.

Camping

Camping is allowed on Elliott and Boca Chita Keys; both have tentsites, cooking grills, and bathrooms. They are only accessible by boat. Elliott Key has fresh water and showers. Boca Chita has no fresh water.

The concession will bring groups out to the camping areas on Elliott or Boca Chita Keys for overnight camping from autumn through spring. The fee for the boat depends upon the group size. Make arrangements at least a few weeks in advance.

Concession Tours and Rentals

The Biscayne Aqua Center concession offers ways for almost everyone to enjoy the coral reef. At the store at Convoy Point, you can reserve space on the glassbottom boat or the snorkel and dive boat. While there are regularly scheduled tours, you can also arrange special group tours in advance. You should make reservations and check schedules in advance for all trips, either in person or by phone: 305-230-1100. All trips leave from Convoy Point and may be cancelled due to weather.

The daily snorkel trip departs at 1:30 PM and the cost of the trip includes equipment. The trip lasts four hours, and about half of that is in-the-water time. *Do not touch the corals*, because touching can kill them. Enjoy watching the colorful angelfish, parrotfish, blue tangs, and butterflyfish. You may even see a complacent nurse shark.

The concession maintains certification facilities. Certified divers can go on the two-tank dives. You'll see some of the thousands of patch reefs that have formed on the oceanside near Elliott Key. A patch reef is a small, circular coral reef (usually only a few hundred yards in diameter) surrounded by a ring of sand.

The concession has a 53-foot glassbottom boat that can carry 49 passengers. The boat was custom-built for the reef, with recessed propellers to prevent turbulence to and siltation of the reef. The 28-inch draft is small for a boat that size and allows it to venture into very shallow water without scraping the coral. A National Park Service interpretive ranger will be on board each trip to narrate about the reef. The 3-hour trip leaves at 10:00 AM daily and is wheelchair-accessible.

Canoeists can rent 17-foot aluminum canoes by the hour, half day, whole day, or overnight. For an extra fee, you can rent a car-top carrier and take the canoe outside the park. For a small additional fee, basic canoeing instruction is also available (enough to get a newcomer going).

Miscellaneous

Food sold here is limited to snacks and soft drinks. There is limited food service at the adjacent county park. The nearest food store or restaurant is in the town of Homestead, about nine miles west.

Best Time of Year

January to April have the fewest insects and the driest weather. Ocean water temperature and clarity are best from April to October (for swimming, snorkeling, and diving) but they are generally good year-round. Glassbottom boat trips are good any month, since the reef is more protected from heavy seas here than off Key Largo. High winds and winter cold fronts can cause boat tours to be canceled. A popular sailing regatta is held near the park every year on Columbus Day weekend.

Pets

Allowed on a 6-foot leash; not in buildings, on concession boats, or on Boca Chita.

DRY TORTUGAS NATIONAL PARK

Flung far out into the Gulf of Mexico are the rest of the Florida Keys. Few visitors realize that the Keys don't end at Key West—just the road does. Almost 70 miles farther west, and another world away, is a small cluster of seven coral islands known as the Dry Tortugas. Fort Jefferson, the "Gibraltar of the Gulf," is located on one of these islands.

Ponce de León was credited with discovering the islands for the Old World in 1513. He named them *Las Tortugas* (Spanish for "The Turtles") because of the numerous sea turtles he found there. The adjective "Dry" was added later to warn mariners that there was no fresh water on the islands. Located strategically in the shipping path between Central America and the United States, the islands became the sanctum of pirates for several centuries. When Florida became part of the United States in 1821, so did the Dry Tortugas.

In 1846, the U.S. Corps of Engineers began to build the fort (named after Thomas Jefferson) on 16-acre Garden Key. Although construction continued for three decades, the fort was never completed. Still, it was the largest seacoast fortress from Maine to Texas at that time, with a perimeter of a half-mile. The

8-foot-thick, 45-foot-high walls contain 16 million hand-made bricks. During the Civil War, Fort Jefferson became a military prison for army deserters. The most famous political prisoner was Dr. Samuel Mudd, accused of conspiring to assassinate President Lincoln. His misfortune was that he set the broken leg of the fugitive John Wilkes Booth. Although sentenced to life imprisonment, he was pardoned after saving the army garrison from a yellow fever epidemic. His predicament is still echoed by the popular phrase "Your name is Mudd!" The Navy took over the fort for a refueling station in 1889. President Franklin D. Roosevelt proclaimed the fort and adjacent islands a national monument (known as Fort Jefferson National Monument) in 1935 for their historic and educational values. In November 1992, the monument achieved national park status in recognition of its exceptional natural resources.

But enough of the human history. Let's talk about birds. Just as the islands are located in the middle of the shipping lanes, so they are also located in the middle of the migration flyways between North and South America. For as long as the lonely coral islands have poked their heads above the water, sea birds and land-dwelling migrants have found a haven on them. Nesting birds start arriving in March, and by April, up to 100,000 terns have eggs on Bush, Hospital, and Long Keys. Most are sooty terns, but brown noddies and roseate terns also nest here. Gulls, other terns, shorebirds, raptors, frigatebirds, boobies, and accidentals from the West Indies can all be found most of the year. In 1832, John James Audubon visited the Tortugas to study the spectacular bird life.

Not to be outdone, the scene underwater is equally spectacular. Excellent snorkeling and scuba diving sites abound. The clear shallow waters are perfect for the growth of coral and associated reef fish. Four endangered species of sea turtles—the hawksbill, green, Atlantic Ridley, and leatherback, as well as the threatened loggerhead—have been found here.

Effective July 2001, the new Tortugas Ecological Reserve was established in the waters northwest and southwest of the park. Boaters entering these waters may need permits. Call Florida Keys National Marine Sanctuary for details (305-743-2437).

If you don't mind primitive camping, this is the place to do it. There is so much to see for such a small group of islands. It's also the ideal place to relax—cellular phones and fax machines don't work out here!

Location, Mailing Address and Phone

Accessible only by private boat, chartered boat, ferry, or seaplane. Several private concessions run seaplanes from the Keys and southern Florida cities to Dry Tortugas. Call the Florida Keys and Key West Tourist Bureau, the Florida Board of Tourism, or the Greater Key West Chamber of Commerce (see Other Sources of Information for phone numbers) for the current list of licensed operators. You can also send for the list of charter tour operators by contacting the Superintendent's Office at Everglades National Park. A commercial ferry began operating in 1996: Tortugas Ferry at 800-634-0939, 7 days/week; for a modest extra fee, campers can arrange to have the ferry pick them up on its next trip 1 or 2 days later (carrying camping equipment onto the ferry is easier than onto a small seaplane). Boats take 3 to 5 hours and the water can get uncomfortably rough, causing trips to be canceled often. Seaplanes are much quicker (about 45 minutes), but occasionally it is too rough for seaplanes to land. The standard seaplane trips are half-day or full-day, but overnight trips can be individually negotiated.

The Florida Audubon Society sponsors a guided birding trip to Dry Tortugas every April or early May, coinciding with spring migrations and tern nesting (see Other Sources of Information for how to contact Florida Audubon). Reserve early, for this is a popular trip.

Superintendent, Dry Tortugas National Park, P.O. Box 6208, Key West, FL 33041. Dry Tortugas has no phone.

Facilities and Activities

Visitor center, self-guided tour, birding, fishing, swimming, snorkeling, scuba diving, campground. No entrance fee, but small fee for camping.

Note: Visitors must bring all their own provisions. This

includes drinking water and food; no fresh water available. No lodging available; overnight stays on land require camping. All garbage must leave with you. The fort, visitor center, and campground are on Garden Key.

Visitor Center

The Visitor Center contains historical exhibits, an interpretive slide program, and books for sale. Ranger-led programs are offered in the winter. Check the Center for the schedule. Ask for the bird checklist here; it's very thorough. Snorkel equipment can be borrowed from the Visitor Center.

The Fort

The half-mile self-guided tour leads you around the historic fort. Ignore the sign that says it takes a half hour for the trip. It's just too fascinating to breeze through that quickly. Interpretive signs guide you inside and outside the brick fortress, through bastions and narrow stairwells, past the ammunition magazine, and even into Mudd's spartan cell. Calcified water percolates through the ceiling in places, creating mini-stalactites and corresponding stalagmites inside the building. The fort was never completed because of the invention of the rifled cannon, which could penetrate even the 8-foot-thick walls. Old and new cisterns can be seen. The old ones cracked from settling, letting in salt water. The original lighthouse stands defunct. From the roof of the fort (accessible by stairs), the view across the water is spectacular.

Entirely surrounding the fort is a brick sea wall constructed as added protection to the fort, much as the coral reefs protect the islands. Between the fort and the seawall is a moat containing quiet, sheltered water. You can walk on top of the sea wall for its entire length and see into the clear water on both sides. Non-swimmers will be treated to a view of marine life almost as good as a snorkeler's view if the water is calm. Bring a strong flashlight if you're staying at night, and try looking into the moat after dark. The wind often dies down after dusk, making the water calmer. The nocturnal creatures emerge, and wonderful views of active conchs, lobsters, crabs, shrimp, moray eels, urchins, and sea stars can be seen.

Loggerhead Key

About two miles west of Garden Key is the largest of the seven islands. Boaters are permitted to dock at Loggerhead and climb the 180 steps to the top of the functioning lighthouse. It affords a glorious view of the Dry Tortugas. The island was named after the loggerhead turtles that nest on the sandy beaches in the summer. The nests are carefully protected by park rangers.

Birding

Birders from around the country and many other countries come to the Dry Tortugas to see seabirds and migrating land birds. There are 285 species known to occur here. Many are accidentals from far away, appearing briefly after getting blown off course from a cold front or tropical storm. The late winter cold fronts blow flocks of weary migrants onto the islands. The exhausted birds perch listlessly on branches, recovering strength enough to feed. This is when binoculars just get in the way. The metaphor "the trees were dripping with warblers" is appropriate after cold fronts.

From March to October, tens of thousands of sooty terns and brown noddies can be watched from Garden Key. Most nest on Bush and Long Keys, only a few hundred yards from Garden Key. A strong spotting scope will give an impressive view of the nest islands from Garden Key.

In October and November, the north winds bring migrations of raptors (such as merlins, peregrine falcons, sharp-shinned hawks, and broadwings), warblers, and shorebirds. All are hoping to rest, feed, and store up energy for the remaining marathon flight across the havenless water to Cuba and beyond.

Snorkeling and Swimming

Snorkeling and swimming is exceptional around the outside of the sea wall on Garden Key. Snorkelers will find a rich variety of marine life in a mere three or four feet of water. Colorful fish, lobsters, sea cucumbers, conchs, corals, and so on are all easily visible. Look for loggerhead and hawksbill sea turtles feeding in the seagrasses. Scuba divers must bring their own diving equipment, but snorkeling equipment can be borrowed at the Visitor Center.

Boating and Fishing

Many sailboaters find the Dry Tortugas a great destination from cities on both coasts of Florida. Motor boaters usually "jump off" from Key West. If you bring your own boat to the islands, make sure you have the Dry Tortugas NOAA Chart #11438 to navigate safely around the shallow reefs. No permit is necessary to anchor within the park boundaries. The waters between Key West and the Tortugas can get rough during the winter or during summer thunderstorms, so check the forecast before casting off. No fuel or provisions of any type are available at the islands; you must be completely self-sufficient. There are no overnight slips in the Dry Tortugas. Mooring at the dock on Garden Key is limited to two hours during daylight. Boats must be anchored in designated places at night. Water skiing and jet skiing are not permitted.

Between March 1 and October 1, nesting and fledging birds have priority over Bush Key, and the island is closed to human visitation. Also, because sea turtles nest on East, Middle, Bush, and Loggerhead Keys, these islands are closed from sunset to sunrise from May through September. Hospital and Long are closed year-round.

Fishing is excellent, but even out here a Florida saltwater fishing license is required (must be purchased before your arrival). Florida residents must obtain a license to fish from a boat (not needed for dock fishing). No bait is available other than what you catch. Lobster and conch are protected from harvest and spearfishing is prohibited. Snappers, groupers, grunts, and tarpon are often caught. A fish cleaning table is located at the dock on Garden Key. If you're not an angler, bartering for fresh fish is worth a try (steaks are good trade items).

Campground

A more peaceful, picturesque, relaxing setting for camping can't be found in Florida. Your tent is pitched under a palm tree, birds "drip" from the trees, and with a mere two skips you're slipping into the warm coral reef waters. Even better, your office can't reach you.

Camping is permitted only in the designated camping area on Garden Key. Picnic tables, grills, and saltwater toilets are provided. Camping is on a first-come first-served basis, since there are a limited number of sites. Groups of 10 or more must obtain a permit in advance by writing to the Superintendent. All supplies must be packed in and all trash must be packed out. There are no showers.

Best Time of Year

For birding: April to September for nesting terns; spring and autumn for migrants; year-round for sea birds. For snorkeling: the water is warmest and calmest in summer. For fishing: year-round.

Pets

Allowed on leash. Not allowed inside the fort or left unattended.

EVERGLADES NATIONAL PARK—OVERVIEW

The name "Everglades" conjures up images in tourists' minds of vast tangled jungles with vines and snakes dripping from the trees. Park rangers frequently hear visitors comment, "This isn't like I pictured." Indeed, the Everglades does have vine-covered jungles, but they are not vast, and the snakes don't drip from trees. The "jungles" are mostly in the form of isolated tree islands and mangrove stands. The two major habitat types are the open freshwater marshes and the coastal mangroves.

The Everglades is a unique ecosystem—there is no other like it anywhere in the world. That is why so many people (starting with Ernest Coe in 1928) led the fight to protect it, culminating with the dedication of this national park in 1947.

Many other honors have been bestowed upon it: The park was designated an International Biosphere Reserve in 1976;

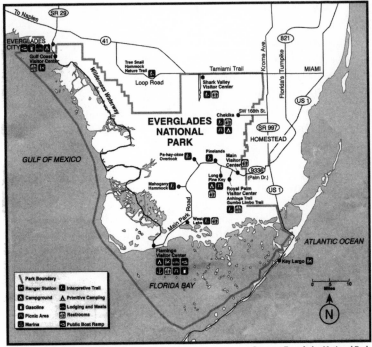

Courtesy Everglades National Park

Everglades National Park

UNESCO, the United Nations Educational, Scientific, and Cultural Organization, named it a World Heritage Site in 1979; and in 1987 it was named a Wilderness of International Significance. Two canoe trails were designated as National Trails in 1981. There is no doubt the Everglades has played and will continue to play a major role in Florida's mental and environmental health.

Everglades National Park plays another unique role. It was the first national park to be established at the mouth of a waterway, rather than at the source. Most parks are at the headwaters of rivers (like Glacier, Yellowstone, Grand Teton, and Yosemite), where the water is pure and the main administrative problem is the overabundance of visitors. Everglades National Park is at the end of a water system that has environmental insults thrown at it every step of the way, causing major ecological problems.

Less than 20 percent of the original Everglades region is contained within the park boundaries. The boundary encompasses 1,506,539 acres of wilderness: 572,200 acres of marsh; 220,200 acres of coastal areas; 230,100 acres of mangroves; and 484,200 acres of Florida Bay and the Gulf of Mexico. This total acreage includes the newest addition (dedicated in 1989) to Everglades National Park, the "East Everglades," a 107,600-acre freshwater marsh northwest of Homestead. This undeveloped area was cut off from the natural flow of water by levees and canals, which in turn blocked water to Shark River and Taylor Sloughs. The acquisition of this land will mean sheet flow can be restored, and it is a major step toward saving the southern Everglades. Included in the newly acquired area is the former Chekika State Recreation Area in Homestead.

Thirteen species of animals found in the park are federally endangered. They are the American crocodile, green sea turtle, Atlantic Ridley sea turtle, hawksbill sea turtle, leatherback sea turtle, Cape Sable seaside sparrow, snail kite, wood stork, Florida panther, West Indian manatee, Key Largo wood rat, Key Largo cotton mouse, and Schaus' swallowtail butterfly. The red-cockaded woodpecker has been extirpated from the park. The rich variety of plants and animals includes approximately 400 species of birds, 25 mammals, 60 amphibians and reptiles, 125 fish, 120 trees, and 1000 flowering plants. More than 25 types of orchids grow in the park.

The 137-mile coastline attracts many people for the saltwater fishing. Others come for the excitement of seeing alligators, flocks of wood storks, and other fascinating animals. Still others come to camp in the solitude of the Ten Thousand Islands. Visitation has steadily increased from 123,405 people in 1950 to close to one million each year recently.

The duration of your stay depends on how much time you have, since you can easily fill a two-week stay. If you have only a day in the winter, you should at least see the Anhinga and Gumbo Limbo Trails at Royal Palm. If you have only a day in the summer, you may be better off canoeing away from land and the mosquitoes at Flamingo or taking a boat tour of the Ten Thousand Islands at Everglades City. A two-day trip should include an overnight stay at the quiet outpost of Flamingo, with a canoe trip or boat tour. Hopefully, you will have at least a week, with time to see Royal Palm, Flamingo, Shark Valley, and Everglades City. Take advantage of the ranger-led trips and programs to learn about the Everglades. Wildlife observing, canoeing, fishing, hiking, and photographing opportunities are excellent.

Because of the magnitude of the park's resources and facilities, each area will be described separately below.

Location, Mailing Address and Phone

There are four land entrances (Florida City, Shark Valley, Everglades City, Chekika). Key Largo has just a ranger station (MM 99 Overseas Hwy. bayside), although plans are in the works for an Interpretive Center. The main park entrance is west of Florida City on SR 9336 about 10 miles southwest of the intersection of SW 344th St./Palm Drive and US 1. Chekika, Everglades City, Flamingo, Long Pine Key, Royal Palm, and Shark Valley are regions of the park that are covered separately below.

40001 SR 9336, Homestead 33034-6733; 305-242-7700. This address is for all regions and entrances of the park. www.nps.gov/ever.

Facilities and Activities

Camping, nature trails, hiking trails, birding, canoeing, bicycling, boat tours, tram tours, boat and canoe rentals, bicycle rentals, ranger activities, freshwater and saltwater fishing, boating, wildlife observation areas, visitor centers, lodging and restaurant, marina, gift shops. There are no airboat tours in the park.

Literature is available in Spanish, German, French, Japanese, Italian, and Dutch at the main and Shark Valley Visitor Centers. Visitors should stop at the Visitor Center serving the area they are about to explore to gather the tour schedules, trail maps, and other helpful materials. Most of the park's facilities are accessible to the handicapped and assistance is available. Visitor Centers are located at the main park entrance, Royal Palm, Flamingo, Shark Valley, and Everglades City. Operations (such as tours and naturalist programs) are reduced during the summer, so call ahead to confirm schedules.

Camping

Three campgrounds (Long Pine Key, Flamingo, and Chekika) provide basic camping facilities. Camping stays are limited to 14 days. Although the campgrounds are open year-round, the summer heat, insects, and thunderstorms can be intense. Few people brave an overnight camping stay. Summer camping (approximately May 1 to mid-November) is free, but sites are reduced in number (never a problem) and ranger assistance is reduced.

Long Pine Key

The Long Pine Key campground turnoff is about 6 miles from the main entrance. The 108 sites have minimal facilities (no showers).

Camping is pleasant under the shady slash pine trees. You're more likely to be kept awake by a barred owl than by your neighboring campers. The lake next to the loop road usually has alligators. Miles of hiking trails through the pinelands originate from the campground.

Flamingo

At the far end of the Main Park Road is another campground. The 235 drive-in sites are more open and sunny than Long Pine Key. It has water and bathrooms plus a sewage dumping station. This is the only camping area with showers. But be prepared— they are cold water only and they are "open air," so take your shower before a cold front hits!

The 60 walk-in sites are great for tent camping. Picture a large grassy field sprinkled with palm trees, perched next to Florida Bay. The parking lot where you leave your car is at most a few hundred yards away. You can pick a spot near your car or near the bay. From your tentsite, you can see reddish egrets lurching drunkenly for prey in the shallow water, a bald eagle stealing food from an osprey overhead, a corn snake sliding down from an arboreal hiding place, and dolphins spouting plumes of vapor as they surface. Red-bellied woodpeckers love the coconut palms and can

A boater sets up his campsite at the Rodgers River Bay chickee.

easily be identified by their trilling calls. Each site has a grill and table, and bathrooms are nearby; showers at the drive-in sites are walking distance away. The walk-in sites are closed in summer.

Chekika

This newly-acquired campground north of Homestead is reached from SR 997. There are 20 sites, obtained on a first-come basis, plus a group site for which reservations can be made.

Backcountry Sites

There are 41 designated primitive backcountry sites from Everglades City to Flamingo and three in Florida Bay that are accessible only by canoe or motor boat. These are either chickees, ground sites, or beach sites. Two additional sites along the old Ingraham Highway can be reached by hiking.

The chickees (named after the Miccosukee word for house) are 10-foot by 12-foot wooden platforms on stilts over water, in areas where there is no high ground available. They are suitable for self-supporting tents or open-air sleeping. The chickees have roofs and chemical toilets. The maximum group size is six people. Some are double chickees, with enough room for two groups. One chickee at Pearl Bay (a four-mile canoe trip from the Main Park Road) is adapted for wheelchairs: it has an accessible toilet, railings, stair ramp, and a boat slip for canoe stability.

The ground sites are on relatively high ground away from the coast. Some are located on old Indian middens (like Willy Willy), which explains the higher ground. They have docks, chemical toilets, and picnic tables, but no pavilions. Beach sites are on beautiful shell beaches, with open views and cooling breezes, but no tables and most have no toilets. Remember to pitch your tent well above the high tide line.

The backcountry sites are within easy canoeing distance from each other (some are as little as a mile apart). However, conditions can be difficult (high winds, strong currents, heavy rains, getting lost), so you must get a backcountry permit from a ranger at the Flamingo or Everglades City Ranger Stations.

Camping is permitted in Florida Bay at three sites only: North Nest Key, Carl Ross Key, and Little Rabbit Key. These are beach sites and the permits may be obtained from Flamingo or Key Largo Ranger Stations. Length of stay limits vary for each site from one to seven nights during the peak visitor season (December 1 to April 30). During the summer, mosquitoes and no-see-ums can make camping unbearable, so visitation drops off; however, you still need a permit. Call the Key Largo Ranger Station (305-852-5119) to inquire about permits.

Campfires are permitted only at some beach sites below the storm surge line. Driftwood on the ground may be used for fires. At all other sites, fires are permitted only in camping stoves; no grills are provided at the sites. Particularly at the ground and beach sites, raccoons spell trouble for your food—they are relentless in their pursuit of it. You should have a hard-sided cooler (styrofoam does not work) or a way to keep food out of reach of the raccoons. Raccoons will also chew through soft-sided water containers, particularly in the dry season.

Lodging

The only lodging within the park is at Flamingo. All other main visitor areas are near enough to towns to be easily accessible to motels.

The Flamingo Lodge (phone 1-800-600-3813 for reservations or 239-695-3101 for information; www.flamingolodge.com), located between the marina and the campground at Flamingo, offers 102 air-conditioned rooms with full services, including a laundromat. The screened-in pool, for lodge guests only, represents the only safe swimming in the park (gators and sharks prevent swimming in the fresh and salt waters, respectively). The lodge also maintains 24 family-oriented cottages. Each cottage contains a fully-equipped kitchen (refrigerator, stove, oven, dishes, utensils), so you need only bring your food. The full-service dates are November 1 to April 30, and reduced services are May to October. The peak rates are from December 15 to March 31, lower rates are April 1 to April 30 and November 1 to December 14, and lowest rates are May 1 to October 31. Summer weekend rates are slightly higher than weekday rates. No pets are allowed in the lodge or cottages.

The restaurant at Flamingo flaunts a spectacular view of Florida Bay, with eagles, pelicans, and egrets visible during dining (theirs and yours). It is the only restaurant this author keeps a bird list for! The atmosphere is so relaxing and unique that people drive from Miami just to have dinner here. Make reservations early in the day in the winter. Like the lodge, summer visitation drops off so much that the restaurant is closed around mid-April to early November. Salads, pizza, sandwiches and drinks are available year-round at the Buttonwood Lounge (located beneath the restaurant) and the marina serves snacks.

Fishing

About one third of Everglades National Park is water, and fishing has always been popular. Noncommercial fishing is permitted in the park and must follow park fishing regulations. A freshwater license is needed to fish in Nine-Mile Pond and all waters northward along the Main Park Road or to possess freshwater fish caught in brackish waters. This license must be purchased outside the park, since none are sold within the park. You will need a saltwater license for Florida Bay, the Gulf of Mexico, Long Sound, Little Blackwater Sound, and Blackwater Sound. You can purchase a saltwater license at the Flamingo Marina (same phone as Flamingo Lodge above).

Due to mercury found in largemouth bass, the park has issued the following warning: "Do not eat bass caught north of the Main Park Road. Do not eat bass caught south of the Main Park Road more than once a week. Children and pregnant women should not eat any bass." This warning does not apply to saltwater fish. Some of the main freshwater ponds are posted with warning signs. Too bad the otters and gators can't read.

Areas closed to fishing for wildlife protection include the ponds by the main Visitor Center and Royal Palm Visitor Center area and trails, Taylor Slough, Mrazek Pond, Eco Pond, along the Shark Valley tram road, and at the Flamingo Marina during daylight hours.

Saltwater anglers may land any one of the following fish: snook, spotted seatrout, redfish, mangrove snapper, sheepshead, and black drum. Tarpon, ladyfish, and shark are also good possibilities, as well as dozens of other species. Guides are available for hire by calling the Flamingo Marina.

Boating

The boat ramps (fee charged) are located at Flamingo (Florida Bay side and Buttonwood Canal side), Paurotis Pond, West Lake, Little Blackwater Sound, and Everglades City. Southern Florida Bay is accessible from the Keys via boat ramps at marinas or at public ramps and may have a fee.

Some areas are off-limits to boats (including canoes). Boats are prohibited from landing on all of the little mangrove islands in Florida Bay, with the exceptions of Carl Ross, Little Rabbit, North Nest, and Bradley Keys (Bradley Key only during daylight hours). This is to protect the nesting birds and other wildlife. A crocodile refuge exists in northeast Florida Bay; therefore, there are seasonal restrictions on when boats are allowed in the waters of Little Madeira and Joe Bays or in the waters of the back bays from Little Madeira Bay east to US 1. Boats are allowed to land on any of the keys in the Ten Thousand Islands, except the southern part of Pavilion Key.

Motors are prohibited from some parts of the park, including all freshwater lakes. Prohibited brackish areas include the canoe trails of Bear Lake, Noble Hammock, Coot Bay Pond, and Mud Lake, Raulerson's Marsh, the southern part of Hell's Bay canoe trail, and the creek at the southeastern end of West Lake through to Garfield Bight. On West Lake, only motors of 5.5 horsepower or less are permitted. "No Wake" zones exist around Everglades City, Flamingo, and Key Largo. Waterskiing and "jet-skiing" are prohibited throughout the park. Coast Guard regulations require that all watercraft carry a personal flotation device, quickly accessible, for each person on board.

The Marina at Flamingo, operated by a concession, has gas pumps and slips with water and electric hookups for at least 50 boats. Skiffs, kayaks, canoes, and bicycles may be rented at the Marina.

Birding

The vastness of the park, the warm climate, and the rich variety of habitats and plants contribute to the exceptional birding enjoyed by visitors to Everglades National Park. As of 1990, the park's bird list included 350 species. Birds from temperate North America and the tropical Caribbean thrive in South Florida. Tropical storms blow accidentals from far out at sea.

There is no telling where an interesting bird may show up. The following easily accessible places are the most reliable to start with: Anhinga Trail, Mahogany Hammock, West Lake, Snake Bight Trail, the mud flats in front of the Flamingo Visitor Center, Eco Pond, and the Shark Valley Tram Road.

The use of audiotape recordings to attract birds is prohibited within the park. Such tapes interfere with the birds' natural activities. Binoculars may be rented at the Flamingo Marina and the Shark Valley tram office.

Pets

Must be on a six-foot leash, must not be left unattended; not allowed on trails, in buildings, in amphitheaters, or on boat and tram tours.

EVERGLADES NATIONAL PARK— MAIN PARK ENTRANCE

From the north: take Florida's Turnpike Extension south to the end in Florida City. Turn right onto SW 344th St./Palm Drive and follow the signs on SR 9336 to Everglades National Park. From the Keys: Take US 1 to first traffic light in Florida City at SW 344th St., turn left and follow the signs on SR 9336. U.S. fee area.

Facilities and Activities
Main Visitor Center

The Main Visitor Center is located on the right, before the Entrance Station, and is open 8:00 AM to 5:00 PM daily. Information for any part of the park can be obtained here. A large selection of books about the Everglades (natural and human history) is for sale. Hurricane Andrew destroyed the original Visitor Center in 1992 and the new state-of-the-art one opened in late 1996.

Outside the Visitor Center are two marshy ponds that attract many birds. Spend a few minutes, especially early in the morning, and you might see alligators, wading birds, and ospreys, with swallow-tailed kites present from March to August.

EVERGLADES NATIONAL PARK— ROYAL PALM

Enter the park from Florida City on SR 9336. Turn left off the Main Park Road about two miles past the Entrance Station.

Facilities and Activities

Visitor center, birding and other wildlife viewing, nature trails, photographic opportunities, ranger programs.

Royal Palm was the nucleus of the new national park in 1947. It was the site of the first state park in Florida, formed in 1916 by the Florida Federation of Women's Clubs to preserve the fabulous hammock at Paradise Key with its stately native royal palms. The state gave it to the National Park Service in 1947.

Visitor Center

Static displays by the very creative artist Charles Harper illustrate the intricate web of life in Taylor Slough. You must look closely at each display to catch all the characters in the web. It will take only 5 or 10 minutes to study the displays. The small gift shop sells Everglades books, field guides, film, and insect repellent. Restrooms are available. Vending machines dispense snacks and drinks.

Anhinga Trail

Certainly the most famous trail in the park, the Anhinga Trail is one of the most famous trails in the National Park system. One of the reasons is the ease in reaching it from a major metropolitan area. Another is the ease of walking it. Most thrilling of all is the reward of fantastic views of wildlife found few other places in the country.

What makes this trail so attractive to wildlife? If you look on the official Everglades National Park map, you'll see that Taylor Slough flows through the Royal Palm area. The slough is a region of slightly deeper water than the surrounding area. During the dry season, much of the water in the Everglades disappears through evaporation, transpiration through plants, and run-off

Anhinga chicks are easily observed from Anhinga Trail.

to the sea, but water always remains in the Taylor and Shark River sloughs. Wildlife is forced to concentrate around these watering holes. The Anhinga Trail passes right over the water where these concentrations are. Through the years, the animals have become habituated to the presence of humans on the trail. They seem to know that the wingless two-legged creatures stay within a certain territory and won't bother them. In fact, the anhinga (the bird the trail was named for) even nests within plain view of the trail! Visitors have observed courtship displays, eggs, fluffy pink chicks, and awkward fledglings without disturbing the birds. Caution is advised whenever wild animals dwell so close to visitors. Stay at least 15 feet away from any animal.

The wildlife concentrations begin around November or December, depending on the local water levels. From January to

April, visitors may be treated to excellent views of alligators, frogs, snakes, turtles, gar fish, ospreys, anhingas, herons, bitterns, raccoons, deer, marsh rabbits, and much more. The anhingas generally nest beginning in January or February. Look for these birds swimming gracefully underwater, then watch them climb onto a branch and spread their wings to dry and warm themselves. During the winter, the pond at the start of the trail is a sure place to find alligators.

The trail is only a half mile long, but you won't want to hurry around it. Most of the trail is actually a boardwalk. The only part over dry land is where the old Ingraham Highway (the original route of the Homestead-to-Flamingo road) passed. Notice the cypress dugout canoe in the pond by the Visitor Center. You can watch anhingas spear bass underwater, purple gallinules step lightly on lily pads and rummage for insects, and soft-shelled turtles glide silently by. Look for black racers, rough green snakes, and water snakes. Short-tailed hawks have been seen soaring overhead from October to March.

You will be comforted to know that, since the trail is mostly open, mosquitoes are less pesky here than on most other trails in the park. The trade-off is that it is often very hot in the sun. So, just as mamma says not to salt your food before you taste it, refrain from applying insect repellent until you get to the trail and are sure you'll need it. Bring a sun hat and sunblock, though.

The openness of the trail is due to the fact that it courses through the sawgrass marsh. This is an excellent place to see sawgrass close up and even touch it. Beware of its telltale name—the blade's edge can cut your skin like a knife. Other common plants are willow, coco-plum, and pond-apple.

Photographing opportunities are wonderful, and you don't even need a supertelephoto lens (unless you want a photo of an alligator's eye). Because the habitat is open, slow-speed film is usually sufficient. An inexpensive instant-type camera will work well here.

Check the announcement board by the Visitor Center for the schedule of ranger activities. Rangers give talks in the shade by the Visitor Center and lead groups around the trail every day. This trail is easily accessible to the handicapped.

Gumbo Limbo Trail

A few yards to the right of the start of the Anhinga Trail is the beginning of the Gumbo Limbo Trail. Quite the opposite of the Anhinga Trail, the Gumbo Limbo is cool, shady, and buggy. This narrow paved footpath, also a half mile long, wanders through the Paradise Key hammock. The hammock is densely vegetated by West Indian hardwood hammock trees, orchids, bromeliads, ferns, and climbing vines, lending a jungle feel to the trail. Look for tree snails, anole lizards, and golden orb-weaver spiders. Some common plants are strangler fig, lancewood, poisonwood, wild-tamarind, and pigeon-plum.

The unusual name of this trail comes from a tree of the same name. Plenty of gumbo-limbos inhabit the hammock, displaying their satiny bronze bark to the visitors. Although the hammock is lush with epiphytic plants, you won't find them attached to gumbo-limbos. This is because the bark is smooth and flakes off too easily, like birch bark, so the plants can't get a good grip. Epiphytes like to grow on fissured and firmly attached bark.

Hurricane Andrew severely damaged this hammock. Almost every branch was stripped of its leaves and epiphytes, and many large limbs were broken. The gumbo-limbos rebounded well and formed the foundation for the rest of the hammock's recovery.

Because the vegetation grows densely, the mosquitoes find a haven from intense sun and debilitating breezes in the summer. Photographers will have a more difficult task in capturing the plants and animals on this trail. Most of the animals are the small types (that is, songbirds and tree snails rather than great blue herons and alligators). The filtered sunlight will make metering tricky, and the closeness of the subjects will make focusing harder. Slow-speed film, tripods, and even flash units are handy here. Handicapped-accessible with caution.

Best Time of Year

December to April. The anhingas nest from late January to April.

EVERGLADES NATIONAL PARK—
LONG PINE KEY

Enter the park from Florida City on SR 9336. Turn left at the sign for Long Pine Key past the Entrance Station on the Main Park Road.

Facilities and Activities

Campground, picnic area, fishing pond, nature trails, and bicycling.

The main draw for people to Long Pine Key is the campground (see "Campgrounds" above). But there are other reasons to go, even if you're not camping. Forty-three miles of shady trails offer excellent hiking and bicycling (get the trail map from the Main Visitor Center). Botanizing is exceptional, with about 30 species of plants found here and nowhere else. Located in a large stand of slash pines, the habitat is maintained by periodic prescribed burns conducted by the National Park Service.

Long Pine Key Trail

Just before the fee station at the campground entrance is the beginning of this trail (look for Gate 4 on the side of the road). The gate is locked and only Park Service vehicles are allowed past it; human feet, bicycles, and horses are the permitted alternatives. The trail is an unpaved fire road that the rangers occasionally use, so it is wide, hardpacked, and passable by bicycle. In the summer, there can be large puddles from rain and large clouds from mosquitoes. Winter is beautiful hiking weather and the trail will most likely be dry. From Gate 4 to the end of the trail at the Main Park Road (Gate 8), the trail is seven miles long. You can return the same way, walk along the Main Park Road, or find another (but longer) footpath back.

The trail heads west from Gate 4. It passes alternately through tall pine stands and open marshes. There are a few turns, and occasional side trails intersect, but the main trail is obvious. Besides the slash pine, you should see the small satinleaf trees, one of the most beautiful tree species in the park. The leaves are dark green above and shiny bronze underneath. When the wind blows, the satiny undersides shine in the sun. Other common species are beauty berry, rough velvetseed, tetrazygia, and willow bustic. The trail ends at the small Pine Glades Lake, near Gate 8 on the Main Park Road. It is five miles along the main road from Pine Glades Lake to the turnoff to Long Pine Key Campground.

Pinelands Trail

This trail is located 2.1 miles west of the entrance to Long Pine Key Campground on the Main Park Road. Look for the sign "Pine Land" with a parking lot on the right. The trail is a half-mile paved loop through typical slash pine habitat. Although the trail is gentle enough to walk on, the ground beside the trail is treacherous. The soil is shallow, and the limestone substrate rock pokes through numerous places. The limestone is pock-marked from dissolving by rainwater mixed with acidic plant matter. Most solution holes are very small, hardly noticeable. Occasional ones are a foot or more across and several feet deep. Picture the early explorers trying to hike across this unforgiving land. The larger solution holes serve as refuges during the dry season for small fish and other aquatic organisms. The holes may be the only places left in the dry season with drinking water for deer, panthers, northern bobwhite quail, and other terrestrial creatures.

About 25–40 percent of the pines were killed by Hurricane Andrew. The taller ones snapped, but the younger ones were probably more flexible.

The predominant shrub-like palm forming the understory is saw palmetto. Look also for tetrazygia, wild-tamarind, satinleaf, Florida trema, and beauty berry. The trail is punctuated with interpretive signs about the plants and animals and the role of fire in the ecosystem.

Other Trails

Several other trails originate at the Long Pine Key Campground. One starts at Gate 3, directly opposite the gate for the Long Pine Key Trail above (Gate 4). This trail runs east, with two right turns along the way. The first right turn takes you on a three-mile round-trip hike. The second right is a five-mile round-trip. Both require walking a short distance on a paved road (Research Road).

Research Road

Formerly called "Long Pine Key Road" by the locals, this 4-mile stretch of paved road (accessible from Royal Palm Road) leads to the Research Center for Everglades National Park. The Research Center is the working office for the many biologists and hydrologists who are seeking ways to understand and protect the Everglades.

The road is a popular wildlife crossing. You may see a white-tailed deer, bobwhite, gray fox, pygmy rattlesnake, Everglades racer, barn owl, or glass lizard. Panthers and black bears have been seen on this road within the last few years. However, there may be no more panthers in this area now.

Hidden Lake

Named for its seclusion, this lake is not on the main tourist list. You can find it by turning off the Main Park Road onto the Royal Palm Road, then turning right towards the Research Road, and going straight past the turnoff for the Research Center (see sign for Hidden Lake). The road becomes unpaved. Look for Gate 13 off the left side of the road 0.3 miles past the turnoff to Research Road. Park your car and walk the short distance in to the pond. The pond is good for quiet wildlife observations. There are no facilities, no interpretive signs, and no provisions for handicapped people. Programs at the nearby Interpretive Center are for school groups by reservation only.

Old Ingraham Highway

The original highway, built in 1922, was the first land link to Flamingo. Before that, Flamingo residents traveled by boat, usually to Key West for supplies. When the Park Service rerouted part of the road, they closed this section to vehicular traffic. It is now a good hiking and biking road.

To find the start of the road, turn off the Main Park Road at Royal Palm, make the first right (as if you're going to the Research

Center), but keep going straight past Research Road. Pass the gate for Hidden Lake on the unpaved road. At one mile past the turnoff for Research Road, Gate 15 crosses the road and blocks through traffic for vehicles. The only vehicles allowed are the Park Service and utility companies (the latter maintain the power lines along the road). The road continues for 11 miles.

This road through the marsh would not be here but for the grace of the canal that parallels the road, created by digging for fill. Look through the trees on the north side of the road and you will see the canal. The canal is the reason you may see semi-aquatic animals cross your path, such as otters, alligators, water snakes, anhingas, and turtles. It's a good hike to take in the dry season, when wildlife is concentrated around watering holes. The road may be flooded in the wet season.

At the end of the road, the trail appears to end. However, the persistent hiker can continue on a small foot path for three more miles to the Main Park Road at Sweet Bay Pond. These last three miles were bulldozed to allow the water to flow across the marsh. The power lines disappear underground here. Don't attempt this last three-mile section unless it is a very dry year.

Two backcountry campsites are along this road: Ernest Coe (at about 4 miles) and Old Ingraham (at about 10 miles). There are no facilities, not even water, and no ground fires are permitted; backcountry permits are available at main visitor center.

EVERGLADES NATIONAL PARK— MAIN PARK ROAD FROM ROCK REEF PASS TO BUTTONWOOD CANAL

Stay on the Main Park Road from the Main Park entrance.

Facilities and Activities

Many people see Everglades National Park only from a road, usually from this one. The National Park Service has established stops along the road at all the main habitat types to provide people with convenient places to view the land. Some of the stops have only interpretive signs, but some have trails with interpretive signs. Allow extra time on your drive to Flamingo to stop at these trails.

Rock Reef Pass

This is marked by a sign on the road bragging that the elevation is three feet. Although Coloradans may snicker, this is not an insignificant landmark. In this flat land, just barely above sea level, *every inch* counts. On both sides of the road, the trees grow on this narrow strip of higher land. From the air, this narrow band of trees looks like an anaconda snaking through the marsh. It is the slight extra elevation above the adjacent marsh that keeps the trees' roots dry enough to grow here and not in the adjacent marsh. Changes in the Everglades are indeed subtle!

Pa-hay-okee Overlook

A short boardwalk (0.2 miles) leads to a two-story observation platform that overlooks the sawgrass prairie. In fact, the name Pa-hay-okee means "Grassy Waters" in the Seminole language. The panoramic view includes tree islands (hammocks), wading birds, and hawks. It is an excellent spot for using your binoculars, spotting scope, and camera. At certain times of the year, brush fires and thunderstorms can be seen in the distance.

Along the boardwalk leading to the platform, look over the railing into the sawgrass for the shells of the apple snails (*Pomacea paludosa*) about 1.5 inches in diameter. These are the famed snails that the endangered snail kites feed on almost exclusively. Also look for their pearl-like egg clusters clinging to a plant stem near the water's surface.

Interpretive signs explain the ecology of the sawgrass prairie. The observation platform and the trail were rebuilt after Hurricane Andrew destroyed them. The larger trees lost limbs, but the marsh shows little or no remnant damage.

Along the Main Park Road near Pa-hay-okee Overlook, you will start to see stunted cypress trees. These are dwarf pond-cypress that may be over 100 years old but only 15 feet tall. Their

Mahogany

growth is limited by the depth of water and soil under them; generally, the taller cypress grow in deeper water and soil. Most visitors see these trees in the winter when they lack their foliage. The needles are dropped in the autumn at the start of the dry season, theoretically to conserve moisture.

Mahogany Hammock

To many people, Mahogany Hammock is what the Everglades is supposed to look like—dense and jungly, with vines strangling every tree. This is a fascinating trail, one of the most interesting places in the park that's easily accessible. The trail is actually a boardwalk, a half-mile long, through the interior of one of the largest tropical hardwood hammocks in the park. The hammock's name is derived from the huge mahogany tree along the boardwalk that is the U.S. champion (that is, the largest mahogany in the United States). There are also numerous smaller mahoganies in the hammock. Hurricane Donna in 1960 did more damage to this area than Andrew, which passed just north of the hammock.

At the "doorway" into the hammock, notice the clump of skinny palms with fan-shaped leaves. These are the state-threatened paurotis palms, native to southern Florida and restricted to the transitional (brackish) marshes between the fresh water and the estuary.

Notice the bromeliads, orchids, and ferns growing in the upper branches of the mahoganies and live oaks. This microhabitat of plants creates places for treefrogs, anoles, insects, and snakes to find food, water, and hiding places without ever descending to the ground. Most of the ferns in the upper branches are resurrection ferns. In the dry season, these ferns dehydrate and wither into brown leaves that look dead. But a soaking rainfall will saturate these plants and allow them to "resurrect" into vibrant, green, growing plants.

As you stroll through the hammock, keep an eye peeled for anoles, warblers, and tree snails. The snails may be on a tree trunk or on the boardwalk. Don't even touch a tree snail, for touching it may cause it to break its moisture seal, which in the dry season will kill it. In winter, white-crowned pigeons are occasionally found feeding here; they are common in the summer. The hammock is also a reliable place to see and hear barred owls. Be patient, and look and listen quietly for them.

If you visit in the dry season, the vines, ferns, bromeliads, and orchids will make the hammock look luxuriant. However, the summer rains really spur the growth in the hammock, and the lush vegetation in July, August, and September is phenomenal.

From June to September be prepared for mosquitoes. The boardwalk is accessible by wheelchair; proceed counterclockwise for easiest approach to the two moderately steep inclines.

The pines across the Main Park Road from Mahogany Hammock are a traditional roost for bald eagles. At dawn, they depart the pines, heading south to the lakes and bays. At dusk, they return from the south, and you should see the eagles as they approach. December and January are the best months and evening is the best time for viewing the eagles.

In the summer, a few sandhill cranes return to the marsh

around Mahogany Hammock. Look for them along the Main Park Road near the Mahogany Hammock turnoff.

Paurotis Pond

This small artificial pond was named for the paurotis palms on the island. The pond has a ramp for small hand-propelled boats and picnic tables at the pond's edge. This pond sometimes offers views of wood storks, which have nested on the spoil islands in recent years, and a variety of other wading birds.

West Lake

A nature trail (handicapped-accessible) and canoe trail originate here; see page 117 for canoeing information. The nature trail is a boardwalk (less than 0.5 miles long) that bisects a mangrove stand. The four tree species collectively known as mangroves can be seen from the boardwalk. During the wet season, this section can be very buggy. The boardwalk ventures out onto the open water and refreshing breeze of West Lake. In late winter, hundreds of ducks of at least half a dozen species can be seen. Alligators, coots, and wading birds are commonly seen. In fact, West Lake is a great place to sit and watch the water—a lot goes on because of the abundant life beneath the water's surface. Redfish, snook, mullet, and other fish need this brackish lake for feeding.

Interpretive signs along the trail explain the mangrove ecosystem. The only restroom facilities between Long Pine Key and Flamingo are located here.

Snake Bight Trail

The old road to Snake Bight formerly served a fishing camp on Florida Bay. The road is 1.8 miles long and terminates at a boardwalk on the edge of Florida Bay. The boardwalk is an exceptional place for birding most of the year. It is tidally influenced, rather than seasonally influenced, meaning you must catch the right tides for good birding. An outgoing tide is best; a high tide is worst. Shorebirds and wading birds (including roseate spoonbills) use this shallow, rich, protected edge of the bay as a feeding ground. It is here that the best views of flamingos have been seen from land over recent years.

Along the trail are excellent opportunities to view wildlife. Alligators find this trail a convenient place to rest. If you see one, keep your distance, since it can fool you with its sluggish appearance. Snakes are common, and treefrogs can be found in the bromeliads. Warblers and mangrove cuckoos are active here. Bobcats prowl frequently. Perhaps the best known inhabitant of the Snake Bight Trail is the mosquito. If mosquitoes are anywhere around, they'll show up here first.

From December to April the road is also used by the concession for tram tours (inquire at gift shop). The trams have mosquito netting over the windows and a narrator to explain the sights. Just prior to the first tram tour of the year, the Park Service mows the vegetation that has grown on the road since the previous year. For several months before the tours commence, vegetation can get tall, so watch out for chiggers. Bicycling is permitted.

Mrazek Pond

Park Ranger Vincent Mrazek must have had a glorious view of wading birds as he gazed out over this pond in the 1950s and 1960s. Judging by the activity almost 40 years later, it must have been quite a sight. Mrazek Pond is one of those special birding spots that almost every local birder and every birder who has been to the park knows about. Finding it and getting to it couldn't be easier. The pond is immediately alongside the Main Park Road.

The birds seem to habituate to people watching quietly from the grassy shore, so it's easy to observe them feeding and resting. Some of them get too close to focus a telephoto lens! In fact, Mrazek Pond is known even more as a photographic hotspot than for birding. Probably more photos of wading birds have been published from here than from Anhinga Trail, which is saying a lot. The nice part is that you don't have to lug your camera gear far.

The bad news is that the avian activity doesn't last all year. The peak months are December to March, when water levels in the park are dropping. Sometimes the activity is reduced to a hectic few weeks during those months, when it seems like every wading bird from Cape Sable to Taylor Slough is visiting. You're likely to see great egrets, snowy egrets, great white herons, great blue herons, little blue herons, tricolored herons, roseate spoonbills, wood storks, white ibises, green-backed herons, white pelicans, black skimmers, common moorhens, rails, blue-winged teal and other ducks. The birds disappear when their feeding frenzies have depleted the fish populations. In drought years, the pond may dry completely in late winter. You also may see alligators, turtles, and maybe even a bobcat.

Coot Bay Pond

Just past Mrazek Pond is the small channel known as Coot Bay Pond, leading from the Main Park Road to Coot Bay. In late winter and spring, it is a good place to watch ducks and wading birds. There are picnic tables and there is a place to launch canoes.

Rowdy Bend Trail

This old road winds through stands of buttonwood trees and coastal prairie for 2.6 miles and ends at the Snake Bight Trail. Buttonwoods were used by the early South Florida settlers for making charcoal for cooking. Cactus and yucca grow here because of the lack of fresh water. Wet and buggy in summer. Not recommended for bicycles.

Christian Point Trail

Remnants of a buttonwood forest are evident along the trail, where the weathered trunks that once surrendered to a hurricane lie prone on the coastal prairie. The trail is 1.8 miles one way and ends at the western part of Snake Bight. Ospreys are usually seen along this trail. Keep your eyes open for a rare indigo snake, the longest snake in Florida.

Best Time of Year

December to May for the trails; they are usually too buggy and wet the rest of the year.

EVERGLADES NATIONAL PARK—FLAMINGO

Go to the end of the Main Park Road, 38 miles from the main park entrance.

Flamingo was a quiet fishing village in the late 1800s. No roads led to it; it was accessible only by boat. Families built houses on stilts and farmed small patches of land. A few of the crops they grew were bananas, tomatoes, sugar cane, and squash. They made charcoal from buttonwood trees for shipment to Key West. Every few years a hurricane would level most of the houses and destroy the crops, so the village never grew very large. In fact, after the road from Florida City was completed in 1922 and villagers discovered a way *out*, more people left than arrived. It may go without saying that living with the mosquitoes was pure torture much of the year. Smudge pots inside the houses were a way of life.

Some Flamingo residents made a living by plume hunting. Many of the colonies of birds the plume hunters sought were near Flamingo. Around the turn of the century, the killing of egrets, herons, and spoonbills for their feathers was very lucrative. The long breeding plumes of the great egret brought $32.00 an ounce (more than gold cost). In 1905, National Audubon Society warden Guy Bradley, who lived in Flamingo, was shot to death by plume hunters while protecting a colony of birds. His death stirred a major crusade, sparked several years earlier by women outraged that the birds were killed for so worthless a purpose. In 1910, the governor of New York signed a landmark bill making the sale of plumes illegal in that state. The political attack against the center of the plume market in New York City effectively curtailed much of the slaughter.

The town was named in 1893, when residents had to identify the post office they had requested. Knowing their town was unique and rather hellish, they wanted to name it something exotic and distinctive. A flock of a thousand flamingos, probably from the Bahamas, had been seen on Cape Sable a few years previously and lent their name to the town. Since then, only a handful of flamingos are seen occasionally in Florida Bay.

Since 1947, when the Park Service became caretakers, the village has included only Park Service and concession employees, their families, and tourists. Flamingo was not affected by Hurricane Andrew, other than being cut off from the rest of the world by the damage up the road.

Facilities and Activities

Campground, hiking trails, boat tours, tram tours, bicycling, naturalist programs, canoeing, visitor center and museum, boat rentals, canoe rentals, houseboat rentals, bicycle rentals, fishing, boating, boat ramps, birding and other wildlife viewing, lodge, marina, and restaurant. Concession: write Flamingo Lodge, Marina and Outpost Resort, #1 Flamingo Lodge Hwy., Flamingo 33034 or call 1-800-600-3813 for reservations or 239-695-3101 for information on all rentals.

During the winter season, the rangers lead numerous walks, slogs, canoe trips, and lectures. At the amphitheater next to the walk-in campsites, expert scientists and naturalists present slide shows every evening. Schedules can be found at the ranger station information desk. The campground and lodge were discussed above (see "Camping" and "Lodging").

Marina and Store

The marina is open daily year-round. It offers automobile and boat fuel pumps; boat ramps to the Florida Bay side and to the Buttonwood Canal side; rental skiffs, canoes, kayaks, houseboats, binoculars, and bicycles; boat tours; and the marina store, which is more like a general store, with groceries, basic boating and camping equipment, fishing bait and tackle, books, and souvenirs. The snack bar at the marina store is useful in the summer when the restaurant is closed. There are restrooms and showers. Boaters can pay for overnight docking here (electric hook-ups available).

Reservations are accepted for canoes. Skiffs may be used only on the Whitewater Bay side (not in Florida Bay). For a total water experience, you can rent a houseboat that sleeps 6–8 people for up to a week. Houseboat renters can rent a canoe for a discount and bring it on the houseboat for exploring shallow places.

Boat Tours

There are three types of boat tours, all operated by the concession (fees charged). The very large capacity "Bald Eagle" and "Pelican" pontoon boats operate in Florida Bay and Whitewater Bay and cruise for 1½ and 2 hours respectively, with a naturalist narrating and pointing out wildlife. The six-passenger "Everglades Queen" seeks out the shallower backwaters for three hours. The boat captains know where to find interesting wildlife. The sailboat "Windfall" is a 57-foot sloop that sails into Florida Bay for the sunset every evening in the winter. Reservations are required for all boat tours.

Visitor Center Complex

The Visitor Center complex near the marina includes a ranger station, museum, observation deck, and gift shop, as well as the restaurant and lounge. Go to the ranger station if you need to plan a backcountry trip or get a permit. Information on ranger-led activities is also posted there. In summer, the ranger station desk may be closed, and you may have to self-register for a backcountry permit. Next to the ranger station is the small museum with exhibits of local Everglades ecology.

The observation deck is a great place to be at low tide. Wading birds and shore birds are abundant and easily observed. Pelicans, ospreys, terns, skimmers, cormorants, and gulls round out the complement of birds. In most years, a pair of bald eagles nest on a small mangrove island just offshore and are visible from the deck. Peregrine falcons hunt for shorebirds and ducks over the mud flats in the winter. Bottle-nosed dolphins are frequently seen in the bay by Flamingo.

The Gift Shop (beneath the restaurant) has a wide assortment of books, gifts, and souvenirs. It is closed in summer, usually from May 1 to October 31. Register for the tram tours to Snake Bight here. The tours operate three times a day from about mid-November to Easter. The trip lasts 1½ hours.

Walking Trails
Bear Lake Trail

Go to Bear Lake Road on the west side of the Buttonwood Canal and turn north. The trail head is at the north end of Bear Lake Road, 1.8 miles from the Main Park Road. This unpaved road may be closed to vehicles if the potholes are bad. The trail parallels the Homestead Canal through dense mangroves and other hardwoods. The canal was so named because it connected Cape Sable with Homestead. The fill for the trail was obtained from dredging the canal in the 1920s. Birding will probably be concentrated on passerines and other small woodland birds, particularly warblers in winter. Photography will require fast film and short lenses. The trail is 1.6 miles one way.

Eco Pond

Located between the marina and the campground on the main road, this eight-acre freshwater pond is an excellent place for observing wildlife. The treated effluent from Flamingo is discharged into this shallow evaporation pond. The half-mile

Butterfly orchid

loop trail circumnavigates the cattail-dominated pond. From the observation platform at the beginning of the trail, you can watch herons hunting for fish, gators hunting for herons, and raccoons hunting for just about anything. The ramp leading to the observation platform was completed in January 1992 for handicapped-accessibility. Eco Pond is a popular roost for white ibis and roseate spoonbills, so try to be there at sunset or sunrise. Look for rails, smooth-billed anis, painted buntings, baby gators, frogs, and bobcat tracks around the pond.

Guy Bradley Trail

If you're looking for a shortcut by foot or bicycle from the campground to the marina, take this one-mile trail located at the eastern end of the campground by the amphitheater. It meanders partly along the shore and gives a good view of the mud flats at low tide where you may see a reddish egret. Marsh rabbits often feed along the trail.

Bayshore Loop

This trail begins at the very western end of the drive-in campground Loop C, where the Coastal Prairie Trail starts. It's a 0.4-mile unmarked loop that goes from the Coastal Prairie Trail to the shore of Florida Bay. To find it, turn left at the sign "Coastal Prairie Trail" that's part way down the Coastal Prairie Trail. Florida box turtles are frequently seen. In summer, it is muddy and overgrown. It's a convenient walk from the campground.

Coastal Prairie Trail

This trail, which follows an old roadbed beginning at the western end of campground Loop C, goes through buttonwood forests and coastal prairie. There is little shade and the breeze never seems to reach here. It is often hot, humid, buggy, and wet. On a cool winter day, none of these are a problem, and the trail is delightful. Salt-tolerant plants (like saltwort, glasswort, prickly-pear cactus, sea purslane, yucca, and coral bean) dominate. A hardy backpacker can hike to Clubhouse Beach at the trail's end (7.5 miles) to camp. The white sand beach is beautiful, and with the prairie behind and the mangroves on either side, you can feel quite isolated. Bring plenty of drinking water; there are no facilities.

Canoe Trails

Nine Mile Pond

This is a nice trip for the summer months, when the water level is high, since mosquitoes are less prevalent here. The trail is a 5.2-mile loop and takes about four hours to complete. The National Park Service distributes an excellent printed guide for this trail that is coordinated with numbered signposts, so be sure to ask for one at the Visitor Center. Watch for immature bald eagles here. Motors are prohibited.

Noble Hammock

The trail originally was used during Prohibition by bootleggers going to their stills in the hammocks. The two-mile loop is marked with numbered floats and takes about three hours. Low water may present a problem during the dry season. Narrow passages and tight corners make this trail tricky for novices. Motors are prohibited.

Hell's Bay

You'll understand the origin of this trail's name when you paddle your way through the dense mangroves, cutting through spider webs, clouds of mosquitoes, and branches masking the trail. The trail is marked with floats. The distance is three miles to Lard Can, the first campsite (about two hours). About a half-mile farther is the Pearl Bay Chickee, and about two miles past Pearl Bay is the Hell's Bay Chickee. Not for novice canoeists.

West Lake

A 7.7-mile trail starts from the launch by the West Lake Interpretive Shelter. The trail first crosses a long stretch of open lake, making for windy paddling much of the time. The marked trail progresses through a series of smaller lakes connected by creeks and terminates at Garfield Bight. The Alligator Creek campsite (no improvements) is located at Garfield Bight. Allow about seven hours travel time one way. The Shark Point campsite on Florida Bay is two miles farther.

Coot Bay

There are three places to launch a canoe headed for Coot Bay: at the Flamingo Marina, at the north end of Bear Lake Road, and at Coot Bay Pond. Launching from Flamingo adds about 2 miles, but the Bear Lake Road may be closed; therefore, Coot Bay Pond may be the shortest route. The Buttonwood Canal is straight and easy paddling, a good choice for novice canoeists or windy days. Coot Bay is open and can be windy. Canoeists can continue to Mud Lake then circle back via the Bear Lake Canoe Trail to Bear Lake Road. That loop is 4.8 miles long.

The bay is named for a past era when coots, aquatic chicken-like birds, were abundant here. They fed on the aquatic vegetation that was wiped out when the canal was built because the canal allowed saltwater intrusion. The salinity has been reduced since 1982, when the "plug" (a concrete dike) was installed at the Florida Bay end of the canal to prevent further intrusion.

Bear Lake

As with the Coot Bay Trail, there are three possible launch sites: the Flamingo Marina, at the north end of Bear Lake Road, and at Coot Bay Pond. The Bear Lake Road requires a 200-yard portage, but the road may be closed. From the Bear Lake Road portage, it's 1.6 miles to Bear Lake along a narrow mangrove-lined canal. The canal was dug in 1922 to drain Cape Sable and provide access to the Cape. Motors are not permitted on Bear Lake Canal.

Cape Sable

Experienced canoeists who desire a two- to three-day camping trip can continue past Bear Lake to Cape Sable. The total distance from Bear Lake Road to Cape Sable is 12 miles and includes a second portage on East Cape Canal. Parts of the western stretch can be impassable during the dry season (check with a ranger). The destination is a campsite on East Cape, which means a paddle of about one mile on open Gulf of Mexico waters (not recommended for novices). Camping on Cape Sable is very remote and peaceful. Aside from an old dock, there are no reminders of civilization. Look closely at the sand on the beach; it's made of broken shells, not quartz like most other beaches.

Florida Bay

Canoeing on Florida Bay can be wonderful or miserable, depending on the weather and tides. Check with a ranger or concession employee about those two factors before setting out into Florida Bay. Winds and tides can be very strong and thunderstorms can make it hazardous to be out in the open. Low tides can strand you for hours. The concession will not rent canoes for the Florida Bay side on windy days.

On calm days, when the water is called "flat" by the locals, canoeing on shallow Florida Bay presents an unbeatable way to see flocks of wading birds and shorebirds. Dolphins are frequently seen around Flamingo. Manatees and sea turtles are possibilities. Small sharks (such as black-tipped, bonnethead, and lemon) are common; their dorsal fins break the water's surface, revealing their presence. They pose no threat to people in canoes, but it is not advisable to wade in the shallow water.

Much of Florida Bay, including the Flamingo area, is covered by seagrass. There are three common kinds of seagrasses here: turtle grass (*Thalassia testudinum*), manatee grass (*Syringodium filiforme*), and shoal grass. Turtle grass, with flat blades up to a half inch wide, is grazed by green sea turtles. Manatee grass, which (along with other seagrasses) is grazed by manatees, has leaves that are round in cross-section. Shoal grass, with very narrow flat leaves, is important as an early colonizer of disturbed underwater sites.

During daylight hours, boaters are permitted to land on Bradley Key. This is a worthwhile and easy destination. The island was named for Guy Bradley, the Audubon warden who was killed nearby while protecting a colony of wading birds from plume hunters. Boaters may not land on any other island in this area. Another destination is Snake Bight, the cove to the east of

Flamingo. At low tide, hundreds of wading and shore birds gather to feed on the mud flats laden with invertebrates.

Boating

Flamingo is a popular launch site for small, shallow draft motor boats. There are two ramps: the Florida Bay ramp and the White-water Bay ramp on the Buttonwood Canal.

Although Florida Bay was once connected to Whitewater Bay by the Buttonwood Canal, passage is now blocked by the dike that keeps salt water from intruding into the mostly fresh canal. A boater who wishes to pass through Flamingo from one bay to the other, and who doesn't have a boat trailer at Flamingo, must have the boat mechanically hoisted over the dike at the marina (fee charged).

Florida Bay is shallow and laced with mud banks. At low tide, much of the bay is exposed, and the sight of thousands of wading birds and shorebirds feeding on the invertebrates and trapped fish is spectacular. The shallow water attracts small sharks, rays, dolphins, sea turtles, and occasionally a manatee. Local boaters learn to "read the water." That is, they can tell by the size of the waves and the water's color if they are about to hit a shoal. A newcomer to Florida Bay boating should get a nautical chart at the marina and stick close to port. Running aground is not just an inconvenience for the boater—it's destructive to the seagrass beds.

Fishing

All year long the lure of saltwater fishing draws people to Flamingo. Locals make frequent weekend trips for sport or to stock their freezers. For those who prefer shallow calm water and light tackle to deep sea fishing, Florida Bay is the perfect place. An easy (but not cheap) way for a novice to fish is to hire a fishing guide through the Flamingo Marina.

The most sought-after food fish are snook, redfish, spotted seatrout, black drum, mangrove snapper, tripletail, and sheepshead. Other popular targets are tarpon and ladyfish. The warm shallow waters of Florida Bay are a rich nursery for invertebrates (such as shrimp, crabs, lobsters, and mollusks) and larval fish. This gives the larger gamefish plenty to feed on.

In recent years, a combination of habitat destruction and sport fishing pressure has severely stressed the Florida Bay fisheries. Some guides claim the problem is with the commercial fishermen outside the park. However, on any one weekend day or holiday, several hundred recreational boats may be in the bay fishing. These boats are taking the fish that may be ready to spawn in the estuary. The toll on the scarred seagrass beds and on the thousands of fish that were caught and kept (plus the "stress-and-release" fish that may not spawn that year or even survive) every weekend all year cannot be ignored.

Best Time of Year

December to April for most activities. Mosquitoes and heat keep many people away in the summer.

EVERGLADES NATIONAL PARK—CHEKIKA

From Florida City, go north on SR 997/Krome Ave. about 9 miles to SW 168th St./Richmond Dr. Turn left, go 6 miles to SW 237th Ave., then right for 0.6 miles.

This is the most recent addition to Everglades National Park. The 640 acres that was formerly Chekika State Recreation Area was turned over to the National Park Service on October 1, 1991. This encourages visitor access to the eastern part of the Everglades to see a tropical hardwood hammock surrounded by sawgrass marsh. Visitors traveling between the main park entrance and Shark Valley or Everglades City will find a convenient place to camp or have a picnic lunch.

The area was named for the famous Seminole, Chief Chekika. Chekika was hanged in 1840 in a nearby hammock by Lt. Col. William Harney in revenge for several earlier attacks by the Seminoles.

As late as 1903, local Indian families camped in the high ground of the hammock. In 1943, oil prospectors drilled 1,250 feet into the underlying aquifer and struck water instead of oil. The resulting artesian well released 2.5 million gallons of sulphurous water a day. The deep well was later capped to prevent the ground water, having one type of chemical composition, from mixing with surface water, which has a different composition. Now the water is recirculated by pumping, so it looks like a spring. Chekika was hard hit by Hurricane Andrew and was not reopened for many months.

Facilities and Activities

Campground, nature trail, boardwalk, fishing and picnicking. U.S. fee area.

The Hammock Trail is a short footpath through a hardwood hammock, labeled with interpretive signs (not handicapped-accessible). A boardwalk crossing the sawgrass is also labeled with interpretive signs. The pond was created by directing the artesian well into a natural depression. See "Campgrounds" above for information on camping.

Best Time of Year

December to April for most activities.

EVERGLADES NATIONAL PARK— SHARK VALLEY

On Tamiami Trail, 18 miles west of the intersection of the Trail with Krome Ave./SR 997. Phone 305-221-8776 for National Park Service information; 305-221-8455 for concession information (tram tours, bicycle rentals).

Shark Valley is at the northern boundary of Everglades National Park. It provides access for visitors to the Shark River Slough, a wide but shallow and slowly moving body of water that supports much wildlife. It is easily reachable from Miami and Naples. Too many visitors to Everglades National Park head only to Flamingo or Royal Palm and miss this part of the Everglades. A trip around the Tram Road to the Observation Tower, whether by tram or bicycle, is a good way to see alligators and wading birds. Hurricane Andrew edged past here, causing major damage, although not as severe as farther south.

Facilities and Activities

Visitor center, bicycling, bicycle rentals, nature trails, birding and other wildlife viewing, naturalist programs, tram ride, and observation tower. Open 8:30 AM to 6 PM. U.S. fee area.

Visitor Center

This small center contains educational displays and items for sale, including local human and natural history books, slides, videos, and film. At the Visitor Center, you can obtain the schedule for the many ranger-led programs offered. These include a 3.5-hour bicycle tour to the observation tower, a three-hour get-your-feet-wet "Slough Slog" to a gator hole or hammock, a 45-minute walk on an elevated boardwalk, or a 20-minute sit-down talk next to the Visitor Center.

Vending machines for chips, snacks, and soft drinks provide the only food on the premises. Across the Tamiami Trail from the entrance station is a restaurant, run by the Miccosukees, which serves Miccosukee and American food. The marsh behind the restaurant is a good place to check for snail kites.

Trails
Tram Road

The main "trail" is the 15-mile loop road that leads to the Observation Tower. The road was built by Humbel Oil (now Exxon) in 1946 for oil drilling. It is paved and is seven miles on the western side and eight miles on the eastern side. Plenty of gators, including babies, can be seen at close range, such as in the culverts on the side of the road (but keep at least 15 feet away). Wood storks, deer, otters, water snakes, snail kites, and many other animals can be seen. The road intercepts Shark Slough and is the only way most people will get to see the slough. A slough is a slow-moving channel in the marsh that has slightly deeper water than the rest of the marsh. It holds water longer (has a longer hydroperiod), looks greener from the air, and serves as a refuge for wildlife when other areas dry up. Shark Slough is the largest slough in the park.

The only motorized vehicles allowed are the tour trams and official vehicles. Visitors can travel the road one of three ways: taking the tram, riding a bicycle, or walking. Due to the openness and heat, not many people choose to walk the entire length, although many people walk shorter segments. The tram is the most popular way.

The two-hour tram tours are run by the concession seven days a week all year (weather permitting). The tram makes a half-hour stop at the Observation Tower (see below) and riders are encouraged to disembark and ascend the ramp to the tower. Occasional stops are made elsewhere if the guide sees something interesting, but riders must stay on the tram. Reservations are suggested from December to March. Tickets are available at the Tram Tour Office (fee charged). Call first for departure times, since they vary seasonally. In the busy season, the schedule includes moonlight and early morning tram tours.

An excellent way to see and feel the Everglades more closely is by bicycle. Many people ride the 15-mile road. Visitors can bring their own bicycles or rent them from the concession. Specify if you want a bike with a basket for carrying your field guides and lunch. Bicycling is easy on the flat terrain, but it can get very hot. Bring plenty of drinking water and a sun hat. Don't attempt to bicycle if there are thunderstorms around. You will not be safe from lightning on a bicycle as you would be in a car, and there is little protective cover along the road. Allow at least two to three hours to pedal the route.

Bobcat Trail

A short walk from the parking lot is a 0.25-mile handicapped-accessible boardwalk that connects the two legs of the Tram Road. The boardwalk trail leads to the bayhead habitat and is punctuated by interpretive trail signs. A small gazebo midway along the trail provides a place to rest and enjoy the quiet. Look for rails, particularly the king rail, along the boardwalk.

Otter Trail

A 0.5-mile walk along the western leg of the Tram Road (from the parking lot) will bring you to the start of the Otter Trail, which is about one mile long. It is a narrow footpath through a hammock, also with interpretive signs, and emerges on the same side of the Tram Road.

Observation Tower Trail

Originally built as a fire tower, the current observation tower was remodeled in the 1960s for park visitors. A long spiral ramp (handicapped-accessible) now leads to the top of the 65-foot tower, which yields a glorious panoramic view of the Shark Slough. This is one of the more popular photography spots in the park. During the spring months, the drying of the glades forces gators, turtles, fish, and other wildlife to concentrate in the water at the base of the tower. Several dozen gators may be seen at once. The trees surrounding the tower also serve as a diurnal roost for yellow-crowned night herons. At the base of the tower are restrooms and drinking water.

The Tower Trail, a small side trail near the base of the Observation Tower, is 0.25 miles long. It is good for observing butterflies and great blue herons and for photography.

Best Time of Year

December to April (the dry season) because wildlife will be concentrated in the water along the road and the weather is cooler. In the summer, high water levels may drive snakes, frogs, and mammals onto the roads and trails where they are more visible.

EVERGLADES NATIONAL PARK— EVERGLADES CITY

The Gulf Coast Ranger Station in Everglades City is on SR 29, 4.8 miles south of the intersection with Tamiami Trail. For park information, call 239-695-3311 or 305-242-7700. For concession information (boat tours, canoe rentals), call 239-695-2591 or 1-800-445-7724, or write Everglades National Park Boat Tours, P.O. Box 119, Everglades 34139.

Tucked up in the northwest corner of Everglades National Park is a region called the Ten Thousand Islands. Named for the myriad of small, irregularly shaped mangrove islands, this area is popular with canoeists and anglers. It is a vast wilderness in which it is easy to find solitude. Wildlife abounds here. Manatees, dolphins, alligators, rays, sharks, sea turtles, spoonbills, and white ibises are visible at certain times of the year. This is a water-oriented area; there are mangrove islands but no land for trails. You'll just have to find a boat if you want to see this area. Everglades City was not affected by Hurricane Andrew.

Facilities and Activities

Canoeing and canoe rentals, boating, fishing, boat tours, visitor center, and gift shop. No entrance fee.

Visitor Center

The Visitor Center is also the ranger station where boaters and canoeists get back-country permits and maps. There are two audio-visual presentations available on request. The Visitor Center is located on the second floor of the building and is not accessible to the handicapped. Handicapped people should ask on the first floor for park information.

A concession operates the gift shop on the first floor and sells souvenirs, Seminole crafts, and a small assortment of books. Vending machines dispense sandwiches, snacks, and drinks. For more substantial meals, there are restaurants across the street.

Boat Tours

Two boat tours (fee charged) make it easy for visitors to see the Everglades coast by water. The "Ten Thousand Island Boat Tour" is a 1¾-hour trip through the coastal mangrove islands and estuaries. The concession will assist with wheelchairs.

Canoeing

Canoeing is an excellent way to see the Ten Thousand Islands. Trips of several hours to several days can be planned. This is the northern terminus of the Wilderness Waterway, a 99-mile canoe trail to Flamingo (see "Wilderness Waterway" below).

All canoe trips should be carefully planned in advance. Proper safety equipment includes a Coast Guard-approved personal flotation device for each person. The Coast Guard recommends all boaters bring a current NOAA nautical chart covering their route and vicinity. The chart for the Everglades City area day trips is #11430 ("Lostmans River to Wiggins Pass"). For the Wilderness Waterway trip, you would also need #11432 ("Lostmans River to Shark River) and #11433 ("Whitewater Bay"). The National Park Service recommends each person bring at least one gallon of water per day planned, plus enough for one extra day. Since strong tides can greatly impede your progress, check with a ranger for the local tide schedule.

Day trips don't require a backcountry permit, but it is best to check with a ranger before departing for the latest information on tides, winds, and storms. Tides can be very strong, and combined with a head wind, it can be impossible for a strong canoeist to make headway. There aren't many places to pull over and rest either. The mangroves can be confusing to navigate if you deviate from a marked trail or visibility decreases. However, with careful planning, you can make sure the tides are with you and enjoy a most delightful canoe trip.

Day Trips

The National Park Service distributes printed guides with maps for canoe day trips. The trips will be briefly described in the next two paragraphs for advanced planning, but you should ask the Park Service for these guides when you arrive or send for them earlier (request the canoe guides for Everglades City). You can bring your own canoe or rent one at the concession at the Ranger Station. You can launch at the Ranger Station or at Outdoor Resorts on Chokoloskee Island (Outdoor Resorts also rents canoes).

The Sandfly Island trip will take about 2½ hours paddling time (round-trip). Sandfly Island is about two miles from the Ranger Station, across open water. It will take longer if you circumnavigate the island. There is a dock at the near end, with a nature trail on the island, so get out and stretch your legs. The Chokoloskee Bay Loop is almost entirely open water with no reliable place to land and rest. It is also about 2½ hours paddling time.

If you prefer an "inland" canoe trip, you can choose several routes through narrow mangrove and sawgrass channels. You can leave either from an access road on the Tamiami Trail (about 11 miles east of Everglades City), from the Gulf Coast Ranger Station, or from Chokoloskee. The Turner River trip takes about five hours from Tamiami Trail to Chokoloskee and is not a loop (so an upriver return or alternate transportation back to your car must be planned). From Everglades City or Chokoloskee, you can take a shorter loop through Halfway Creek and Left Hand Turner River. This will take about three hours, depending on wind and tides. Due to the intense mosquito population, the inland trips are best avoided in summer.

There are other nice routes for day trips that you can plan yourself using a nautical chart. The rangers at Gulf Coast Ranger Station will be glad to help you plan a route.

Overnight Trips

Numerous combinations of routes can be used to plan overnight trips. In fact, there are too many to describe here. The backcountry chickees and campsites are strategically placed by the Park Service for overnight convenience (see "Backcountry sites" under "Camping" above). As mentioned above, you need a permit from a ranger to stay at a backcountry site. During the busy winter season, you will have a better chance of getting the backcountry camping site of your choice if you avoid holidays and begin on a weekday.

Wilderness Waterway

For those super-adventurous, super-experienced canoeists with 7–10 days available for serious canoeing, there is the Wilderness Waterway. It's a 99-mile marked canoe trail between Everglades

City and Flamingo. Even though the numbers on the markers begin at Flamingo, the trail can be traveled just as easily from the other direction.

While paddling along the waterway, you'll pass seemingly endless miles of mangroves. Concealed in the tangle of living trunks and prop roots are the skeletal ghosts of giant mangroves, destroyed in the hurricanes of 1960, 1965, and 1992. Some died by having their branches stripped bare of leaves.

Occasionally, a shell mound will create enough elevation for a change of vegetation. The shell mounds were built by the Calusa Indians, who lived along the southwest coast possibly as early as 1450 B.C. These indigenous people depended on shellfish, primarily oysters, clams, and conchs. They piled the empty shells into huge mounds. Some were burial sites, some were refuse piles, and some were structured for habitation. The latter mounds reached extraordinary proportions. The town of Chokoloskee, at the northern end of the Wilderness Waterway, is built on a 150-acre shell mound that is 20 feet high. Sandfly Island, west of Chokoloskee, is a 75-acre shell mound. While clams have since been depleted by canneries early in the 20th century, the oysters are still abundant. This will be gratingly obvious every time your canoe scrapes over an oyster bar.

The trail bisects some of the wildest country left in the eastern United States. That is why people who are looking for solitude and wilderness head for this unique trail. It is also why anyone who undertakes this journey must be experienced, well-prepared, and willing to take a risk. Risks are mostly in the form of strong tides, high winds, choppy water, lightning, sun exposure, hypothermia, lack of drinking water, and getting lost. The last one is not a problem if you keep the markers in sight. If you explore off the trail or encounter poor visibility, you can easily get confused in the tangle of mangrove islands. As for drinking water, there is no source from Everglades City to Flamingo. All boaters must carry their own in heavy duty (preferably hard-sided) containers that won't puncture and will be secure from raccoons. During the dry season, the lack of fresh water can drive raccoons and other animals to seek it from humans. Raccoons can chew through soft-sided containers.

The campsites (chickees and ground sites) are spaced at irregular intervals along the trail. Some are as little as a mile apart and some have almost ten-mile gaps. Since most campsites are slightly off the marked trail, they can be difficult to find. They are marked on the NOAA nautical charts #11430, 11432, and 11433. Be sure to get the Park Service brochure "Backcountry Trip Planner" that explains where the campsites are.

A long-distance trip like this must be planned well in advance. Since the trail is not a loop, you will need to arrange transportation from your destination back to your car, unless you plan to paddle the 99 miles back! The drive around by land between Flamingo and Everglades City is about 3½ hours.

Plan your Wilderness Waterway trip carefully. The Park Service brochure "Introduction to Canoeing the Everglades" includes an excellent checklist of items to carry. You'll have to get permits for the campsites (see "Backcountry Sites" under "Camping"). You can also buy a book called "A Guide to the Wilderness Waterway of the Everglades National Park" (by William G. Truesdell) from The Florida National Parks and Monuments Association. Write to the Association at 10 Parachute Key #51, Homestead 33034-6735 or call them at (305) 247-1216 for ordering information.

Fishing and Boating

Fishing is extremely popular around the Ten Thousand Islands. Snook, cobia, redfish, spotted seatrout, and mangrove snapper are some local favorites. Fishing guides can be contacted by calling the Everglades City Chamber of Commerce at 239-696-3941. Boats can be launched at the Baron Marina on SR 29 in Everglades City (239-695-3591) or at Outdoor Resorts in Chokoloskee (at the end of the causeway between Everglades City and Chokoloskee; 239-695-2881).

If you bring your own boat, you had better be good at reading the local nautical charts. The water is so full of shoals, it's almost impossible to drive in a straight line. During extremely low tides, boating to or from Chokoloskee may be impossible for several hours.

Best Time of Year

Generally, November to April. Winter has fewer mosquitoes, cooler temperatures, less rain, and more wading birds. In the summer, though, waters are calmer for boating. Some National Park Service programs may not be run during the summer.

FLORIDA PANTHER
NATIONAL WILDLIFE REFUGE

The National Wildlife Refuge system was established first and foremost to protect wildlife and their native habitats. A secondary objective is to allow public access where it is compatible with the primary goal. Thus, some refuges are not accessible to the general public or are barely so. Florida Panther is one of those. The 26,400-acre refuge was established in 1989 to protect the panthers and is generally closed to the public. However, the staff has found a way to share the refuge while preventing disturbance to the big cats. They offer guided tours of the refuge to small groups on a limited basis. These are not family recreational outings or birding trips, but rather educational trips to learn about the panthers.

The refuge is located at the northwest corner of I-75 and SR 29. It encompasses the northern end of Fakahatchee Strand, which consists of cypress and subtropical hardwoods. It shares its eastern boundary with Big Cypress National Preserve. The flatness of the terrain, like so much of south Florida, allows most of the refuge to have standing water during the wet season—from several inches to three feet. Slight rises in the limestone substrate allow for variations in vegetation communities. Thus, there are wet prairies, mixed hardwood hammocks, slash pines, and palmettos.

The refuge staff is actively involved in the recovery of the panther in south Florida. The refuge forms the core of several panthers' home ranges. Others travel across the refuge between Big Cypress National Preserve and Fakahatchee Strand State Preserve. Other species of special interest at FPNWR are the Florida black bear, Everglades mink, fox squirrel, bald eagle, Florida grasshopper sparrow, wood stork, and indigo snake.

This refuge also oversees Ten Thousand Islands National Wildlife Refuge, part of a large area of mangrove islands on the Gulf Coast near Everglades City. It is a relatively new acquisition and management plans are underway. No visitor facilities are planned, but visitor access by boat is permitted. Call FPNWR for more information.

Location, Mailing Address and Phone

Headquarters in Naples: Located at the southeast corner of the intersection of I-75 (Exit 15) and SR 951; office is in the Comfort Inn. Refuge: open by appointment only; located approximately 20 miles east of Naples.

3860 Tollgate Blvd., Suite 300, Naples 34114; 239-353-8442; http://floridapanther.fws.gov

Facilities and Activities

Guided tours by reservation only for a limited number of small groups (call a few weeks ahead). No fee.

A refuge employee will take small groups on a 2-hour educational tour of panther habitat and will describe the panthers' life history, how biologists study them, and what panthers need to survive in the wild. It is not likely that a panther will be seen.

Best Time of Year

Winter for cooler, drier weather, but summer is also nice and may offer greater ease in securing a reservation.

Pets

Not allowed.

J.N. "DING" DARLING
NATIONAL WILDLIFE REFUGE

One of the greatest tributes a conservationist can receive is to have a national wildlife refuge named after him. Thus, the great conservationist J.N. "Ding" Darling, founder of the National Wildlife Federation, has become immortalized in a refuge he helped create through his initiation of the "Duck Stamp" program.

The 6,354-acre refuge protects several tracts of land. The largest (Darling Tract) consists of mangroves and mud flats on San Carlos Bay. Migratory and wading birds frequent the two brackish impoundments within this tract. Over half of the Darling Tract is designated a Wilderness Area. The popular Wildlife Drive goes through part of the Darling Tract. The 100-acre Bailey Tract in the interior of the island is a freshwater wetland. Native dune plants thrive on the three-acre Perry Tract on the Gulf side of Sanibel Island. The 176-acre Buck Key offers canoeing around shallow mangrove flats.

About 800,000 visitors each year come to see such birds as the magnificent frigatebird, white pelican, reddish egret, roseate spoonbill, mottled duck, black skimmer, American oyster-catcher, and bald eagle. Alligators are commonly seen, and occasionally a crocodile is found on the Wildlife Drive. This is the northern limit for crocodiles on the Gulf coast. West Indian manatees regularly visit the refuge in the winter and eastern indigo snakes are seen occasionally year-round. Atlantic logger-head turtles and Atlantic ridley turtles dwell in the adjacent marine waters.

Birders from all over the continent come to "Ding" Darling in the winter. It is touted as one of the greatest birding hotspots in the country. Visitors to the refuge should allow a day for driving or biking the auto route, canoeing, and hiking the short trails. While you're in the neighborhood, stop in at the Sanibel-Captiva Conservation Foundation for more hiking (see separate entry).

The island of Sanibel has a beach resort atmosphere and has scenic charm. It is considered one of the best shelling places in the world. The island is very popular with tourists in winter, so expect crowds and reserve lodging accommodations well in advance. The crowds are gone in summer.

The refuge also manages several other undeveloped national wildlife refuges accessible only by boat: Pine Island (548 acres, 16 islands), Matlacha Pass (512 acres, 23 islands), Caloosahatchee (40 acres, 3 islands), and Island Bay (20 acres, 5 islands). They are bird nesting areas and have visitor restrictions. Contact "Ding" Darling's office for more information.

Location, Mailing Address and Phone

To Visitor Center: From I-75, take Exit 21 and go west on Daniels Parkway (which becomes Cypress Lake Dr.) Turn left onto McGregor Blvd./CR 867 and follow to Sanibel Island by crossing Sanibel Causeway (toll). On Sanibel, turn right onto Periwinkle Way, right onto Tarpon Bay Rd., and left onto Sanibel-Captiva Rd. Proceed to refuge Visitor Center 2 miles on right. To Concession (at Tarpon Bay): Follow directions above onto Tarpon Bay Rd., then straight north to Tarpon Bay. http://dingdarling.fws.gov

Visitor Center: 1 Wildlife Drive, Sanibel, Fl 33957; 239-472-1100

Concession: 900 Tarpon Bay Road, Sanibel Island 33957; 239-472-8900; www.tarponbay.com

Facilities and Activities

Wildlife Drive (auto route), wildlife observation, tram tour, bicycling and bicycle rentals, canoeing and canoe rentals, fishing and guided fishing, Visitor Center. Open sunrise to sunset. Wildlife Drive is U.S. fee area; gate opens at 7:30 AM and closes a half-hour before sunset; closed on Fridays. Visitor Center core hours are 9 AM to 4 PM, closed Fridays and Federal holidays. Fee charged for tram tour and canoe rentals.

Wildlife Drive

This is the main visitor access to view wildlife. The self-guided route is five miles long and passes salt marshes, mangroves, brackish and fresh water impoundments, and mud flats. The best time to see foraging birds is at low tide. An observation tower provides a good photography vantage.

Almost 240 species of birds have been seen on the refuge, and many can be seen along this route. Bald eagles and Arctic peregrine falcons are occasionally seen. Wading birds such as reddish egrets, snowy egrets, great egrets, white ibises, great blue herons, little blue herons, tricolored herons, roseate spoonbills (especially in spring), and wood storks can be seen. Ospreys are year-round residents (look for nests). Peregrines are fall and winter visitors. Waterfowl (such as mottled ducks, blue-winged and green-winged teal, northern pintails, northern shovelers, American widgeons, hooded and redbreasted mergansers) are found from December to April. Many species of shorebirds overwinter and are residents.

Nature Trails

The Indigo Trail is two miles each way and starts at the Visitor Center. It runs along a dike through mangroves. The Shell Trail is a 0.3-mile interpretive loop trail to an Indian shell midden. It is located at end of the Wildlife Drive.

The Bailey Tract is a 100-acre freshwater wetland area offering a network of 1.75 miles of hiking trails. Alligators and wading birds may be seen. To find it, take Tarpon Bay Road south from Periwinkle Way (opposite direction from the concession).

The Perry Tract is a three-acre tract that features native dune vegetation on the Gulf of Mexico side of Sanibel Island. Long stretches of pristine beach are accessible from here. To reach it from the causeway, take Periwinkle Way west, turn left onto Casa Ybel Rd., then left onto Algiers Rd.

Visitor Center

This fine new center (opened in 2001) offers exhibits, a short video program, and an excellent selection of natural history books and gifts. Rangers and volunteers offer many types of programs (inquire at desk for schedule).

Tram Tour

The tram offers visitors a two-hour guided tour of Wildlife Drive. It operates from the concession at Tarpon Bay Recreation Area on Tarpon Bay Road, just east of the refuge visitor center. The tram reduces the number of cars using Wildlife Drive. It does not run on Fridays.

Bicycling

Bicycles are allowed on Wildlife Drive. Indeed, this is a wonderful way to see some of the more discrete creatures. The concession at Tarpon Bay rents bicycles.

Canoeing

The Commodore Creek Trail is a 2-mile loop trail. It is reached by the Tarpon Bay Recreation Area on Tarpon Bay Road. From the boat launch, go west along the shore of Tarpon Bay for ¾-mile to the trailhead. The trail winds through beautiful red mangroves and seagrass and mud flats, offering views of wading birds, shorebirds, fish, crabs, and other wildlife.

The Buck Key Trail is a 4-mile marked loop trail on Captiva Island. To reach it, drive west on Sanibel-Captiva Road to Captiva Island, about nine miles past Tarpon Bay Road. The access is 'Tween Waters Marina (private), which also rents canoes. From the marina, paddle southeast about ¼-mile to Buck Key. The trail sometimes follows canals that were dug for mosquito control. The island is heavily vegetated with mangroves along the shore and hammocks in the interior. Avoid travel during low tide, since the canoe trail may be impassable.

Visitors may also launch canoes (or other non-motorized boats) from the right side of Wildlife Drive (the bay side) at marked locations.

The concession at Tarpon Bay rents canoes and kayaks. It also rents canoes with electric trolling motors.

Fishing

People may fish by launching small boats at the Tarpon Bay Recreation Area (launch fee charged) and fishing along the mangrove edges. Fishing is also permitted from the banks along

Wildlife Drive. The concession offers guided fishing trips. Red-fish, seatrout, and snook are three species of fish caught locally. Freshwater anglers can try the Bailey Tract (see above). Crabbers find blue crabs along Wildlife Drive and in the shallows around the mangroves by boat. Observe all refuge regulations for fishing and crabbing.

Best Time of Year

Winter is best for wintering birds and weather. Fall and spring are good for migrating shorebirds, raptors, warblers, and so on. Summer is best to see manatees off Tarpon Bay and Wildlife Drive.

Pets

Allowed on a 6-foot leash.

NATIONAL KEY DEER REFUGE

It was a close call. The diminutive Key deer (*Odocoileus virgini-anus clavium*, a subspecies of white-tailed deer) had reached the perilously low population size of about 50 individuals, when protection came in the form of a refuge created specifically for them. The islands had never supported great herds of the deer and human interference had whittled the numbers down by hunting, habitat destruction, automobile collisions, and other hazards. With the establishment of the refuge in 1957 came total protection from hunting, reduced speed limits, and regulations preventing harassment. The population has partially recovered, largely due to the persistent efforts of Jack Watson, the first warden of the refuge. Watson tirelessly and fearlessly pursued poachers and succeeded in getting them convicted. The present population is estimated at 700–800 deer.

The small size of these deer can be attributed to island living. Since the islands provide limited food and fresh water, the smaller deer thrive. Key deer bucks weigh about 80 pounds and does average about 64 pounds, the size of large dogs. Other than that, they look like their larger northern cousins.

Since this is a refuge for wildlife (part of the National Wildlife Refuge system), and most of the 8,542 acres is covered by the Gulf of Mexico, you won't find visitor facilities as in a national park. The Watson Trail and Blue Hole wildlife observation spot are all that were created for visitors. The deer may be found wandering anywhere on Big Pine or No Name Keys. With patience and careful looking, you will see these beautiful animals.

A special word of caution: drive very slowly and carefully around Big Pine and No Name Keys to protect the deer. They are too often killed by cars. Also, do not feed or entice the deer. Besides the improper diet they might receive, they learn to associate humans (and thus houses and cars) with food. Besides, there's a $250 fine! A sign on US 1 near the refuge keeps the grim tally of the year's deer mortality. Ten to fifteen percent of the population may be killed by cars in a single year. Free-ranging dogs are also deadly. Observe the deer quietly from a distance, and you will be rewarded by seeing more natural behavior.

The refuge also manages several other undeveloped refuges in the Keys: Crocodile Lake, Great White Heron, and Key West. These are primarily shallow water areas with mangrove islands that serve as vital habitat for seabirds, wading birds, sea turtles, and many other animals. Access is resticted or prohibited in most areas. Call Key Deer Refuge for information.

Location, Mailing Address and Phone

To Headquarters: On US 1, go to traffic light on Big Pine Key at MM 30.5 (Key Deer Boulevard). Turn right and go 0.1 miles on Key Deer Blvd. to shopping plaza on right; refuge office is on south side of shopping plaza. To Blue Hole: go north on Key Deer Boulevard 3.2 miles to sign saying "Blue Hole Observation Pool Entrance." Parking lot is on the left. To Watson Hammock Trail: go 0.3 miles past Blue Hole on Key Deer Blvd. Look for small sign saying "Wildlife Trail Entrance." Parking lot is on the left.

P.O. Box 430510, Big Pine Key 33043-0510; 305-872-2239. http://nationalkeydeer.fws.gov/index.html

Facilities and Activities

Nature trail, wildlife observation area. No entrance fee.

The headquarters building, open on weekdays, is where the administrative offices are located. There are a few visitor displays, and refuge personnel will be happy to answer your questions. If you arrive after hours, you can obtain a refuge map outside the office door or at the nature trail entrance. The map will show the most likely places to see the deer. Wander around the roads marked on the map in early morning or late afternoon and evening and you'll have a good chance of seeing a deer.

Blue Hole Observation Area

Formerly a rock quarry mined for road construction, this gaping hole now contains fresh water, a rare commodity in the Keys. The fresh water, which sits atop a layer of salt water, attracts many terrestrial animals that come to drink, including the deer. Freshwater aquatic animals, uncommon elsewhere on the Keys, may be found here. These include alligators, frogs, soft-shelled turtles, and largemouth bass. It's a good place to photograph (you need only lug your equipment a few yards from your car) or just sit and watch the wildlife parade.

Watson Trail

The trail was named for Jack Watson, the first refuge manager, and is about 0.6 miles long. As the name "Big Pine Key" suggests, the island is wooded with slash pines (*Pinus elliotii var. densa*), and so is this trail. The varietal name refers to the high specific gravity of the wood. Enough light gets through the canopy to allow the understory hardwoods to outcompete the pines. Under natural conditions, that doesn't happen, since wildfires suppress the hardwoods.

Under the pines are saw palmetto, wax myrtle, sawgrass, blackbead, buttonwood, key thatch palm, silver palm, and sweet acacia, to name some species along the trail. From May to October, expect to see white-crowned pigeons flying around. They feed on mast from figs and poisonwoods in Watson's Hammock, which the trail passes near. Also look for old, small ditches cut through the limestone years ago and stocked with mosquitofish for mosquito control. The ditches are treacherous to Key deer fawns that drown while trying to cross them.

The trail is flat, surfaced with a very thin layer of gravel, and wide enough for a wheelchair.

Best Time of Year

The deer are visible any time of the year. Early morning and late evening are the best times.

Pets

Allowed on a leash. However, dogs are a major threat to the deer (even on a leash, because the deer get accustomed to their presence and lose their fear of unleashed dogs), so it is preferable to leave them at home.

The Atlantic bottle-nosed dolphin is a common fishlike mammal of shallow south Florida marine waters, such as Florida Bay. [Larry Lipsky]   **1**

Two Key deer nuzzle each other on Big Pine Key. [Larry Lipsky]   **2**

Isolated Lignumvitae Key is relatively pristine.
[Larry Lipsky]   **3**

A visitor studies the view of the mangroves from the observation tower at Long Key State Park.
[Larry Lipsky]   **4**

The common salt marsh mosquito gorges itself on human blood. Actual body size is about one-quarter inch.
[Grover L. Larkins]   **5**

A male snail kite balances on a branch as it eats its staple food, the apple snail. [Rob Bennetts] **6**

A sawgrass marsh extends to the horizon, while two alligators bask in the foreground. [Larry Lipsky] **7**

Greater flamingos occasionally appear in Florida Bay. Those pictured were at Sandy Key in Everglades National Park. They are not known to nest in the wild in Florida. [Grover L. Larkins]

A sleek river otter emerges from the water at Shark Valley.
[Grover L. Larkins]   **9**

A limpkin, which can be recognized at night by its piercing cry, wades in swamps feeding on snails.
[Grover L. Larkins]   **10**

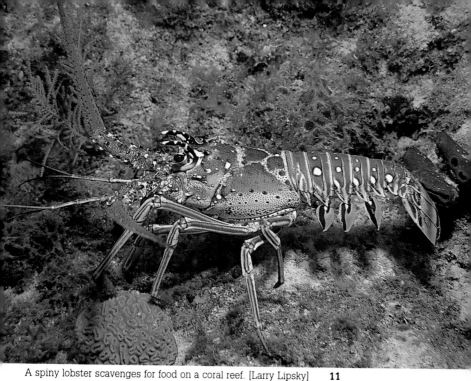

A spiny lobster scavenges for food on a coral reef. [Larry Lipsky]   **11**

One of the most captivating fish of the coral reef is the queen angelfish, named for the halolike marking on its forehead. [Larry Lipsky]   **12**

In its head-up and motionless stance, the American bittern camouflages beautifully with the reeds and grasses of its typical habitat.
[Grover L. Larkins]   **13**

A bald eagle devours its finned prey.
[Grover L. Larkins]   **14**

A female alligator guards her nest, a mound of decomposing sawgrass, rushes, and other aquatic plants. [Susan D. Jewell]   **15**

The spectacular roseate spoonbill uses its spatulate bill to sift through muddy water for small fish and shrimp. [Larry Lipsky]   **16**

A survivor in stone if nothing else, this Florida panther surveys the damage to the Gumbo Limbo hammock at Royal Palm (Everglades National Park) caused by Hurricane Andrew. Note the two fallen royal palms on the grass. [Susan D. Jewell]   **17**

Dulled in color beside the vivid red fire sponge, the bluestriped grunts, French grunts, and yellow goatfish school together on a coral reef. [Larry Lipsky]   **18**

This large tree is-
land in the southern
Everglades is
surrounded by
sawgrass.
[Susan D. Jewell]
19

Atop a nest of sticks, an osprey dines on a fish. [Larry Lipsky]   **20**

Fakahatchee Strand State Preserve staff have intentionally set this low-energy, carefully watched fire to keep ground debris from accumulating and causing an uncontrollable destructive fire. [Susan D. Jewell]   **21**

The town of Tavernier is surrounded by mangroves. The narrow undeveloped mangrove island in the background contains a channel that early settlers blocked at both ends to trap manatees (Cowpen's Cut). [Larry Lipsky] **22**

The Florida Keys are renowned for their spectacular sunsets, owed partially to the humid air. Here, two brown pelicans glide over Florida Bay near the old Florida East Coast Railroad tracks. [Larry Lipsky] **23**

An American crocodile basks on an algae-covered rock in the C-111 canal. Note the gray skin color, the narrow snout, and the protruding fourth tooth in the lower jaw that distinguishes it from an alligator.
[Grover L. Larkins]
24

ed touch yellow kills a ow" is the adage that rns of the poisonous al snake. Note the and yellow bands t touch each other d the black nose nfirming this is a al snake.
over L. Larkins]
25

The West Indian manatee is such a slow-moving creature that algae can grow on its back.
[Larry Lipsky]　**26**

A better adjective could not be found to describe the striking colors of the painted bunting, which winters in south Florida. Pictured is a male of the species; the female is a drab greenish yellow. [Grover L. Larkins]

27

A sea wall protects Fort Jefferson on Garden Key in Dry Tortugas National Park. In the clear shallow moat between the fort and the sea wall, many fascinating marine animals can be observed. [Susan D. Jewell]   **28**

A wood stork flashes its wings to startle prey, making foraging easier. [Grover L. Larkins] **29**

In the open cypress marshes of the Everglades, a hefty cowhorn orchid flowers in the spring. [Susan D. Jewell] **30**

This burrowing owl, with its characteristically long legs, stands beside its burrow that contains litter the owl collected.
[Larry Lipsky]   **31**

A male anhinga preens its feathers. The colorful eye ring indicates it is in breeding condition.
[Larry Lipsky]   **32**

A hungry brood keeps this female anhinga busy at the Anhinga Trail (Everglades National Park). Her fluffy chicks stick their heads into her mouth to retrieve the fish she's swallowed.
[Grover L. Larkins]   **33**

Of the many orchids native to Florida, the grass-pink (*Calopogon*) is one of the most beautiful. [Grover L. Larkins]   **34**

Brown noddies perch on prickly pear cactus on Bush Key at Dry Tortugas National Park. [Susan D. Jewell]   **35**

Birders and photographers gather on the bank of the famed Mrazek Pond (Everglades National Park) to watch wading birds feeding on the concentrations of fish. [Larry Lipsky]
36

Barred owls are a common sight at Mahogany Hammock and Corkscrew Swamp. Their "who-cooks-for-you" call can be heard often at night. [Grover L. Larkins]

37

Black skimmers, here at rest, feed by flying barely above the water, skimming the surface with their long lower bills to feel for fish. [Grover L. Larkins] **38**

VI
NATURAL AREAS:
STATE LANDS

FLORIDA CANOE TRAILS

The Florida Recreational Trails Act of 1979 authorized the state to establish recreational, scenic, and historic trails for the public. One network of trails is for canoeing. There are 36 such trails in the state trail system. The rivers and creeks were chosen for their scenic quality, variety of habitats, and distribution around the state. Almost 950 miles of waterways lace the state. Four trails are in the geographic area covered by this book.

The state trail designation does not mean that they are the only waterways worth canoeing. For example, lakes and larger rivers are not included but may be excellent for canoeing. Nor does it mean that they are only for canoeing; for example, motorboats are permitted. The waterways are publicly owned but often flow through private property, meaning that the stream banks are privately owned. Canoeists are responsible for making sure that they don't trespass. Water conditions vary with weather and season. After heavy rains, current flow may increase dramatically. During the dry season, water levels may be low enough to cause short portages.

Two of the four trails in our area are described in the state park section: Estero River is under "Koreshan State Historic Site" and Blackwater River/Royal Palm Hammock is under "Collier-Seminole State Park." One is described under "Riverbend County Park." The following is the description of the remaining trail, which does not flow through any park described in this book. The access points listed have parking areas. For more information and a trail map, contact the Department of Environmental

163

Protection, Greenways Management and Trails, Mail Station 795, 3900 Commonwealth Blvd., Tallahassee 32399-3000 (phone 904-487-4784) and specify the name of the trail.

Hickey's Creek

Half of this four-mile trail is on the Hickey Creek and half is on the Caloosahatchee River. Hickey Creek flows gently through a subtropical hammock. The river is wide and open, exposing canoeists to wind, waves, and motorboats. The creek is narrow and sheltered. There are two accesses. One is at the bridge over Hickey Creek on SR 80 (1.1 miles east of Franklin Lock Ramp, near Ft. Myers Shores), but there is really no place to park except the shoulder. The other is on the Caloosahatchee at the Franklin Lock Ramp, which is operated by the U.S. Army Corps of Engineers (U.S. fee area). From the north, the lock is off CR 78, just east of the Telegraph Creek Bridge. From the south, it is off SR 80, 7.2 miles east of I-75 at Old Olga Road. Launch on the upstream side of the river. A good quiet trip for beginners would be to launch at the SR 80 bridge, then go upstream (south) on Hickey Creek for two miles to the bridge at Bateman Road and return. Look for crested caracaras, bald eagles, ospreys, and wading birds.

LAKE OKEECHOBEE HOOVER DIKE TRAIL

To some hikers, reaching the summit of a mountain is the ultimate challenge. For Floridians, who have no mountains in their state, the challenge is met by circum-hiking Lake Okeechobee. The 110-mile trail is situated on the Hoover Dike, the levee that encloses the 750-square-mile lake (the second largest lake entirely within U.S. borders). It is one of the loop trails of the Florida Trail Association and is designated a Florida National Scenic Trail.

The dike was named for President Herbert Hoover, who ordered construction of the dike after the 1926 and 1928 hurricanes killed about 2000 people. They drowned when a wind-driven wall of water overflowed the natural bank of the lake, flooding Belle Glade. Since then, the dike and its associated water control structures have been used to control water levels in the lake, and the lake has been maintained at a lower level. Because of the reduced water levels, a once-familiar landmark to boaters—the "Lone Cypress"—guides no more. Its distinctive spreading crown now shades a roadside historic marker a half-mile from the lake!

The South Florida Water Management District maintains the dike and the control structures. The SFWMD continues to make improvements to the trail for hikers. For example, they provided a fenced walkway around a pump station near Belle Glade to save hikers a 9-mile detour.

Location, Mailing Address and Phone

Several access points are A) Moore Haven Recreation Area - Off US 27 in Moore Haven, one section west of the Caloosahatchee River Canal and one section east of the canal, B) Okee-Tantie Recreation Area - On SR 78, about 6 miles southwest of the town of Okeechobee. On the lake shore, north side of the Kissimmee River, C) Pahokee Recreation Area - Near the intersection of US 441 and SR 15/715 in Pahoke, D) Port Mayaca Recreation Area - Off US 441 in Port Mayaca, on the north side of the St. Lucie Canal.

South Bay Access Area: Off US 27, just northwest of South Bay.
For More Information:
Florida Trail Association, Inc. P.O. Box 13708 Gainesville 32604; 904-378-8823 or 1-800-343-1882 (Florida only)
S. Florida Water Mgt. Dist. P.O. Box 24680 W. Palm Beach 33416; 561-686-8800 or 1-800-432-2045

Facilities and Activities

Hiking, bicycling, camping, wildlife observation.

Veterans of the loop hike comment that it is an interesting trip. There are approximately 50 access areas, half of which are listed on the SFWMD recreational guide. Primitive camping is permitted along the levee or hikers may stay at fish camps. The mostly treeless trail is 20 feet above the surrounding land, offering dry footing and wide vistas of the surrounding country-side. If it hasn't been mowed in a while, the grasses may be tall. The lake, marshes, cattle ranches, and citrus groves comprise parts of the view. On the south shore, 2.2 miles east of the Miami Canal and 3.8 miles west of the railroad tracks in South Bay, is a bald eagle nest in an Australian-pine that is visible from the dike.

The lack of shade necessitates a warning to all trail users; bring plenty of drinking water and sun protection, even in the winter. In winter, it's difficult to predict whether the temperature will be 80° or 40°, so be prepared for both.

Hiking

Before going on a long hike (or bike), hikers should acquire the "South Florida Water Management District Recreation Guide to Lake Okeechobee" brochure/map from SFWMD in West Palm Beach (call or write). It lists the camping sites and facilities, where water and groceries are available, and access points and parks.

The Florida Trail Association sponsors an annual trek around the lake, dubbed the "Big O Dike Hike". It's held the week of Thanksgiving (from the Saturday before to the Sunday after) to allow for the 8 days the trip takes (a pace of 10–15 miles/day). The FTA makes all the necessary arrangements. Contact them in Gainesville for more information.

Bicycling

Bicycling is also permitted on the entire trail and is an excellent alternative to hiking. Mountain bikes would be appropriate, since the levee may be rough. With a bicycle, you can easily leave the trail and wander into one of the small lakeside towns for food, lodging, or just exploring. Plan around three days for a comfortable trip.

Best Time of Year

Winter, because of the cooler weather and lack of thunderstorms.

Pets
Permitted if under control.

WATER CONSERVATION AREAS

While part of the remaining true Everglades is contained within Everglades National Park and A.R.M. Loxahatchee National Wildlife Refuge (which contains Water Conservation Area 1), the rest is managed by the state as Water Conservation Areas (WCAs) 2 and 3. WCA 2 (134,400 acres) lies just south of Loxahatchee, and WCA 3 (584,700 acres) lies between WCA 2 and Everglades National Park. The conservation areas were created in the 1950s and 1960s by building levees and canals around them to control the surface water. They are now managed for multiple uses, including water storage, habitat protection, recreation, and hunting. WCA 2 and 3 are managed by the Florida Fish and Wildlife Conservation Commission as the Everglades and Francis S. Taylor Wildlife Management Areas. Hunting, frogging, and off-road vehicles are permitted. No environmental education facilities are available. Boating access is gained at ramps along Alligator Alley, Tamiami Trail, and US 27. Some ramp locations along the eastern boundary:

WCA 2:

at the west end of CR 827/Lox Road in Palm Beach County
  Markham Park in Broward County (see "Broward County Parks")

WCA 3:

Holiday Park in Broward County (private)
  Milton E. Thompson Park and Campground (county), 16665 NW 177 Ave., Miami 33192; 305-821-5122
  Contact the FFWCC at 561-640-6100 for more information.

BAHIA HONDA STATE PARK

The Spanish influence in this area is obvious by the name of the park, which means "deep bay." Indeed, the channel at the west end is one of the deepest natural channels in the Florida Keys. The bridge that spans it is correspondingly high, since the deeper the water, the higher the waves will be. The 635-acre park preserves many plant species of West Indian origin. One of the largest remaining stands of silver palm is found here.

Flagler's railroad passed through Bahia Honda, and remnants of the hurricane-torn tracks still rise above the park. Because of its height above the water, the old bridge is a good scenic observation spot.

This is Florida's southernmost state park. The park encompasses lagoons, beach dunes, coastal berms, mangroves, submerged marine habitats, and tropical hardwood hammocks. Several rare and unusual plants are found here: satinwood, manchineel, silver palm, key thatch palm, and the endangered small-flowered lily thorn (or spiny catesbaea).

Location, Mailing Address and Phone

MM 36.9, US 1 on Bahia Honda Key; 12 miles south of Marathon. 36850 Overseas Highway, Big Pine Key 33043; 305-872-2353. Concession: 305-872-3210

Facilities and Activities

Nature trail, birding, campground, swimming, picnicking, boat ramp, marina, cabins, fishing, windsurfing, kayak, bicycle, and snorkel rentals. Admission fee. Fees for camping, cabins, rentals, and boat trips are extra.

There are three camping areas with 80 sites for trailers and tents. Six cabins can accommodate eight people each; linens and utensils are provided. No pets overnight.

The concession runs daily snorkel trips to the coral reef at Looe Key. Looe Key is part of the Florida Keys National Marine

Sanctuary. Swimming and snorkeling are excellent from the beaches on the ocean and bay sides.

At the marina, charter boats and fishing guides are available for hire. There is a boat ramp and overnight docking facilities. The concession store sells marina supplies and limited groceries.

In the autumn, Bahia Honda is a good place to watch for migrating birds. The birds fly south along the chain of keys, resting, feeding, and searching for a way to cross the big water.

Silver Palm Trail

This is a short loop trail, about a 15-minute walk, near the swimming beach on the Atlantic side. A printed trail guide follows the numbered posts, explaining the hammock and dune ecology. The shrubby silver palms are common along the way because they are protected here. Elsewhere, silver palms are stolen from their natural settings to be planted in peoples' yards. The silvery undersides of the fronds are indeed beautiful.

Other plants along the trail, such as bay-cedar and black-torch, are typical of Keys beaches. Sea oats and sea-grape, seen along the beach, are state-protected dune stabilizers. Animals include land crabs and white-crowned pigeons in the hammock and wading birds in the lagoon.

Best Time of Year

For migrating raptors, shorebirds, and warblers, March, April, and September to November. For wintering birds, December to April. For diving and snorkeling, April to November.

BILL BAGGS CAPE FLORIDA STATE RECREATION AREA

Cape Florida is part of a large barrier island that protects the mainland. Beaches and dunes are a natural part of the Cape. In 1992, the island was put to the test when Hurricane Andrew blew ashore about 15 miles south. The southern tip of Cape Florida was at the outer edge of the northern eye wall. Virtually every tree in the park was blown down. These were primarily the unwanted Australian-pines, which are clearly not hurricane adapted. The park staff took this opportunity to initiate major habitat restoration. They cleared all the downed exotics, removed the surviving exotics, and replanted native species (e.g., sea-grape, geiger tree, cabbage palm). The result is a spectacular improvement of this park as a natural area.

In 1966, the state bought 406 acres at the south end of Cape Florida and named the new park after a Miami newspaper editor instrumental in getting the area protected. Because of the Cape's proximity to the dangerous shoals and reefs of the Atlantic Ocean and Biscayne Bay, a lighthouse was built in 1825. Through the bitter Seminole Wars, the lighthouse was alternately lit and darkened. It survived Andrew and underwent major renovations in 1996 to restore it to its appearance in 1825, when it was relit after a long darkness.

The waters around Biscayne Bay have attracted a rather unusual situation. If you go to the seawall at the southwest corner of the park and look out into Biscayne Bay, you'll see the famed neighborhood known as "Stiltsville." Through the years, people have built houses on stilts in the bay, obviously accessible only by boat.

Cape Florida is primarily a recreational area, with Miamians flocking to the beaches in the summer and the picnic areas on holidays. For a few months in the fall, Cape Florida shines as a birding hotspot. Because migrating birds, particularly warblers and raptors, follow the coastline from the north, they often congregate on the south end before venturing across the water. You may see as many as 20 species of warblers in one day when unfavorable winds or weather frontal systems concentrate migrating birds at coastal sites. Shorebirds frequent the long stretches of beaches.

Location, Mailing Address and Phone

At the southern end of Key Biscayne (southeast Miami). From the southern end of I-95, take the Rickenbacker Causeway south to

the park entrance.
1200 S. Crandon Blvd., Key Biscayne 33149; 305-361-5811

Facilities and Activities

Swimming, nature trail, birding, picnicking, fishing, bicycling and rentals, kayaking and rentals, historic lighthouse, snack bar. This is a day-use park. Admission fee.

A self-guided nature trail cuts through a hammock for about a half mile one way near the swimming beach. Interpretive signs explain about the native vegetation and habitat. A bicycle path circumnavigates most of the park, but joins with the road for a short stretch. The beautiful swimming beach is on the Atlantic Ocean side and is about 1.25 miles long. The seawall along Biscayne Bay is a popular fishing place. Anglers can catch snappers, groupers, jacks, snook, and other game fish.

The 95-foot lighthouse is an interesting historic site. Tours inside are given periodically during the day (fee charged). The lighthouse area is a good place to watch for migrating birds. It's possible they use the lighthouse as a navigational aid, as mariners do.

Best Time of Year

September to November for migrating birds. Year-round for all other activities, such as swimming and fishing.

CAYO COSTA STATE PARK

Put your walking shoes on, because you can't drive around this park. No roads span the Pine Island Sound to this 2,100-acre pristine park, which still resembles its appearance 500 years ago. The park includes parts of three islands: LaCosta, North Captiva, and Punta Blanca. LaCosta contains the docks, campground, and trails. Shelling is very popular on the miles of sandy beaches as it is on all the barrier islands in the area. The habitat includes pines, oak-palm hammocks, and mangroves. This is a popular stop for southbound shorebirds in August and September.

Location, Mailing Address and Phone

Accessible only by boat. Commercial ferries include Kingfisher Cruise Lines in Punta Gorda (941-639-0969) and Tropic Star Cruise Boat in Bokeelia (239-283-0015).

c/o Gasparilla Island State Park, P.O. Box 1150, Boca Grande 33921; 239-964-0375

Facilities and Activities

Primitive camping, rental cabins, hiking, swimming, shelling, picnicking.

Five trails lace the north end of the main island. The campground contains tentsites and 12 rustic cabins. Reservations are accepted for the cabins. No pets overnight.

Best Time of Year

Summer for boating and swimming, late summer for migrating birds, winter for shelling and camping.

COLLIER-SEMINOLE STATE PARK

Everywhere you turn in this part of the state is something with the Barron Collier name. Barron Collier owned a million acres locally in the 1920s. Part of his holdings included a rare stand of native royal palm trees. Collier reserved this stand for a park. It became a state park in 1947. Before Collier owned the land, it was the home of the Seminole Indians. Some still live nearby. The park's name partly honors these Native Americans.

One of the most impressive historical features in the park is the "walking dredge" displayed near the entrance station. This dredge, a huge contraption, was used to dig the Tamiami Canal in the 1920s. The 60-foot-long machine had legs that spanned the width of the yet-to-be-dug canal. The dredge would scoop the ground between its legs, then "walk" along, scooping as it went. The dredged material would be placed alongside the canal and sculpted into a road. Other walking dredges were used to build other canals in south Florida.

The park's 6,423 acres contain diverse habitats: tropical hardwood hammocks, mangroves, cypress swamps, salt marshes, and pine flatwoods. Thus, the wildlife is also diverse. Some of the rare and endangered species of Florida that have been seen here are the bald eagle, wood stork, brown pelican, red-cockaded woodpecker, crocodile, manatee, black bear, and mangrove fox squirrel.

The tropical hardwood hammock contains trees typical of the coasts of the West Indies and Yucatan. Royal palms, which may reach 100 feet tall, grow in this hammock. The mangroves are mostly found in a 4,760-acre wilderness preserve within the state park. This relatively untouched preserve can be explored by canoe.

The park was on the extreme northern edge of Hurricane Andrew. Damage was minimal. Some trees were knocked down. Oaks were uprooted and branches were broken off. Most royal palms withstood well, but some were beheaded.

Location, Mailing Address and Phone

On Tamiami Trail (US 41), 17 miles south of Naples, near Marco Island; 8.4 miles east of SR 951, 15.6 miles west of SR 29.
20200 E. Tamiami Trail, Naples 34114; 239-394-3397

Facilities and Activities

Self-guided nature trail, hiking and bicycling trails, interpretive center, fishing, canoeing and kayaking, boating and boat ramp, guided boat tours, campground, and primitive camping. Admission fee. Fees for camping, boat tours, and canoe rentals are extra.

The 130 campsites are split into two campground areas, one popular for tenting and one for recreational vehicles; pets allowed overnight. One-hour guided pontoon boat tours through the mangroves on the Blackwater River are run year-round. Some ranger-led programs are available only during the winter. Paddleboats can be rented for use in the boat basin. There is a boat ramp at the boat basin from which motorboats can run the Blackwater River to the Ten Thousand Islands.

Interpretive Center

The Interpretive Center is a tiny building that is of more interest than the exhibits it houses. The building is a cypress log block house, a replica of the type used locally during the Seminole Wars by the defending whites. Its six sides were made of limestone rocks on the first floor and cypress logs on the second. The interpretive exhibits on local natural and human history are located in the small room downstairs.

Walking Trails

The Royal Palm Nature Trail

This 0.9-mile self-guided trail wanders through tropical and temperate hardwoods. Large royal palms, Jamaica dogwoods, and gumbo-limbos grow along the trail. The cabbage palms are hosts for the epiphytic golden polypody and rare shoestring ferns. The trail is partly boardwalk and partly hardpacked dirt (not wheelchair accessible). Interpretive signs line the trail. A dead-end spur of boardwalk leads to a small observation platform overlooking the salt marsh. During the winter, songbirds that migrated from the north use the hammock for foraging.

Collier-Seminole Hiking Trail

This trail is relatively unknown because it's not on the state park map. It starts on US 41, 0.7 miles east of the park entrance. The small gate on the north side is unmarked. This is because hikers must first register at the entrance station to gain access through the locked gate.

The 6.5-mile loop trail passes primarily through pine flatwoods and cypress swamps. There is a primitive backpackers' campsite about three miles from the gate. Carry at least a gallon of drinking water per person for an overnight stay.

Royal palm

Canoeing

The mangrove Wilderness Preserve is accessible by canoe (rentals available). The trail is 13.5 miles long and has a primitive campsite for an overnight stay. In the winter, rangers lead three-hour guided canoe trips to Mud Bay, part way along the canoe trail. Manatees are occasionally seen along the trail. Wading birds are common.

Best Time of Year

November to April. The nonmosquito season.

DUPUIS RESERVE STATE FOREST

The 21,875 acres of Dupuis Reserve State Forest contain a variety of habitats: pine flatwoods, wet prairies, cypress domes, and marshes. Bald eagles, wood storks, limpkins, bobcats, deer, armadillos, and many other kinds of wildlife may be seen.

The reserve, straddling Martin and Palm Beach counties, was purchased in 1986 by funds from "Save Our Rivers", a program maintained by the South Florida Water Management District to protect water resources. It is managed as a limited multi-use area, allowing hiking, hunting, and horseback riding. The Florida Trail Association created and still maintains the hiking trails. The DuPuis Horsemen's Association developed and maintains the equestrian trails.

Cattle and sheep ranching operations by former owner John H. DuPuis (pronounced doo-pwee') are evident by the park-like understory and the drainage ditches and fences still crossing the land. The SFWMD is gradually filling ditches to restore the natural hydrology of the land.

Location, Mailing Address and Phone

Take the Beeline Highway/SR 710 to SR 76. Go west on 76 about 6 miles. Look for Gate #2 on your left; this is the hikers trailhead parking lot. Gate #3 is for horseback riders. Alternate route: take SR 441 to Port Mayaca, turn east onto SR 76 and go about 5 miles to gates (on right).

561- 924-5310 (SFWMD) for hiking information

561-640-6100 (Florida Fish and Wildlife Conservation Commission) for hunting dates

Facilities and Activities

Hiking, wildlife viewing, primitive backpack camping, horse trails. Entrance fee; extra fee for camping. Gate open dawn to dusk; may be closed on weekends during hunting season in the autumn and winter (call FFWCC for hunt schedule).

Hiking

Four loop trails give hikers a choice of four distances: 4.3, 6.8, 11.5, and 15.5 miles. You can easily plan an all-day hike. These trails are for hiking only; the horse trails are separate. The trails are flat, grassy, occasionally wet (especially in the summer and autumn), and can be bumpy because of feral hog rootings. The canopy is open slash pines and live oaks (little shade) with frequent cabbage palms. The understory is an open grassy parkland and saw palmetto clumps. Some plants you may encounter are round-leaved sundew, bog bachelor-button, gallberry, white sabatia, celestial lily (endangered), glades lobelia, and spider orchid.

Wildlife abounds for the observant. Deer, bobwhite, wild turkeys, raptors, gray foxes, and bobcats are common. Bald eagles, sandhill cranes, alligators, and indigo snakes may also be seen. Waterfowl and wading birds feed in the marshes.

Camping

The distance from the trailhead to the West Route primitive campsite is 5.7 miles and from the trailhead to the East Route primitive campsite is 9.7 miles. Campers must pay a small fee at the gate. There is no potable water.

Horse Trails

There are three loop trails, with the shortest at 7.2 miles long and the longest at 16.5 miles long. These trails are located in the same general area as the hiking trails (which they occasionally cross), so the habitats are similar. However, the horse trails are placed on the more upland places within the area. Camping and use of the horse barn are allowed at the Equestrian Center by the parking lot (extra fee).

Best Time of Year

From December to April for the driest trail conditions.

Pets

Allowed on leash.

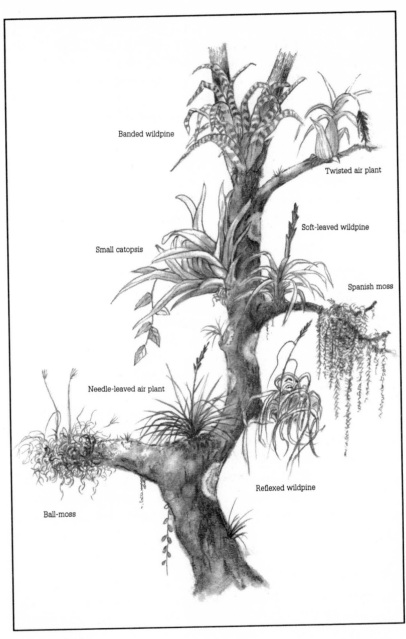

Banded wildpine

Twisted air plant

Soft-leaved wildpine

Small catopsis

Spanish moss

Needle-leaved air plant

Reflexed wildpine

Ball-moss

Bromeliads

FAKAHATCHEE STRAND STATE PRESERVE

Fakahatchee Strand State Preserve is a priceless addition to the state park system. It extends from Alligator Alley on the north end to Everglades National Park and the Ten Thousand Islands on the south. The strand, approximately 20 miles long and varying from 3 to 5 miles in width, is part of the Big Cypress Swamp. The 74,000-acre preserve, the largest unit in the Florida park system, contains the largest stand of native royal palms and the greatest variety of native epiphytic orchids, bromeliads, and ferns in North America. Many rare plants are found here. Currently there are 38 native ferns, 38 native orchids, and 14 native bromeliads.

Although it is now one of the wildest areas left in Florida, traces of old logging operations that ended in the 1950s are evident. The old roads used for logging cypress trees are called "trams" now by the locals. The only old growth cypress left in the preserve are at Big Cypress Bend. Natural plant communities in the preserve include mixed hardwood swamps, swamp lakes, wet prairies, cypress forests, pine rocklands, oak-palm islands, fresh water marshes, saltwater marshes, and mangrove swamps. Because of this diversity, about 140 bird, 21 mammal, 24 reptile, and 14 amphibian species have been documented in the preserve. Fakahatchee Strand is one of the last strongholds for the Florida panther. Black bears, Everglades mink, bald eagles, and wood storks also live in the preserve.

During the dry season, you can easily spend a day hiking the trams and walking the Big Cypress Bend boardwalk.

Location, Mailing Address and Phone

There are two main accesses. Big Cypress Bend is on the Tamiami Trail, 7 miles west of the junction of Tamiami Trail and SR 29. It is right next to the Indian Village. To find the Headquarters and Janes Scenic Drive from Tamiami Trail: turn north onto SR 29, drive 2.5 miles to County Road 837 in Copeland. Then turn left onto County Road 837 and drive 1.1 miles, bearing sharply right at the fork in the road, to a small building on the right that is the Fakahatchee Strand State Preserve headquarters (next to the fire tower). If the office is closed, pick up a brochure outside and continue up the road. Almost immediately the road becomes Janes Scenic Drive.

P.O. Box 548, Copeland 34137; 239- 695-4593

Facilities and Activities

Boardwalk, scenic drive, hiking trails, bicycling, guided walks (3rd Saturdays from Nov.–Feb., reservations required), birding. Note: This preserve is not developed for visitors. No food, water, restrooms, or other facilities are available. Write in advance for the vertebrate checklist (birds, mammals, amphibians, and reptiles). No admission fee.

Big Cypress Bend

This 2,000-foot (one way) boardwalk is an impressive addition to the state park system. It rivals Corkscrew Swamp Sanctuary's boardwalk on a smaller scale. If you are in the area to see Everglades City, for example, it is well worth a stop at Big Cypress Bend. It has been designated a National Natural Landmark. The boardwalk ends at a central slough with deeper water. Interpretive signs along the way explain about the slough that the boardwalk passes over, the massive old growth cypress trees, the abundant and fascinating epiphytes, other plants, and wildlife. Preserve brochures are available at this location also. Handicapped-accessible.

W.J. Janes Memorial Scenic Drive

Janes Scenic Drive is a well-graded gravel road about 11 miles long. Unless you really know your way around the abandoned roads at the far end (formerly part of the Golden Gate Estates, now Picayune Strand State Forest), consider the road a dead end. The Golden Gate Estates was a large-scale development fiasco that left a maze of dozens of unfinished roads in an otherwise wilderness area.

The speed limit is 30 mph to protect the wildlife, such as black bears, deer, panthers, foxes, turtles, and snakes. The lack of automobile traffic makes Janes Drive a good road for trail bicycles.

Hiking

The trams (old dirt logging roads) are scattered at intervals along Janes Drive. They are marked by locked gates, preventing vehicular passage. Most of the trams are overgrown and difficult to hike. Seven of the 20 trams have been partially cleared, meaning at least the first few miles of the roads have been cleared of regrowth, and passage by foot is easy. The cleared trams are Gates 2, 7, 12, 15, 16, 19, and 20. Even on the uncleared trams, the trails are obvious, since they are higher than the surrounding land. For specific information on the cleared trams, call the preserve headquarters.

The trams pass through many types of habitats, such as hardwood hammocks and swamps. Some of the more picturesque, such as Gate 7 (4.4 miles from the headquarters), open onto wet prairies. Because of the variety of habitats, it's possible to see many types of wildlife.

Guided Walks

The giant preserve is understaffed, leaving a paucity of natural history programs in this fascinating region. Also, conditions are often too hot and buggy in summer to lead walks. From November to February rangers lead monthly walks through the strand. Call in advance for reservations. Limit 15 people. Be prepared for some wet slogging—you may find yourself in waist-high water!

East River Pond

Paralleling the Tamiami Trail is a canal that was created by "borrowing" fill to build the road. Occasionally, more fill was needed and large pits were dug. The pits have filled with water and become ponds. One such pond is in Fakahatchee Strand State Preserve. To find it, drive 5.2 miles west of the intersection of SR

29 on the Tamiami Trail. A small brown sign for the preserve indicates the dirt turnoff on the left.

You can fish here and even launch a small boat. The pond is loaded with alligators. During the early summer (April–June), tricolored herons and snowy egrets may be seen in the mangroves in the pond. They are visible from the water's edge with a spotting scope and provide a good photographic opportunity.

Best Time of Year

February, March, and April for the driest conditions on the tram roads. November to April for Big Cypress Bend (best concentration of wildlife).

Pets

Not allowed on the Big Cypress Bend boardwalk; allowed elsewhere on a 6-foot leash.

GASPARILLA ISLAND
STATE RECREATION AREA

Development has squeezed much of the life out of this beautiful barrier island. All that remains of the original habitat is some beach and dunes. The wildlife that is left survives out of instinct and luck, not because of any assistance given by the park service. During the fall, migrations of shorebirds, raptors, and other birds follow the coastline and end up at Gasparilla temporarily. Shellers try their luck here, although its not as productive as Sanibel. The white "sugar" sands are dazzling.

Gasparilla was named for the pirate Gaspar (actually, "Little Gaspar"), who supposedly hid on the island between attacks. Charlotte Harbor was and still is excellent for shipping because of its depth. The town of Boca Grande reflects this fact in its name, which means "Big Mouth" in Spanish, referring to the deep port.

Location, Mailing Address and Phone

Gasparilla Island, located in Lee County, is accessible by land by the Boca Grande Causeway at the island's north end; take either CR 771 or 775 to the causeway (private toll) at Placida, then follow Gulf Boulevard south to the park.

c/o Gasparilla Island State Park, P.O. Box 1150, Boca Grande 33921; 239-964-0375

Facilities and Activities

Swimming, shelling, shorebirding, fishing. Admission fee.

Part of the interest of coming to this park is the drive to the island. Along the causeway, mud flats harbor shorebirds and wading birds, especially when the tide is out. White pelicans winter on the bay side.

Several sections of bathing beaches are located periodically along the road to the end of the island, each one with portable toilets. Check each place for birds and shells.

The lighthouse at the southern end of the island houses a small interpretive center with exhibits of shells, sea life, butterflies, and local history. It is only open the last Saturday of each month.

Best Time of Year

Autumn and during outgoing tides for shorebirds, summer for swimming; after a storm in winter for shelling.

HUGH TAYLOR BIRCH
STATE RECREATION AREA

When attorney Hugh Taylor Birch came to Florida from Chicago in 1893, he settled in the small village of Ft. Lauderdale. By the time he died, urbanization surrounded his 180-acre seaside estate. Birch donated his barrier island property to the people of the state as a recreation spot for all to enjoy. The park preserves some of the last coastal hammock habitat in Broward County.

Two self-guided nature trails, a small freshwater lagoon for canoeing, and access to a swimming beach on the ocean are the attractions.

Location, Mailing Address and Phone

From I-95, take Exit 30 to Sunrise Boulevard and go east 3.8 miles to entrance.

3109 East Sunrise Blvd., Ft. Lauderdale 33304; 954-564-4521

Facilities and Activities

Nature trail, canoeing, canoe rentals, Visitor Center, swimming beach, group campground.

A leisurely 20-minute walk will take you through the coastal hammock on the Beach Hammock Trail. Here you'll see pond-apple, sea-grape, Spanish stopper, marlberry, mastic, coontie, and torchwood plants labeled. The coontie is a reminder that this was one of the last strongholds of the atala butterfly larvae, which feed on the plant. The short Exotic Plant Trail has a brochure indicating native and exotic plants. The exotics include kalanchoe, oysterplant, banyans, and Australian-pine.

The Visitor Center was formerly Birch's house. It now contains natural and cultural history exhibits. Canoes are available for rent for use on the 0.6-mile-long lagoon.

Best Time of Year

No preference.

J.W. CORBETT WILDLIFE MANAGEMENT AREA AND HUNGRYLAND SLOUGH

Formerly timber company land, the 60,224 acres of Corbett encompass slash pine flatwoods, hardwood hammocks, freshwater marshes, and dense cypress domes—a transition between the uplands of central Florida and the Everglades. The Hungry-land Slough, which has standing water at least 9 or 10 months of the year, flows slowly through the center. Part flows east into Loxahatchee Slough and part flows west into Allapattah Slough. The lower portions of these sloughs once flowed into the Ever-glades. At present, canals surround Corbett, but the Florida Fish and Wildlife Conservation Commission is trying to restore the hydroperiods. The FFWCC has been managing the area for hunting since 1948. The Florida Trail passes through Corbett and a boardwalk built for nature observing invites non-hunters.

Native people constructed mounds around 500 B.C., and the Calusa lived in the area until around A.D. 1500. Between the 1500s and 1800s, the Seminoles roamed in small bands locally. They were chased into the slough by non-natives until they were starving and had to surrender. The area became known to local cattlemen as "the hungryland".

Corbett provides habitat for many types of wildlife besides the deer, small game, and feral hogs that draw the human hunters. The endangered Bachman's sparrows and red-cock-aded woodpeckers reside here. A 3,000-acre sawgrass area pro-vides habitat for snail kites. This is one of Palm Beach County's better easy-access getaways.

Location, Mailing Address and Phone

One entrance is 25 miles northwest of West Palm Beach via the SR 710/Beeline Highway and the other is 16 miles northwest of West Palm Beach on Seminole Pratt Whitney Road. The latter accesses Hungryland Slough: from the Beeline Highway, go west on North-lake Blvd./CR 809A for 8.7 miles to Seminole Pratt Whitney Road, then right for 2.9 miles to left turn, then 0.7 miles to grassy parking area (passing "Everglades Youth Camp").

Contact Florida Fish and Wildlife Conservation Commission in West Palm Beach for information; 561-640-6100.

Old World climbing fern, an invasive pest, covers cypress trees at
Hungryland Slough.

Facilities and Activities

Boardwalk, hiking trails, camping. Hungryland Slough always open; no fee. Wildlife Management Area Stamp needed for rest of Corbett.

Hungryland Slough Boardwalk and Trail (1.2 miles)—The upland segment of the trail passes through slash pine flatwoods with coco-plums, dahoons, and wiregrasses. Along the boardwalk are cypress accompanied by pond-apples, red maples, bromeliads (needle-leaved wildpine, cardinal air plant, giant wildpine, twisted air plant, ballmoss, Spanish moss), and 13 species of ferns (including strap, swamp, giant leather, chain, royal, bracken, resurrection). The open wetlands are dominated by sawgrass. In the hardwood hammock, where typical fires can't penetrate, are the oaks, paradise-trees, wild coffees, redbays and stoppers. Turkeys roost in the cypress at night, nest in the pine flatwoods, and feed in the hammocks. White-tailed deer, otters, limpkins, wood storks, sandhill cranes, and barred owls may be seen, as well as alligators, corn snakes, indigo snakes, cottonmouths, pygmy rattlesnakes, and green treefrogs.

Florida Trail (14 miles)—This trail goes west from the Hungryland parking lot to Dupuis Reserve (see separate entry). Along the way are three primitive campsites (at 5, 11, and 14 miles). These are available for hikers during the non-hunting season (fee included with WMA Stamp, register at trailhead). The trail goes through seasonally wet pine flatwoods.

Best Time of Year

Do not go hiking on trails (except Hungryland) during hunting season (peak is October-December); Hungryland Slough is open year-round and is away from the hunt area.

Pets

Restricted depending on location and season. Permitted on leash at Hungryland Slough.

JOHN D. MACARTHUR BEACH STATE PARK

While the Palm Beaches continue to squeeze out the surrounding green spaces, MacArthur Beach remains as a precious remnant of the subtropical coastal habitat. The 225 acres of uplands includes the coastal hammock, dunes, and mangroves, while 535 more acres contain underwater habitats. The beach and the reef are on the Atlantic Ocean, while the mangroves are on Lake Worth and Lake Worth Cove. Several nature trails and a pristine beach are the main attractions of this park, which was opened to the public in 1989. About 800 loggerhead, green, and leatherback sea turtles nest on the beach from May through August. Loggerheads are the most prevalent of the three. The lack of artificial lighting on the beach makes this one of the best turtle nesting areas in Palm Beach County. Snorkelers can enjoy viewing loggerhead turtles, tarpon, snook, and barracuda on the reef. Lucky visitors may see a manatee in Lake Worth. Along the 1,600-foot pedestrian boardwalk may be seen all three species of mangroves found in Florida. The mud flats along the boardwalk are also a good place to find wading and shore birds.

Location, Mailing Address and Phone

Located on Ocean Blvd./SR A1A on N. Palm Beach's barrier island; about 1 mile south of PGA Blvd./CR 786 and US 1 and 3 miles north of the bridge on Blue Heron Blvd.

10900 SR 703, North Palm Beach 33408; 561-624-6950; Nature Center: 561-624-6952

Facilities and Activities

Nature Center, nature trails, butterfly garden, swimming, snorkeling, guided programs. Nature center open from 9 AM to 5 PM (closed Tuesdays). Admission fee.

The 4,000-square-foot Kirby Nature Center contains exhibits of artifacts found in Riviera Beach from the Jaega tribe, live snakes, and live mangrove and reef tanks. It offers guided nature walks (year-round) and snorkeling trips (summer). A self-guided trail through the butterfly garden has a variety of native shrubs that butterflies depend on, such as indigo-berry, wild-lime, and fiddlewood.

The pedestrian boardwalk bridges the gap over Lake Worth Cove to the beach. Free trams run periodically from 10 AM to 4 PM to transport people who don't wish to walk. The boardwalk is a good place to look for wading birds and shorebirds on the mud flats.

Two nature trails provide access to the upland habitats. At the north end of the parking lot is the Satinleaf Trail, a leisurely 20-minute walk. The emphasis is on the mixture of temperate and tropical plant species. Satinleaf is one of the tropical ones, as are paradise-tree, mastic, and strangler fig. Temperate species include red bay, live oak, and red mulberry. Other species include pigeon-plum, wild coffee, Spanish stopper, and coral bean. The coastal hammock trail adjacent to the beach contains torchwood, Jamaica caper, blolly, paradise-tree, gumbo-limbo, mastic, and others. Twenty-six species are labeled.

The pristine beach is a prime nesting area for loggerhead, green, and leatherback sea turtles. Night programs are offered in the summer to observe the turtles laying their eggs. Snorkelers can wade from shore to the rock reef at high tide to see such fish as blueheaded wrasse, sergeant major, puffers, jacks, gray angelfish, and stingrays. Manatees are occasionally seen. Snorkelers must have their own "diver down" flag.

Best Time of Year

Summer for snorkeling and swimming, fall-spring for birds (roseate spoonbills April to October).

JOHN PENNEKAMP CORAL REEF STATE PARK

Appropriately, the nation's first undersea preserve is mostly under water. The park protects part of the only living coral reef in the continental United States. Within this marine sanctuary live

40 species of corals and 650 species of fish. The coral reef is very shallow in places, providing excellent snorkeling and scuba diving opportunities. The park's concession services make it easy for almost everyone to see the colorful reef, either by snorkeling, diving, or glassbottom boat. Other water-related activities are available here, including canoeing, fishing, and swimming. Land-bound facilities include camping and interpretive trails.

The park is named for John Pennekamp, a former associate editor of the Miami Herald, who was instrumental in getting Everglades National Park established. The original plans for the national park called for the boundary to extend south of Florida Bay, across Key Largo, and into the Atlantic Ocean, thus including the reef. Opposition from Florida Keys residents, whose homes would be within the new park boundaries, convinced officials that the only way to get the Everglades preserved was to exclude Key Largo and the reef. Fortunately, the reef was made into a state park shortly after.

Due to the intensive human usage of the reef, this glorious ecosystem is showing signs of stress and declining health. Among the culprits are careless anchoring, propellers striking bottom in shallow water, silting of coral by propeller wash, touching of coral by divers, littering, spilling fuel and oil, bilge pumping, and polluting from land sources. The reef is still beautiful, but please do your part to keep it that way.

Location, Mailing Address and Phone

MM 102.5 Oceanside, US 1, Key Largo.

For general park information, write P.O. Box 487, Key Largo 33037 or call 305-451-1202; for concession information, write Coral Reef Park Company, P.O. Box 1560, Key Largo 33037 or call 305-451-1621.

Facilities and Activities

Visitor center, diving and snorkeling, swimming, glassbottom boat trips, campground, canoeing, canoe rentals, nature trails, picnic tables, snack bar, gift shop, dive shop, boat ramp and fuel, boat rentals. State park entrance fee charged; fees for camping, boat tours, and rentals are extra.

Visitor Center

Open 8 AM to 5 PM. This visitor center outclasses all others in the area. The star attraction is the 30,000-gallon saltwater aquarium, called "The Patch Reef Tank," that recreates a coral reef. Visitors can view the tank from all sides. Although the coral is not alive, the fish don't seem to notice. The live occupants include large lobsters, queen and gray angelfish, ocean surgeons, foureye butterflyfish, hogfish, parrotfish, and yellowtail snapper. Lining the visitor center walls are many smaller tanks, including "The Seagrass Community," "The Spiny Lobster," "Threats to the Reef," "The Reef Fish Community," and "The Outer Reef." Static displays explain natural storm protection from the reef and the mangrove community. In the auditorium, 14 different films about the state parks (each 17–45 minutes long) run continuously; there is no set schedule. This is an excellent small seaquarium for all ages and is included with admission into the park. Ask for their bird list, which contains 198 species.

Swimming

There are three designated swimming areas. The main swimming area, near the main parking lot and the visitor center, is somewhat sheltered from the open ocean. It is a roped-off area with an artificial wreck of a Spanish galleon in very shallow water. The wreck attracts grunts, barracuda, hogfish, gray snapper, and other fish, all very easy for the beginning snorkeler to see. In fact, this is one of the few places in the Keys to go snorkeling from shore and see something interesting. Because of the proximity of the swimming area to the muddy mangrove bottoms, upside-down jellyfish flourish here. They are so named because they swim mouth-downward, but flip over when resting on the bottom, exposing their fluttery mantle containing photosynthesizing cells. They can grow to one foot across and can give irritating stings, but they are not a serious problem.

There are two other swimming areas away from the main

parking lot. One is more open ocean where the scuba classes go; the other is a sheltered area.

Snorkeling and Scuba Diving

You can't see the coral reef by snorkeling from shore. The park concession at the dive shop can set you up with everything you need for snorkeling or diving. Snorkeling and diving trips leave several times daily, weather permitting. You should call ahead to make a reservation and check the weather forecast. The calmest water is usually in the morning. The light is best at noon because it is from directly overhead, revealing all the colors just below the water's surface. The afternoon trip is often windiest. You can rent (or purchase) all types of snorkeling and diving equipment at the dive shop. Scuba divers must show their certification cards to rent equipment and go on the diving boat. Remember...don't touch the coral!

In a typical 30-minute dive, snorkel, or glassbottom boat trip, you may see as many as 100 species of fish. These are the fish that are the most abundant, active, and diurnal. Many other species are present but are less likely to be seen on a short trip. Some of the common ones are blue tangs, trumpetfish, angelfish, damselfish, parrotfish, barracuda, grunts, butterfly-fish, and snappers. Moray eels are common but nocturnal, and stingrays camouflage themselves with the sea bottom.

Glassbottom Boat

A good way for nonsnorkelers and nondivers to see the coral reef is on the 2½-hour glassbottom boat trip. It is more appropriately called a glass-sided boat, distinguishing it from the other glass-bottom tour boats in the area. Viewing is excellent. Reservations are suggested. The natural light is best at noon, when the sun's rays are most direct.

The captain will only rarely allow wheelchairs on board; the weather must be very calm, and he will not make a decision until the day of the trip (see "Glassbottom Boat" under "Biscayne National Park" for alternative).

Boating

Motorboats are available to rent, including 19- to 24-foot boats and small sailboats (one-hour minimum rental). Don't anchor a boat on coral—it is illegal and extremely damaging to the reef. Anchor on sand patches.

Canoeing

From the canoe launch by the Mangrove Trail, canoeists can wind through narrow mangrove channels or paddle out to the ocean. Another place to launch is at the concession, where you can rent canoes and kayaks. Canoeing is a good way to see the park. During the winter season (November to March or April), ranger-naturalists lead several-hour canoe trips.

Trails

There are two short nature trails, one through mangroves and one through a hardwood hammock.

The Mangrove Trail is actually a boardwalk that allows you to walk among the mangrove waterways without getting your feet wet. It's a leisurely 15-minute self-guided walk with interpretive signs along the way. It is an excellent place to see red mangroves in their watery environment, particularly for a wheelchair-bound person. There is an observation tower (not handicapped-accessible) about 10 feet above the water that is just tall enough to view across the tops of the mangroves.

The Tamarind Trail (near the Entrance Station) is a leisurely 20-minute walk through a tropical hardwood hammock. It's a narrow dirt trail with many roots and rocks (unsuitable for a wheelchair). It is unmarked and has no interpretive signs. It is best to go with a ranger for a guided tour. You will see such trees as pigeon-plum and gumbo-limbo, plus the wild-tamarind for which the trail was named. Some commonly seen birds are warblers (palm, prairie, blackpoll, yellow-throated, and redstarts) and indigo buntings.

Ranger-naturalists lead daily walks in the winter (end of November to March or April). During the off-season, no guided trips are scheduled, but you can often find a ranger to give you a tour on request. Special groups tours can be arranged year-round.

Campground

Twenty-five of the 47 campsites are available by reservation only (call 305-451-1202 no more than 60 days in advance), and the other 22 are on a first-come basis. It is best to arrive by 5 PM. There is a maximum camping period of 14 days and a maximum of eight people per site. The sites are small, but enough for one or two cars and a tent. No pets overnight.

At one end of the campground is a lagoon-type pond that often has white ibises, great white herons, terns, and other water birds feeding.

Gift Shop and Snack Bar

The snack bar serves sandwiches, drinks, and snacks. The gift shop has a wide assortment of souvenirs.

Best Time of Year

The water temperature from November to April is 70–75°F at the surface. Except during cold fronts, snorkeling is comfortable. Scuba divers usually wear wet suits since the deeper water is colder. In the winter, cold fronts can cause strong winds, occasionally canceling scheduled boat trips. From May to October, the surf temperature is 80–85°. Starting in June, thunderstorms and tropical storms can make water-related activities hazardous. The most reliable months for good weather are April and May. These are also low mosquito months. Migrating birds can be seen and a lot of the winter crowds have gone.

JOHN U. LLOYD STATE RECREATION AREA

In the summer, a constant stream of beach-going traffic is the norm at this park. It slows down a little in the winter, although Sundays are always crowded. The narrow beach must be maintained by beach renourishment projects that pump sand from offshore back onto the beach. This affects the sea turtles that nest here in the summer. The 251-acre park on the barrier island also contains a less crowded mangrove-lined waterway for canoeing and a short nature trail. Mostly local residents use this park.

Location, Mailing Address and Phone

From the north: From I-95, take Exit 26 to Griffin Road/CR 818, east to US 1, then south to US A1A/Dania Blvd., turn left to Ocean Drive, then left again to park entrance. From the south: From I-95, take Exit 25 to SW 60th St./CR 848, east to US 1, then north to US A1A/Dania Blvd., turn right to Ocean Drive, then left to park entrance.
   6503 N. Ocean Drive, Dania 33004; 954-923-2833
   Concession: 954-923-6711

Facilities and Activities

Swimming, snorkeling, nature trail, canoeing and kayaking and rentals, boat ramp, fishing.

Manatees occasionally use the narrow waterway that divides the park. Canoes can be rented from the concession for use on this waterway. The Barrier Island Trail is undergoing restoration with the removal of exotic plants.

Best Time of Year

Winter for fewer crowds and greater chance of manatees and birdlife.

KEY LARGO HAMMOCK BOTANICAL STATE PARK

This parcel of land has more than six miles of trails for self-guided walks and birding. One trail partly coincides with a small road that is part of the abandoned development that also left traces of walls and foundations around. The Department of Environmental Protection manages this land, which is much

A coral rock wall along the trail is a subtle reminder of how close Key Largo Hammock came to succumbing to development.

larger than the area they allow the public to access. The native plants have regrown and have identification tags. This area of the Keys contains the most species of trees found anywhere in the United States, and most of them are West Indian. Some trees and shrubs you'll encounter include snowberry, mahogany, velvetseed, Jamaica dogwood, poisonwood, paradise-tree, willow bustic, and lancewood. Many passerine birds feed and rest here during spring and fall migrations. This is an excellent short hike for botanists and birders.

Location, Mailing Address and Phone

Located on upper Key Largo, 0.4 miles east of US 1 on CR 905.
c/o John Pennekamp Coral Reef State Park, P.O. Box 487, Key Largo, FL 33037; 305-451-1202

Facilities and Activities

Self-guided nature trail, birding, botanizing, occasional guided walks. Open daily 8 AM to 5 PM. No admission fee.

Best Time of Year

Winter for better weather, fall-spring for birding, year-round for plants, spring and summer for flowers.

Pets

Allowed on leash.

KORESHAN STATE HISTORIC SITE

Nature lovers come to this park to canoe on the Estero River. The 305-acre park was actually preserved for its historic merit. In 1893, Cyrus Teed preached his religion of "Koreshanity" to a group of followers who settled with him here. Teed's religion did not catch on, and the last four followers deeded part of their property to the state in 1961. Visitors can stroll around the restored village. The Estero River is designated a Florida Canoe Trail and makes a relaxing canoeing day trip.

Location, Mailing Address and Phone

From Ft. Myers or Naples, take I-75 to Exit 19. Go west on Corkscrew Road, cross US 41, and proceed straight to park.
   P.O. Box 7, Estero 33928; 239-992-0311

Facilities and Activities

Nature trail, campground, canoeing and rentals, boating, fishing, naturalist programs, historic site. Admission fee.

Hiking

A ¼-mile self-guided loop nature trail along the Estero River goes through pine flatwoods and scrub oak. Watch for gopher tortoises. Ask for the park's vertebrate list.

Canoeing

Visitors can rent canoes at the ranger station or launch their own canoes at the boat ramp and head downstream to Estero Bay (about 3 miles). Ask for the canoe map at the entrance station. Then you can follow all the curves of the Estero River, through subtropical hammocks and mangroves and out to the bay. Once in the bay, you'll see Mound Key, the large island to the southwest. Mound Key is an Indian shell mound that is a State Archeological Site. You can paddle about a mile to a cove on the west side of Mound Key. Pull into the cove and you'll find a walking trail that crosses the island. Less experienced canoeists should return to Koreshan after Mound Key (the current is slow enough to permit round-trip travel). If you plan to go back upstream, make sure you memorize the way downstream, so you don't get confused by side channels on your return. Along the way, watch for manatees, dolphins, roseate spoonbills, black-whiskered vireos, and mangrove cuckoos.

Only experienced canoeists with a compass and chart should

The Estero River at Koreshan SP is excellent for canoeing.

attempt to cross Estero Bay, and then only on a relatively calm day. You can explore around other mangrove islands and return to Koreshan, or you can pull out at the ramp at Carl Johnson County Park (about 3 more miles south; see entry for Carl Johnson County Park).

Camping

The campground has 60 well-vegetated sites. From December to April the campground is usually full every day. Reservations are recommended (by phone, up to 60 days in advance). Pets allowed overnight. There is no concession store in the park. Naturalist programs are held at the amphitheater on the bank of the Estero.

Best Time of Year

Winter for canoeing and camping. Insects are rare in winter, which is why Koreshan is so popular then. The insects aren't as bad as other coastal parks in the summer, but still, they are there.

LIGNUMVITAE KEY STATE BOTANICAL SITE (PLUS INDIAN KEY STATE HISTORIC SITE, SAN PEDRO UNDERWATER ARCHEOLOGICAL PRESERVE, AND WINDLEY KEY STATE GEOLOGICAL SITE)

The 280-acre Lignumvitae Key is a mile cruise across the water from the nearest road. Although it has some of the highest (and safest) ground in the Keys (up to 16.5 feet above sea level), it has miraculously escaped development. The Florida Department of Environmental Protection (DEP) took over maintenance of the island in 1971. DEP has preserved the flora in its natural state, making it one of the best remaining examples of a West Indian tropical hammock. DEP staff and volunteers painstakingly removed exotic vegetation that had escaped cultivation from the original residents' landscaping. A few exotic plants have been left around the building for historical value. The only human inhabitant of the island now is the park's manager. Access to the island is by boat only.

The park boundary includes the surrounding waters of Lignumvitae Key, Shell Key, and Indian Key, totalling 10,838 acres. The waters are protected from the collecting of sponges and tropical fish. The use of boat motors are prohibited where the water depth is three feet or less.

The island's name comes from a small tree, the lignum vitae. Lignum vitae, which means "wood of life," is native to Central America, the Antilles, the Bahamas, and extreme southern Florida (mostly the Keys, rarely the mainland). "Wood of Life" was the name dubbed by 16th-century Europeans who thought it was a cure for syphilis and other diseases. The wood, the densest used commercially, does not float. It is so loaded with resins (about 30% of the weight of the wood) and is so self-lubricating that it was once in demand by the shipping industry to make propeller shaft bearings.

Truly blue flowers, such as those borne by the lignum vitae, are uncommon in native North American plants; most of our blue flowers were introduced. The flowers appear in spring and early summer. The tree is small, up to 33 feet tall, and gnarled looking. The opposite, evenly pinnate compound leaves are

Lignum vitae

evergreen. Lignum vitae trees may grow to be 1000 years old, but they are not common enough to be used commercially any more. In fact, they are on the state's endangered species list.

For botanists, Lignumvitae Key is well worth the trip from the mainland and the limited opportunities to get to the island. It is perhaps the most pristine example of native tropical hardwoods left in the continental United States. The historical aspects (such as the tour of the house) are also fascinating.

Three other state park units are managed by Lignumvitae's manager: Indian Key State Historic Site, San Pedro Underwater Archaeological Preserve, and Windley Key State Geological Site. Indian Key is a 10-acre island on the ocean side of the Keys. Originally inhabited by Calusa Indians, it was bought in 1831 by

Jacob Housman, who built a local empire with his wreck salvaging business. Dr. Henry Perrine, an avid botanist, moved there in 1837 and imported tropical plants from Mexico for cultivation. The thriving town (it was the county seat for Dade) was destroyed by retaliating Calusas. All that remains are foundations, overgrown tropical plants, and old roads. San Pedro is named after a 1733 wreck of the Spanish galleon *San Pedro*. Under 18 feet of water, it supports a diverse congregation of fish and invertebrates—a very old artificial reef indeed! It is accessible only by private or chartered boat. Windley Quarry was formerly a commercial quarry from which rock was obtained for building the Overseas Railroad and later, the Overseas Highway. The unique feature of this site is that visitors can descend into the quarry and examine layer upon layer of ancient petrified coral formations. Trails also bring visitors through the hammock, where interpretive signs explain the vegetation, wildlife, and geology. This site is accessible by appointment only. These three units will add an unparalleled flavor of the Keys to your trip.

Location, Mailing Address and Phone

Lignumvitae and Indian Key: accessible only by boat (tour boat or private). To tour boat dock: take US 1 to MM 79.5 on Indian Key Fill, turn into the parking lot with the sign "Lignumvitae State Botanical Site Tour Boat Monroe Landing." Tourboat leaves for Lignumvitae at 1:30 PM Thursday through Monday; for Indian Key at 8:30 AM Thursday through Monday. To San Pedro: No tour boat; private boats can find it by going 1.25 miles south from Indian Key; mooring buoys mark the spot (please tie up to the buoys to prevent damage to the site). Windley Quarry is located on Windley Key, but you must get a gate key from Long Key State Recreation Area.

All units: P.O. Box 1052, Islamorada 33036; 305-664-2540; Tour boat reservations: 305-664-9814

Facilities and Activities

Guided nature walk and tour of historical house, day-use boat dock. Site open from 8:00 AM to 5:00 PM. Closed Tuesdays and

Wednesdays. Fee charged for boat trip and tour. Private boats may dock (free) during daylight hours and passengers can join the 10:00 AM or 2:00 PM guided walks. Tour boat leaves Indian Key Fill at 9:30 AM and 1:30 PM. Most facilities are not handicapped accessible.

Matheson House

This picturesque house was built of coral rock and Dade County pine in 1919 by William J. Matheson, who also donated the original land for Matheson Hammock Park (see page 245). It is furnished with original and period furniture and now serves as a ranger station and museum. The windmill that provided power to the residents still stands next to the house; now a generator does that job. Fresh water was, and still is, obtained from cisterns. Cisterns are tanks that are filled with rain water falling on the roofs of buildings. The rain water is funneled through gutters to the tanks. From the tanks, the water is pumped to a modern plumbing system. Water that collects during the summer rainy season is usually enough to last through the winter dry months. Be sparing on your restroom flushes here. Once the water is depleted in the reservoir tank, there will be no more until the next hard rain. Lignumvitae is one of the few places left in the Keys still using cisterns because aerial spraying for mosquitoes contaminates the water elsewhere; spraying is not permitted over Lignumvitae. The Matheson house was built with the hot tropical climate in mind, and the design reflects careful usage of architectural features that take advantage of the cooling breezes.

Trails

There are several trails on the island, but visitors must remain with a tour guide when on any trail. The tour guides are well acquainted with the native plants. Some of the trees you may see are mastic, lancewood, white stopper, saffron-plum, pigeon-plum, wild coffee, sapodilla, and satinleaf. In the summer (May-October), white-crowned pigeons are easily seen in the canopy feeding on the fruits of the pigeon-plum, poisonwood, and fig trees.

The trails are wide and level enough for wheelchairs. The tour, including the boat ride, takes about three hours.

Best Time of Year

November to April, the dry season, when mosquitoes are fewest (there is no artificial mosquito control here).

Pets

Not allowed.

LONG KEY STATE PARK

Perched atop vestiges of ancient coral reefs, Long Key is rich in West Indian vegetation and marine life. Realizing the natural resource and recreational values of the area, the state began to protect it in 1961, and by 1973 it had acquired 965 acres for the park; 116 acres are submerged.

Local saltwater fishing was an attraction that brought worldwide attention when Henry Flagler (builder of the overseas railroad to Key West) established the Long Key Fishing Club in 1906 after the first bridge was completed. Fishing continues to attract people to the ocean and bay waters around Long Key.

The park has walking and canoe trails for the non-angler. These bring the nature-seeker close to the shallow lagoons where birds feed on the varied marine fish and invertebrates.

Along the oceanside are natural sandy beaches, accessible only by boat. In the summer, these narrow beaches are reserved for nesting sea turtles. Because sandy beaches are rare in the Keys, this is one of the few places around where sea turtles can lay their eggs.

Location, Mailing Address and Phone

Park entrance is at MM 67.6 on US 1 oceanside on Long Key. Layton Trail is difficult to find; it's outside the park entrance, a few

hundred yards north of MM 68 on US 1 bayside. Look for a green historical marker sign "Long Key Fishing Club" and the small "Layton Trail" sign next to it. Park on the shoulder of the road.
   P.O. Box 776, Long Key 33001; 305-664-4815.

Facilities and Activities

Nature trails, canoeing and canoe rentals, campground (no pets overnight), picnicking, swimming, fishing. Admission fee charged at main entrance (no admission fee for Layton Trail). Fees for camping and rentals are additional.

Nature Trails
Golden Orb Trail

This is a one-mile loop trail around a lagoon and beach. Plaques along the way explain the natural history. An observation tower provides a scenic view.

Layton Trail

If you are driving down the Keys and want to take a break to stretch your legs, this is just the place. This short shady loop trail will take about 15 minutes to walk. It goes through a tropical hardwood hammock, rich with native Keys plants, such as wild-lime, Jamaica dogwood, buttonwood, and seven-year-apple. Plaques identify the trees. The trail opens onto the rocky shore of Florida Bay. Not handicapped-accessible.

Canoe Trail

The Long Key Lakes Canoe Trail is a 1.3-mile self-guided canoe trail. It takes about an hour to paddle the loop around the mangroves, seagrass patches, and soft corals. You can rent a canoe here or bring your own. The trail is suitable for novices.

Best Time of Year

November to May, the nonmosquito season.

Canoeing around the estuary at Lovers Key can be a rewarding experience.

LOVERS KEY STATE PARK

Along the barrier islands from Naples to Ft. Myers are many public beaches. Lovers Key is one of the quietest, least developed, and least crowded. This park recently acquired Carl E. Johnson County Park. Now its 700 acres encompass part or all of Black Key, Lovers Key, Inner Key, and Long Key.

Sea-grapes dominate the woody vegetation. A canoe launch (no motors) provides access to quiet red mangrove lagoons around Estero Bay for hours of exploring. Bottle-nosed dolphins and manatees are occasionally observed near shore. Wading birds (including reddish egrets and roseate spoonbills) and shorebirds can be seen in the lagoon at low tide.

Location, Mailing Address and Phone

Located on CR 865/Estero Blvd. between Ft. Myers and Bonita Beaches, 7 miles north of the intersection of US 41 and Bonita Beach Road.

Contact: Lovers Key/Carl E. Johnson State Park, 8700 Estero Blvd., Ft. Myers, FL 33931; 239-463-4588; Concession: 239-765-1880

Facilities and Activities

Beach activities such as shelling and swimming (beware of strong currents while swimming!), boat launch, canoe and kayak rentals. Admission fee includes tram from parking lot to beach.

Best Time of Year

Tourists frequent the beach in winter; summer is quiet.

OLETA RIVER STATE RECREATION AREA

The location right in Miami makes Oleta crowded year-round. This is the largest urban wilderness park in Florida (854 acres). Most folks come to picnic, some come to swim in the lagoon, and some come to bicycle on the short trails. The persistent urban canoeist will find a surprisingly good maze of mangrove-lined waterways to explore. The park is at the northern end of Biscayne Bay and is named for the Oleta River, which intersects the bay. This is the only reason the park is included here. The upland sections of the park are dominated by Australian-pine and other exotics.

Location, Mailing Address and Phone

From I-95, take Exit 17 east (N. Miami Beach Blvd./SR 826), going 1.1 miles past US 1 (where road becomes Sunny Isles Blvd.), to park entrance.

3400 NE 163rd Street, North Miami 33160; 305-919-1846; Urban Trails Concession: 305-947-0302

Facilities and Activities

Canoeing and rentals, swimming, picnicking, primitive youth camping, primitive rental cabins. Admission fee; extra fee for boat tours and rentals.

Canoeing

Canoes and kayaks may be rented at the park's concession. Ask for their canoeing map. Canoes can stick to the protected lagoon waters or venture into Biscayne Bay (also the Intracoastal Waterway here) and then into the Oleta River, which is less than 2 miles away and less than 2 miles long (full round trip is approximately 7 miles). Watch for manatees in the winter. Mullet, tarpon, and snapper are present, as are brown pelicans, white ibises, bald eagles, herons, and egrets.

Best Time of Year

Winter for manatee sightings.

SOUTHERN GLADES WILDLIFE AND ENVIRONMENTAL AREA

The southern Everglades includes much more than the area within Everglades National Park boundaries. One of the adjacent areas has been made available to hikers. The Southern Glades Wildlife and Environmental Area (SGWEA) is state-owned land under the administration of the South Florida Water Management District. It was purchased through the "Save Our Rivers" and "Conservation and Recreation Lands" programs for recreational use. The Florida Fish and Wildlife Conservation Commission enforces the hunting regulations, but the Florida Department of Environmental Protection and the South Florida Water Management District regulate other aspects.

The 26,000 acres contain canals and levees that were created long ago to drain the Everglades and provide flood protection. The dominant habitat is sawgrass marsh with bay heads and cypress domes interspersed.

The SGWEA was on the southern side of Andrew and incurred intense winds. Trees were uprooted, but there were no visitor facilities to be damaged. Most of the large trees killed were Australian-pines.

Location, Mailing Address and Phone

From SW 344th St./Palm Drive in Florida City, drive 5.3 miles south on US 1. Turn right on Dade County Work Camp Rd./SW 424th St. at MM 122.5.

c/o Florida Fish and Wildlife Conservation Commission, 551 North Military Trail, West Palm Beach 33415; 561-640-6100

Facilities and Activities

Hiking, bicycling, fishing, hunting. No visitor facilities. No admission fee.

The two trails, totalling 16 miles, are on top of the levees paralleling the canals. The levees were built with the dredge material from the canals and have been used as access to maintain the canals. No trails, then, were newly cut for the change in management plan. The levees are 4–5 feet above the surrounding marsh, affording an open view and dry footing. The easternmost levee was degraded in 1996 as mitigation for the widening of US 1, so the trail that it formerly supported no longer exists.

The first trail can be found by driving on Work Camp Road 1.8 miles west from US 1. Work Camp Road becomes unpaved and rather narrow and rough after a mile. The trail is five miles long and suitable for all-terrain bicycles. The canal banks are overgrown, so the view is limited. The trail can also be reached from the southern end by driving on US 1 to MM 116.4 and turning east into the C-111 canal area (north side of the canal). Walk under the bridge and follow the canal west to the beginning of the trail. You may see a crocodile along this canal. The second trail, 4 miles long, is approximately 2 miles west of the first trail. The trails connect at their southern ends.

With careful searching, you may see some of the endangered animals that have been reported in the SGWEA: crocodiles, Cape Sable seaside sparrows, snail kites, and wood storks. Also watch for the threatened eastern indigo snakes, bald eagles, least terns, and sandhill cranes. Other animals you may see are bobcats, river otters, white-tailed deer, limpkins, and roseate spoonbills.

In addition to sawgrass, some trees and plants to look for are wax myrtles, redbay, sweet bay, coco-plum, paradise-tree, butterfly orchid, worm-vine orchid, and twisted air plant.

Hunting, fishing, and frogging are permitted. Because this is not a true Wildlife Management Area but an area created for controlled multiple recreational and educational uses, there are more hunting regulations.

Best Time of Year

October through April to catch the migrating and overwintering birds. From June to September, wildlife may use the levee roads as corridors, since everything else may be submerged. Be prepared for mosquitoes. Since this is a hunting area, wear bright clothing in the autumn and winter.

Pets

Allowed.

VII
NATURAL AREAS: COUNTY, CITY, AND PRIVATE

AH-THA-THI-KI MUSEUM

To the Seminoles, it means "a place to remember." Ah-tha-thi-ki, which opened its doors in 1997, is a place where the Seminoles remember who they are and where they came from. The rest of us will learn it for the first time.

This museum, nine years and $10 million in the making, invites visitors into the world of the traditional Seminole culture—how they lived in the Everglades while they were hiding from the persecuting whites. The four exhibit buildings boast a collection of clothing, tools, utensils, photographs, and so on. On the surrounding 65 acres of the Big Cypress Seminole Reservation, visitors can examine the traditional chickees of the type that some Seminoles still live in. Besides the living village, the other planned sites include a fishing camp, hunting camp, burial site, water transportation exhibit, water trails, observation tower, and ceremonial grounds. A boardwalk through the cypress swamp takes visitors into the land that they, like the Miccosukees, hid in for so many years.

The museum is located on the Seminoles' Big Cypress reservation, the largest of the tribe's five reservations. Approximately 430 Seminoles live on the 52,338-acre federal reservation. Florida panthers and black bears still roam this remote land. The tribe was given official recognition by the U.S. government in 1957. They were finally "home," after 150 years of being chased by American soldiers south from their homeland around north

211

Florida, Georgia, and Alabama. They hid in the Everglades, where they thought they were safe. They adapted to their new home by living in small family groups in the heart of the great wetland. They traveled from high ground to high ground by cypress dugout canoes and grew corn, squash, beans, sweet potatoes, and so on. Some contemporary Seminoles still live as their descendants did, in raised chickees in remote areas.

Location, Mailing Address and Phone

Located in Big Cypress Seminole Indian Reservation. Take Exit 14 north from I-75 for 17 miles.

Ah-tha-thi-ki Museum, HC-61, Box 21-A, Clewiston, FL 33440; 863-902-1113 or 954-792-0745 (Seminole office in Davie)

Facilities and Activities

Cultural museum, boardwalk nature trail, living village, gift shop, educational programs, resource library, theater. Tuesday through Sunday 9 AM to 5 PM. Admission fee.

BRIGGS NATURE CENTER & ROOKERY BAY

The Briggs Nature Center is nestled within the 15,000-acre Rookery Bay National Estuarine Research Reserve. It serves as the environmental education arm of the reserve. Although the reserve is administered by the National Oceanic and Atmospheric Administration and the Florida Department of Environmental Protection (DEP), the Nature Center is run by a private nonprofit conservation organization in Naples called The Conservancy of Southwest Florida. The reserve exists through the dedicated efforts of individuals and organizations (such as the National Audubon Society). When the area was threatened with development in 1964, a local conservation movement succeeded in halting it temporarily.

To prevent subsequent development threats, this group was

able to purchase the land and protect it permanently. The Conservancy, Inc. was born of this movement. It continues to be a strong voice for conservation in southwestern Florida (see also NAPLES NATURE CENTER). In 1977, The Conservancy's efforts were rewarded when Rookery Bay was included in the National Estuarine Sanctuary Program.

The protected mangrove estuary is vital to the growth of gamefish, commercial fish, shrimp, crabs, oysters, and snails. These support some of the most stable wading bird colonies remaining in south Florida. Visitors can see some of the sanctuary from the trails and from boats.

Location, Mailing Address and Phone

From Tamiami Trail (US 41), take SR 951 south 3 miles to Shell Island Rd. (look for Nature Center sign); turn right and drive about a mile to the Nature Center.

401 Shell Island Rd., Naples 34145; 239-775-8569; www. conservancy.org

Red Mangrove

Black Mangrove

Facilities and Activities

Interpretive center, nature trails and boardwalk, paddling, guided paddling and boat tours, naturalist programs, boat ramp. Open Monday through Friday 9 AM to 4:30 PM from June through September; same hours Monday through Saturday from October through May, plus Sunday 1 to 5 PM from January through March. Admission fee includes Naples Nature Center.

Nature Center and Boardwalk

The central attraction inside the small Interpretive Center is the pair of 230-gallon saltwater tanks supporting estuarine fish and other animals. Exhibits explain the local wildlife and ecology, and a small section is devoted to nature books for sale. Outside is a labeled wildflower garden for butterflies. You may see Florida scrub jays around the Nature Center, evidence of a research project for which they were transplanted here. Florida scrub jays (a threatened species in Florida) were probably not native to this exact area, but the scrub habitat is suitable and very little remains elsewhere.

The highlight of the Center is the ½-mile boardwalk trail, which is accessible only through the Nature Center. This loop walk enters six ecosystems: oak scrub, wet hammock, brackish pond, fringe mangrove, fringe marsh, and pine flatwoods. There are interpretive signs along the way, but the excellent "Boardwalk Guide" (available inside the Nature Center) accompanies the numbered posts. A covered observation platform overlooks a brackish pond. A short side trail, called "Birdfeeder Trail," lives up to its name. Birdfeeders have been placed by the trail for bird-watching. Allow about an hour for the boardwalk. Wheelchair-accessible. Note: if you go to the Naples Nature Center (see separate entry) earlier the same day, that admission ticket gets you free admission onto the boardwalk here.

Pontoon tours are available Tuesdays through Saturdays from December to April. Guided canoe and kayak trips are offered Thursdays and Saturdays during the same months.

Trails

Two short walking trails are located past the Nature Center at the end of Shell Island Road. Along the road, watch for wildlife on this graded dirt road. Gopher tortoises and yellow rat snakes may be seen. You'll pass the DEP Marine Laboratory Headquarters at 1.6 miles. Two-tenths of a mile past the Lab, the road ends at a small boat ramp, where you can launch a canoe to paddle around the mangroves. The trails begin to the left of the ramp.

The Monument Tower Trail follows an old grassy roadbed about a quarter mile one way to a small stone monument dedicated to two local conservationists. There are no interpretive signs and much of the roadside vegetation is exotic, the result of human disturbance.

The Catclaw Trail turns off near the beginning of the Monument Trail. It was designed as a low-impact interpretive trail. It is also about a quarter mile long and not a loop. There isn't enough dry land around here for longer trails. Some of the trees you'll see are saffron-plum, white stopper, white indigo-berry, and red mangrove. The trail's name comes from another small tree you'll see here, the catclaw. The trees have identification tags.

Best Time of Year

November to April, the nonmosquito season.

Pets

Not allowed.

BROWARD COUNTY PARKS

For more information on the 14 Broward County regional parks: Parks and Recreation Division, 950 NW 38th Street, Oakland Park 33309-5982; 954-357-8100; www.co.broward.fl.us

DEERFIELD ISLAND PARK— BROWARD COUNTY PARKS

This 56-acre island was created by dredging the Intracoastal Waterway. It is maintained as critical habitat for gopher tortoises. Native trees include red mangrove, sea-grape, and cabbage palm, while the exotic Australian-pine dominates. No vehicles are permitted. The county provides free weekly boat transportation and guided walks which last about 2 hours.

Location, Mailing Address and Phone

Located on an island in the Intracoastal Waterway, accessible only by boat. To get to the park's boat ramp for free boat transportation (limited schedule), take I-95 to Exit 37 and go east on Hillsboro Boulevard 2 miles to Riverview Road. Follow signs to dock at Sullivan Park. Private boats permitted.
1720 Deerfield Island Park, Deerfield Beach 33441; 954-360-1320.

Facilities and Activities

Nature trails, guided tours, marina, picnicking. Primitive camping by reservation for non-profit groups. No admission fee. Limited schedule for park boat and tours.

Trails

The Coquina Trail (1/2-mile) goes through a coastal hardwood hammock to an observation platform on the Intracoastal. The Mangrove Trail is ¾-mile and includes a boardwalk. Obtain the free trail guides at the park office.

Best Time of Year

No preference.

Pets

Not allowed.

EASTERLIN PARK—
BROWARD COUNTY PARKS

This 41-acre park is an oasis in an urban setting. Local people generally visit for picnics and recreational activities year-round, while the campground draws some in the winter.

Location, Mailing Address and Phone

Take Exit 32 from I-95, going west on Commercial Street/NW 50 St. Go 0.1 miles, turn left onto Powerline Road, then 1 mile to NW 38th Street. Turn right and go 0.3 miles to entrance.
  1000 NW 38th Street, Oakland Park 33309; 954-938-0610

Facilities and Activities

Nature trail, campground, picnicking. Admission fee on week-ends/holidays; campground fee. Open 8 AM to 6 PM in winter, 8 AM to 7:30 PM in summer.

Trail—The Woodland Nature Trail (¾-mile) goes through an oak hammock and a small section of cypress with treated Brazilian pepper. Native plants include wild coffee, royal palm, strangler fig, and red maple. Obtain the trail guide at the park office for a nominal fee.

Campground—There are 55 sites in this wooded campground, which offers showers and electric hookups. The peripheral noise from I-95, trains, and airplanes can be distracting.

Best Time of Year

No preference.

Pets

Allowed on leash in designated areas.

FERN FOREST NATURE CENTER— BROWARD COUNTY PARKS

Fern Forest is part of a cypress slough which once drained the area from Coral Springs to the ocean at Pompano Beach. It was also part of the cypress strand that stretched from Lake Okeechobee to Fort Lauderdale. The cypress were once logged by the Seminoles. The 254 acres contains 10 habitat types: oak-pine-cabbage palm, mixed temperate/tropical hardwood hammock, maple, ficus-tropical hardwood hammock, cypress-maple, oak-cypress-cabbage palm, prairie, oak-ficus-cabbage palm, tropical hardwood hammock, and exotics (Brazilian pepper-guava). Look for such ferns as resurrection, marsh, leather, swamp, strap, shoestring, golden polypody, and maiden; such trees as gumbo-limbo, cypress (bald and pond), satinleaf, paradise, and wild-lime; such shrubs and other plants as marlberry, wild coffee, firebush, beauty berry, and coontie.

Allow 2 to 3 hours for trails and nature center. Beware that a county ordinance requires the boardwalks to be closed when it's raining because of slipperiness.

Location, Mailing Address and Phone

From I-95, take Exit 34 and go west on Atlantic Blvd. 3 miles to Lyons Rd. Go left on Lyons and proceed to Nature Center.
201 Lyons Road South, Pompano Beach 33068; 954-970-0150

Facilities and Activities

Nature Center, nature trails, interpretive programs, picnic tables. Free admission. Open 8:30 AM to 7:30 PM (trails close at 6:30).

The Nature Center contains exhibits and live reptiles; a few field guides and local natural history books are sold.

Three short trails bring the visitor close to the various habitats of Fern Forest. The Cypress Creek Trail is a 0.5-mile handicapped-accessible boardwalk through one of the last cypress stands in Broward County. The Maple Walk is a 0.3-mile non-wheelchair-accessible trail through a red maple swamp lush with ferns. It can be very wet in summer. The Prairie Overlook Trail (1 mile) goes to a 20-foot-high observation platform over a former cattle pasture now used by gopher tortoises.

Best Time of Year

Fall and spring for migrating passerines; winter and spring for walking on nature trails (wet in summer).

Pets

Not allowed.

MARKHAM PARK—
BROWARD COUNTY PARKS

Markham Park (666 acres) is a truly multi-use recreational park. It has many types of activities but does not shine in any one of them. Some of the more unusual activities include a target range, model airplane field, and personal watercraft area. This does not leave much room for natural areas. If you need a place to camp in Broward County or want access to canoe in the Everglades, this will suffice. The Observatory is open two nights a month.

Location, Mailing Address and Phone

Take SR 84 west almost to the Sawgrass Expressway/SR 869. Entrance will be 1.9 miles west of 136th Ave. at the intersection of 84 and Weston Road.

16001 W. State Road 84, Sunrise 33326; 954-389-2000

Facilities and Activities

Nature trail, campground, canoe and bicycle rentals, observatory, equestrian trails, picnicking, recreational activities. Open 8 AM to 6 PM in winter, 8 AM to 7:30 PM in summer. Admission fee on weekends/holidays; campground fee.

Trail—Don't be fooled by the name "Everglades Nature Trail"—it bears little resemblance to the Everglades, other than a few clumps of sawgrass. Much of the trail is Australian-pine and melaleuca. The trail is not well-maintained and is not worth going out of your way to see. Obtain the trail guide at the park office for a nominal fee.

Campground—There are 86 sites in this wooded campground, which offers showers, electric hookups, and free use of the pool. The noise from boats on the canals and model boats and airplanes on the lake may be bothersome.

Canoeing—The concession rents canoes, paddleboats, and john boats. There are two boat ramps, one on the New River Canal and the other on the L-35A Canal. You can paddle across the L-35A canal, then pull your canoe over the levee and into Water Conservation Area 2A, which is part of the Everglades. From there, you can paddle around the sawgrass, which is far more interesting than the canals and the park's lake.

Best Time of Year

No preference.

Pets

Allowed on leash in designated areas.

SECRET WOODS NATURE CENTER— BROWARD COUNTY PARKS

Nestled between superhighways and a river thoroughfare is a cool green patch of untamed woodland. Three plant communities are found within this 56-acre urban wilderness area: cypress-maple wetland, pond-apple-mangrove wetland, and laurel oak upland. The New River runs along the edge of the woods. The Nature Center features free interpretive programs. The park was opened in 1978.

Location, Mailing Address and Phone

From I-95, take Exit 27 onto SR 84. Go west on 84 for 0.5 miles to Nature Center.

2701 W. State Rd. 84, Ft. Lauderdale 33312; 954-791-1030

Facilities and Activities

Nature Center, nature trails, programs. Free admission. Open every day, including holidays. Opens at 8 AM year-round; closes 6 PM in winter and 7:30 PM in summer.

The New River Trail is a 0.6-mile wheelchair-accessible boardwalk that passes through oak uplands to the New River. Near the river are cypress and maples in the freshwater swamp and salt-tolerant mangroves along the river. Due to the diversion of fresh water upstream, saltwater is creeping farther inland. Look for dying cypress trees, which are the evidence of this. Watch for wading birds year-round in the wetlands. Yellow-crowned night-herons are commonly seen here. Some native plants to look for: firebush, beauty berry, rouge plant, dahoon holly, red and white mangrove, royal palm, and pond-apple. Pickup a trail guide at the office.

The 0.2-mile Laurel Oak Trail visits the oak hammock. Look for the inch-long fiddler crabs that scurry into the small holes in the ground around the boardwalk sections. The larger holes are from land crabs, which are a type of hermit crab.

The Nature Center houses quality exhibits of the local plant communities and wildlife, an aquarium, and live reptiles.

Best Time of Year

Spring and fall for migrating warblers. Year-round for walking on trails.

Pets

Not allowed.

TRADEWINDS PARK (AND BUTTERFLY WORLD)—BROWARD COUNTY PARKS

The unique feature of this county park is the private enterprise that operates the butterfly garden within. The garden is a large screened enclosure where thousands of butterflies from all corners of the world are raised in natural settings. Native food plants are cultivated for the caterpillars and butterflies to feed on. Between the flowers and the butterflies, there is a world of color. Some of the winged jewels will even alight on your head. Educational exhibits are an additional attraction.

The rest of the park offers the usual county park activities, plus a model steam railroad and horseback rides.

Location, Mailing Address and Phone

Take I-95 to Sample Road and go 4 miles west, or take Florida's Turnpike to Sample Road and go short distance west. The park is in two sections, one is on the north side of Sample Road and the other on the south side; most activities, including Butterfly World, are in the south section.

3600 W. Sample Rd., Coconut Creek 33073; 954-968-3880
Butterfly World: 954-977-4400
Stables: 954-968-3875

Facilities and Activities

Butterfly garden, nature trails, horse trails, riding lessons and trail rides, boat and canoe rentals, bicycle rentals and trail, primitive camping for non-profit groups, concession. Admission fee on weekends/holidays. Open 8 AM to 6 PM in winter, 8 AM to 7:30 PM in summer. Additional admission fee for Butterfly World; open 9 AM to 5 PM Monday-Saturday, 1 to 5 PM Sunday.

Butterfly World—What do Sara, Isabella, Julia, and Rosina . . . Zebra, Owl, and White Peacock all have in common? They are colorful species of butterflies that can all be found thriving in the natural settings created for them. The spectacle has to be seen to be believed. Everywhere you look, a butterfly is flitting from plant to plant or resting its beautiful wings. A "nursery" displays live chrysalises that you can watch emerging into adult butterflies. The gift shop has an endless selection of natural history books, gifts, and butterfly-attracting plants for your yard. You can even buy a living chrysalis to take home and watch it emerge. This is a wonderful place for all ages. Allow at least two hours.

Nature trails—A 0.7-mile self-guided boardwalk trail goes through cypress; trail guide is available at the office.

Equestrian activities—There are 3.5 miles of shaded horseback-riding trails. The stable (at the park entrance on the north side of Sample Rd.) has pony rides, riding lessons, and trail rides on weekends and holidays.

Best Time of Year

Butterfly World: year-round, but in winter the warmer days are better (butterflies are less active on cold days).

Pets

Allowed on leash in designated areas.

TREE TOPS PARK—
BROWARD COUNTY PARKS

The live oak hammock, marsh, and pine ridge are the main natural features of this 358-acre park. The oaks are carpeted with bromeliads and epiphytic ferns. The 23-acre marsh has been restored and is edged by a 1000-foot-long boardwalk. The pine ridge rises 29 feet above the surrounding land—not much to brag about, but still the highest *natural* elevation in Broward County (the landfills are much higher!). A pond provides boating and fishing recreation.

Location, Mailing Address and Phone

Take Exit 53 from Florida's Turnpike, go west on Griffin Rd. for 1.7 miles past University Drive. Then right onto SW 100th Ave. for 0.5 miles to park entrance.
3900 SW 100th Ave., Davie 33328; 954-370-3750

Facilities and Activities

Nature trails, observation tower, horse trails, primitive camping for non-profit groups, canoeing and canoe rentals. Admission fee on weekends/holidays. Open 8 AM to 7:30 PM.

There are about two miles of nature trails, some paved and some woodchipped, and over 3.5 miles of trails for horseback-riding. A self-guiding trail booklet is available from the office and marina for the 1000-foot-long Sensory Awareness Trail. One trail goes to the slash pine ridge. The trail to the marsh boardwalk is wheelchair-accessible. The 28-foot-high observation tower brings you to "tree-tops" level.

Some of the native plants you can find in the park are beauty berry, rouge plant, coontie, bromeliads, and swamp fern. Several of the trails, such as the Live Oak Trail near the board-walk, are particularly infested with exotic plants, such as oyster-plant, Brazilian pepper, and (perhaps the worst of all) air-potato. The air-potato is a vine with large heart-shaped leaves that will climb the trunk of a tree and shade the tree to death. Eerie ghost-like images rise from the floor of the woods where the air-potato reigns. The park has hired a full-time staff person who, assisted by volunteers, is responsible for battling the exotic plants.

Concession

The concession is located at the 10-acre pond and rents canoes and paddleboats; it also sells hot dogs, snacks, and drinks. You can launch your own canoe and go to a picnic area on an island in the pond.

Best Time of Year

No preference.

Pets

Allowed on a leash in designated areas.

T.Y. (TOPEEKEEGEE YUGNEE) PARK— BROWARD COUNTY PARKS

Another small (150 acres) urban park frequented by local residents, T.Y. offers a multitude of recreational activities. Canoe rentals are available for the 40-acre lake. The Seminole name means "gathering place."

Location, Mailing Address and Phone

Take Exit 24 from I-95, going west on Sheridan Street/SR 822. Go 0.7 miles to N. Park Road, turn right and proceed to entrance.
3300 N. Park Road, Hollywood 33021; 954-985-1980

Facilities and Activities

Campground, canoe rentals, picnicking, recreational activities. Admission fee on weekends/holidays; campground fee. Opens 8 AM, closes between 6 and 7:30 PM seasonally.

Campground—Most of the 60 sites have electric and water hookups. There are showers, laundromat, and a small camp supply and grocery store. Primitive camping for non-profit groups.

Best Time of Year

No preference.

Pets

Allowed on leash in designated areas.

WEST LAKE PARK (AND ANN KOLB NATURE CENTER)—BROWARD COUNTY PARKS

One of the largest urban parks in Florida, West Lake Park is a relative youngster. The recreational section opened in 1978, but the outstanding nature center complex opened in 1996. Located on the 1500⁺-acre West Lake, this 88-acre complex offers a wide variety of nature-oriented activities. West Lake was created by dredging in the 1920s and is connected to the Intracoastal Waterway; thus it is salt water. Miles of undeveloped mangrove shores beckon canoeists. Ecological restoration activities are ongoing. West Lake is home for many types of fish, crabs, shrimp, and wading birds. If you live in or visit Broward County, this is the place to come to learn and appreciate it.

Location, Mailing Address and Phone

From north or south, take I-95 to Exit 24, go 2.2 miles east on SR 822/Sheridan Street for south section or 2.7 miles east for north section (Nature Center).

1200 Sheridan Street, Hollywood 33019; 954-926-2410
Nature Center: 751 Sheridan Street; 954-926-2480

Facilities and Activities

Nature center, nature trails, environmental education programs, boat tours, canoe and kayak rentals, bicycle rentals, observation tower, gift shop, summer camp, picnicking. Admission fee for south (recreation) section on weekends and holidays. Additional admission fee for nature center, rentals, boat tours. No fee for nature trails, personal boat use, observation tower. Park gates open at 8 AM and close between 6 and 7:30 PM seasonally. Nature Center open 9 AM to 5 PM.

Ann Kolb Nature Center

The theme of the exhibits is the mangrove ecosystem. The 3,500-gallon saltwater aquarium features mangrove plants and animals. The introductory video explains the interactions of the mangrove creatures. The gift shop offers limited nature-related articles and packaged snacks. The 68-foot-high Observation Tower was built with the acrophobic person in mind—very solid and it even has an elevator. A wide variety of educational programs are scheduled. Ask for their species inventory, which includes plants, vertebrates, and invertebrates.

The boardwalk (foreground) at Ann Kolb Nature Center winds through mangroves to West Lake.

Trails

Nature trails and boardwalks—Three walking trails penetrate the mangrove wetlands: Lake Observation (1,374 feet), Mud Flat (1,552 feet), and South (2.3 miles) Trails. All boardwalks on the trails are constructed of recycled plastic. Among the red and black mangrove roots, you may see crabs and white ibises feeding.

Canoe trail—Obtain the canoe trail guide first, since this will serve as your map as well as for interpretation. The trail goes through West Lake's mangrove perimeter, where you may see roseate spoonbills, least terns, black-necked stilts, and yellow-crowned night-herons. Rentals are available at the marina.

Best Time of Year

No preference.

Pets

Allowed on leash in designated areas in south section.

COLLIER COUNTY PARKS
LAKE TRAFFORD COUNTY PARK— COLLIER COUNTY PARKS

This park exists as access to Lake Trafford north of Immokalee. Since the shores of this large lake, almost four square miles, are relatively undeveloped, canoeists should find it a pleasant trip.

Location, Mailing Address and Phone

From SR 29, go west on CR 890 (Lake Trafford Road) to end (3.2 miles).

Contact Collier County Parks and Recreation, 3300 Santa Barbara Blvd., Naples 34116; 239-353-0404.

Facilities and Activities

Canoeing and kayaking, boat launch, picnic tables, fishing pier.

Best Time of Year

No preference.

Pets

Allowed on leash.

CORKSCREW MARSH

The Corkscrew Regional Ecosystem Watershed (CREW) Trust is a private, non-profit organization committed to protecting the watershed around Corkscrew Marsh. It purchases and manages lands within the watershed in cooperation with the South Florida Water Management District. This tract of 6,825 acres was purchased in 1990 by SFWMD and contains uplands as well as the wetlands of Corkscrew Marsh. Approximately 5 miles of trails in several loops are maintained for hikers.

Location, Mailing Address and Phone

From Immokalee, go north on SR 29 to SR 82, turn left and go 5.5 miles to CR 850, turn left and go 1.5 miles to entrance on left.

Contact CREW Trust, Inc., 2301 McGregor Blvd., Ft. Myers, 33901; 239-332-7771. Or South Florida Water Management District, West Palm Beach.

The Flatwoods Trail at Corkscrew Marsh is relatively unknown but is worth a side trip from Corkscrew Swamp Sanctuary.

Facilities and Activities

Hiking trails, guided hikes, primitive camping, birding. No admission fee. Open daily sunrise to sunset.

The trails are in three loops: Marsh Loop Trail, Flatwoods Loop Trail, and Hammock Trail. The first skirts the edge of Corkscrew Marsh, where plains of sawgrass stretch off to the south. The Flatwoods Trail goes through a slash pine community. The Hammock Trail visits a community of live and laurel oaks, red maples, cabbage palms, and ferns. Look for tracks of raccoons, bobcats, armadillos, and other animals along the trail. Primitive camping is available by permit.

Best Time of Year

Dry season (trails can be flooded in wet season)

Pets

Allowed on leash.

CORKSCREW SWAMP SANCTUARY

Corkscrew is owned and managed by the National Audubon Society and is one of the jewels of its sanctuary system. It was made a "Registered Natural History Landmark" by the U.S. Department of the Interior in 1964. The sanctuary's 11,000 acres protects the largest remaining stand of old-growth bald-cypress in the country. Some of the trees are over 500 years old.

The sanctuary would be valuable enough just for protecting the trees, but the real claim-to-fame of the swamp is the wood stork colony that forms almost every year. It has historically been the largest stork colony in the United States. Although the size of the colony has decreased over the years and varies considerably, it is still possible to see 1,000 pairs of storks nesting at the sanctuary in the best years. In 1992, 1800 pairs nested here, with some nests visible from the boardwalk. Nesting depends on water levels in the area; these may fluctuate up to 4.5 feet between the wet and dry seasons. The swamp is accessible by an impressive boardwalk built by the National Audubon Society originally in 1955 and rebuilt in 1995. Alligators are an intimate part of this swamp and are frequently seen.

Location, Mailing Address and Phone

Sanctuary Road is 14 miles south of Immokalee on CR 846 or 15 miles east of I-75 (Exit 17); do not take Exit 19.

375 Sanctuary Rd., Naples 34120; 239-348-9151; www. audubon.org/local/sanctuary/corkscrew

Facilities and Activities

Boardwalk nature trail, birding and wildlife observation, gift shop, educational displays, nature programs. Admission fee. Open 8 AM to 7:30 PM May to November, 7 AM to 5:30 PM December to April.

Visitor Center

The much-needed new visitor center opened its doors in December 2000. It contains a gift shop that sells an excellent variety of natural history books plus beautiful wildlife tee-shirts, note cards, film, wildlife art prints, and so forth. The nearest food is at a convenience store seven miles away.

Next to the Visitor Center is the state-of-the-art "Living Machine," also known as the restrooms. This intriguing design allows 90% of the restroom water to be cleaned on-site by a natural system and recycled directly back to the restrooms. A series of tanks contains bacteria, plants, snails, shrimp, and fish that feed on the nutrients from the water, gradually purifying it. The system is arranged as an educational display, so that the various stages can be clearly seen.

Pick up an illustrated self-guided tour booklet at the Visitor Center before you head out for the boardwalk. Also ask for the bird checklist (189 species) and spend a few minutes in the butterfly garden.

Boardwalk

The boardwalk at Corkscrew is probably world-famous to birders. This 2¼-mile-long serpentine path has given hundreds of thousands of people the opportunity to view a pristine swamp without damaging it. The boardwalk traverses many habitats: bald-cypress, pine flatwoods, hammocks, willows, wet prairies, marshes, ponds, and lettuce lakes. Orchids, ferns, epiphytes, sawgrass, lichens, palms, and hardwoods are among the many plants you'll find here. In June, the wild hibiscus flowers, including the world's only known variety of wild hibiscus with white flowers.

Alligators, Carolina anoles, southeastern five-lined skinks, and cottonmouth snakes are among the many reptiles found here. Mammals include otters and white-tailed deer. Numerous wading birds, warblers during migration, and other birds can be found. Barred owls and limpkins are seen regularly. Many animals become accustomed to humans and walk on the boardwalk themselves.

The chalkboard at the trailhead lists recent sightings of animals. To walk the boardwalk before the sanctuary opens in the morning, make arrangements in advance (send a letter with intended date). At the halfway point is an observation platform that overlooks the central prairie—a beautiful view and a good photographic spot. During the stork nesting season, groups of stork nests can be seen in the cypress surrounding the prairie.

When the boardwalk was rebuilt in 1995, it was widened and lengthened. More importantly, it was replaced with wood from Brazil. The Sanctuary manager thoroughly researched a variety of materials and selected Pau Lope (*Tabebuia serratifolia*). It is rot- and termite-resistant, nearly fire-resistant, twice as strong as pine, and requires no chemicals. Furthermore, the grower practices sustainable forestry and the lumber is milled in Brazil. The new boardwalk is expected to last 100 years.

Truck Tours

Only National Audubon Society chapters (not individual members) are permitted to request truck tours. An Audubon guide will take a minimum of 12 people on the sanctuary's back roads not normally seen by the public. Boardwalk night tours are also available to chapters. Make arrangements in advance.

Best Time of Year

The famous wood stork colony may start forming any time from December to March, if it forms at all. Nesting should be going strong from February through May. You are likely to see storks during this time. In the winter, when the water levels are decreasing, there are concentrations of wading birds, alligators and snakes. Summer visitors will find much of the wildlife dispersed and rainstorms frequent, but many plants are flowering and the vegetation is lush. Mosquitoes are not as obnoxious here.

Pets

Not allowed.

CRANE POINT HAMMOCK (MUSEUM OF NATURAL HISTORY OF THE FLORIDA KEYS)

A major victory for conservation in the Florida Keys came when the Florida Keys Land and Sea Trust acquired the 63.5-acre Crane Point Hammock in Marathon in 1988. This hammock contains probably the last intact virgin thatch palm hammock left in North America. It was a prime site for development on the crowded land-starved island of Key Vaca. The area did not escape development by accident. The Crane family, who bought the property in 1949, were ardent conservationists.

The hammock supports 160 native species of plants, and artifacts of pre-Columbian native people have been found here. The million-dollar museum was completed in 1990. Allow about a half day for your tour of the museum and a walk on the nature trail.

The Florida Keys Land and Sea Trust is a private, nonprofit

organization that acquires natural areas in the Keys to protect habitats and cultural history.

Location, Mailing Address and Phone

MM 50, US 1, Marathon. Look for a small sign on the bay side, opposite the "K-Mart" store.

5550 Overseas Highway, Marathon 33050; 305-743-9100; www.florida-keys.fl.us/cranepoint

Facilities and Activities

Adult and children's museums, artificial lagoon, self-guided nature trail, gift shop. Admission fee.

Museum

The main attraction is the museum housing 20 major exhibits and additional rotating displays of cultural and natural history. In the main building is the "adult" museum, which boasts a 600-square-foot walk-through replica of a coral reef cave. It extends 30 feet above you as you walk through, and you will see mounts of many fish common and not-so-common in the Florida Keys reefs.

Also in the museum is a Key deer exhibit that features a two-day-old fawn that drowned in a ditch dug years ago for mosquito control. Numerous ditches remain in the Keys, a hazard for deer that drown when they try to cross the ditch and cannot climb the steep sides. Strategically placed near the mother and fawn in the exhibit is a taxidermy bald eagle that cleverly shows how diminutive the deer really are.

Exhibits in the main museum depict the 5,000-year human history of the Marathon area. Rare and unusual artifacts of cultural history, some dating back 5,000 years, are highlights. Other exhibits include an authentic dugout canoe, a tree snail display, a satellite photo of the Keys, a crocodile skull and mount, and displays about the ship-wrecking business.

This building also houses a gift shop that vends natural history–oriented jewelry, tee-shirts, hats, and knick-knacks, plus a good selection of local field guides and books on the Florida Keys. The profits go to the Florida Keys Land and Sea Trust for conservation.

As you exit by the rear door of the main building, a walkway passes over an artificial lagoon, where live sharks, snappers, barracudas, parrotfish, and angelfish may be seen swimming around as they might just offshore from the hammock.

The walkway leads to the children's museum, a one-room building created for inquisitive children. Here children can handle the objects in the touch tank and study the fish in the 200-gallon saltwater tanks. Other tanks have horseshoe crabs and sea urchins; a local seashell collection is among the exhibits. One corner of the room is devoted to a "library," where children can plunk down comfortably on the fluffy pillows and read to themselves or each other from the shelf of children's nature books. The museum is a regular field trip destination for local school classes.

Trails

Behind the main building is the beginning of the nature trail. This is a quarter-mile self-guided loop that runs through tropical Crane Point Hammock. A printed trail guide is available at the museum. It explains the ecology of the hammock and some of the native trees you'll see. Many trees along the trail have identification tags. You'll see the Key (or brittle) thatch palm, Florida thatch palm, wild dilly, black ironwood, Jamaica dogwood, and paradise-tree. All the poisonwood trees are labeled, so you'll know not to touch them.

For history buffs, the Adderly House is open to the public. This restored house, built in 1903, is on the National Register of Historic Places and is the oldest house in the Keys outside of Key West. It was built by a Bahamian with home-made concrete and has withstood every hurricane that threatened its threshold. The house is located on a trail behind the museum (a 5-minute walk by a lagoon).

Call ahead for the schedule of programs. Group tours and programs are available if arranged in advance. A possible tour could be a guided walk through the hammock. A program might be on sea life or hammock plants. In other words, the staff is knowledgeable and flexible and will try to work with your group's needs. You must call in advance, preferably at least one week, to arrange a special group program or tour. Fees are dependent on the group size.

Best Time of Year

Any time of year is fine for the museum. The trail is beautiful year-round, with plenty to see, but it may be buggy and muggy in the summer. October, November, March, and April are good months to see migrating warblers and raptors.

Pets

Not allowed.

MIAMI-DADE COUNTY PARKS

For more information on the Miami-Dade County parks contact Miami-Dade Park & Recreation Department, 275 NW 2nd Street, Miami 33128; 305-755-7800; www.metro-dade.com/parks

ARCH CREEK PARK—MIAMI-DADE COUNTY PARKS

The 40-foot oolitic limestone arch that once spanned a small creek and served as a thoroughfare for the Tequesta Indians collapsed mysteriously two hours after the surrounding land was purchased for use as a park in 1973. No evidence could be found linking the collapse to threats by opponents to bomb it if the purchase went through. The area is, nevertheless, a welcomed green haven in an urban environment.

The Tequestas dwelled here from 500 B.C. to A.D 1300. The land was higher and drier than the surrounding land, and it was close to Biscayne Bay and the Everglades. The natural arch formed a bridge that facilitated travel. A midden is visible from the trail.

This replica of a Tequesta chickee is displayed at Arch Creek Park.

Arch Creek is one of the only preserved archeological sites in Miami-Dade County.

Owing to its reputation as one of the greatest natural wonders in south Florida, later residents often used the area for picnics, meetings, and stagecoach rest stops. In 1858, new settlers built a coontie mill to grind the roots into starch, using water from Arch Creek to turn the water wheel.

The small museum was designed as an old Florida pioneer home, with high ceilings, many windows, and a shady porch. It contains historical artifacts found around the bridge and natural history displays. A short trail goes through a mature live oak hammock, which was being overrun by air-potato vines. These vines are being removed by park staff. Among the native plants you'll see are rouge plant, paradise-tree, wild coffee, gumbo-limbo, pigeon-plum, white stopper, and bromeliads. Coontie plantings have encouraged the rare atala butterflies to lay their eggs at Arch Creek. Guided walks are offered on Saturdays.

Location, Mailing Address and Phone

From I-95, take Exit 14 east on NE 135th Street/SR 916 for 2.8 miles; entrance is less than a block before US 1.
1855 NE 135 Street, North Miami 33181; 305-944-6111

Facilities and Activities

Nature trail, historic museum. Open 9 AM to 5 PM. Free admission.

Best Time of Year

No preference.

Pets

Not allowed.

CASTELLOW HAMMOCK NATURE CENTER— MIAMI-DADE COUNTY PARKS

Castellow Hammock, about 110 acres, is administered by the Miami-Dade Park and Recreation Department. It was established as an environmental education center in 1974 and it boasts of a tropical hammock with over 250 species of plants.

Castellow Hammock is probably best known for its wintering painted buntings. People come from all over the country in the winter to watch and photograph these brilliantly colored birds.

Castellow was in the center of the worst winds of Hurricane Andrew. Damage to the hammock and visitor facilities was extreme. The County leveled the remnants of the Nature Center, which has been rebuilt. It took four years of intensive trail work and exotic plant removal to reopen the trail.

Location, Mailing Address and Phone

A ½-mile south of SW 216th St. on SW 162nd Ave. Look carefully for the "Castellow Hammock" sign on the east side of 162nd Ave. 22301 SW 162nd Ave., Goulds 33170; 305-242-7688

Facilities and Activities

Self-guided nature trail. No admission fee.

The bird feeders are frequented by painted and indigo buntings from October through April and white-winged doves year-round. Fortunately, the hurricane appears to have improved the habitat for the buntings, which prefer more open areas than dense hammocks. Before the storm, over 70 species of butterflies and skippers had been identified at and around Castellow. Many are tropical and are found nowhere else in the United States. Hummingbirds regularly visit from September to April.

Nature Trail

The trail through the hammock is a ½-mile one way. It is rocky and narrow (not handicapped-accessible). Some trees likely to be seen along the trail are wild-tamarind, mastic, gumbo-limbo, pigeon-plum, paradise-tree, lancewood, and West-Indian cherry. Look for limestone solution holes along the way.

The bird list for the park includes 126 species of resident and migratory birds. Besides those already mentioned are mangrove cuckoos, smooth-billed anis, scissor-tailed flycatchers, and purple martins.

Best Time of Year

In summer, the graceful swallow-tailed kites roost in the hammock, and in the winter the hammock is a roost for black and turkey vultures. Many warblers feed in the hammock during migration. Buntings and hummingbirds are frequent in winter, and butterflies are common throughout the year.

Pets

Not allowed.

FAIRCHILD TROPICAL GARDEN— MIAMI-DADE COUNTY PARKS

This largest tropical botanical garden in the continental United States is a horticultural gem that showcases tropical and subtropical native and exotic plants. The 83-acre garden, established in 1938, is a nonprofit institution operated for display, education, scientific research, and conservation. Although the county owns most of the land, it isn't technically a county park. Thousands of species and varieties of trees, shrubs, vines, ground covers, orchids, and other epiphytes are established, sometimes in sections emphasizing such plant groups as palms, cycads, bromeliads, and orchids. Don't miss the "Rare Plant House," a collection of difficult-to-grow plants such as breadfruit, orchids, aroids, and giant tree ferns.

Despite the many exotics planted here, there are many natives, and many species which have become naturalized in south Florida. If you want to learn plant identifications better, this is a good place to start. Allow about a half day to walk around (more if you're a hard-core botanist).

The garden was at the outer edge of Andrew's northern eye wall. FTG botanists estimated 60–70% of the total collection of trees and plants was damaged or destroyed. Releafing of the remaining trees occurred within weeks. Staff and volunteers replanted hundreds of fallen trees, particularly palms, within weeks of the storm.

Location, Mailing Address and Phone

10901 Old Cutler Rd., Coral Gables. Take Kendall Dr./SW 88th St. east from Kendall and turn right onto Old Cutler Rd. Fairchild is just south of Matheson Hammock Park.

10901 Old Cutler Rd., Miami 33156; (305) 667-1651

Facilities and Activities

Gardens with labeled woody and herbaceous plants, tram tour, botanically-oriented bookstore, educational programs on plants, snack bar. No picnicking or bicycling. Open 9:30 AM to 4:30 PM daily, except December 25. Admission fee includes tram tour.

If you're a nut for plant books, you'll cotton to the bookstore. It has a wonderful assortment of books for sale—mostly botanical, but also tropical cookbooks, gardening, local history, and wildlife. Many plant identification guides and horticultural books are stocked. The bookstore also serves as a small visitor center and gift shop.

Fairchild Tropical Garden is well-arranged for self-guided tours. The trees and plants have identification labels. Several miles of paved and unpaved walkways cover the area, but you can walk anywhere off the roads for closer examination of the plants.

Guided tours are also available. Tram tours leave hourly; guided walking tours are available seasonally. Special group tours can be arranged (call in advance). Almost all areas (including the bathrooms) are wheelchair-accessible. The tram makes it easy for everyone to get around. The bookstore has several wheelchairs available for loan.

The snack bar serves sandwiches and drinks and has outdoor tables under a huge sapodilla tree.

Best Time of Year

There is something flowering every month of the year, particularly in the summer. Winter is usually more comfortable weatherwise.

Pets

Not allowed.

GREYNOLDS PARK—MIAMI-DADE COUNTY PARKS

A small county park within the urban confines of Miami, Greynolds Park has a special claim to fame. The 240-acre park was renowned for the water birds that nest on the mangrove islands in close proximity to the trails. Such species as great egret, great blue heron, tricolored heron, little blue heron, snowy egret, cattle egret, anhinga, and cormorant commonly nested here. Sometime in the 1980s, the rookery (nesting colony) collapsed for unknown reasons. It is still a good place to see wading birds.

Of further interest is the history of the scarlet ibis's introduction into the park. In the 1950s, a neighbor living adjacent to the rookery imported scarlet ibis eggs from Trinidad and Surinam to place into the nests of the white ibises already nesting there. He hoped that the scarlet ibises would reside at Greynolds when they grew up and would be visible from his yard. The first batch of eggs failed, and a second batch was imported in the early 1960s. Some chicks survived and later mated with the white ibises. The resulting pink or orange offspring have been seen occasionally around south Florida to the present.

Location, Mailing Address and Phone

One entrance at 17530 West Dixie Highway, 0.7 miles south of SR 860/Miami Gardens Dr.; another entrance on NE 22nd Ave., just south of Miami Gardens River Dr.

17530 West Dixie Highway, North Miami Beach 33160; 305-945-3425. Office hours 8:30 AM to 4:30 PM Monday to Friday. Call for schedule of guided walks.

Facilities and Activities

Nature trails, bird roost, guided birding and nature walks, biking paths, boat rentals, paddleboats, picnic tables, snack bar, children's playground, golf course. Admission fee on weekends and holidays. Open sunrise to sunset.

The Lakeside Nature Trail circumnavigates the mangrove pond and islands where the wading birds roost. It is narrow and rocky, not handicapped-accessible; other trails, however, are accessible.

A bird checklist, containing over 130 species, is available from the office. This is a good place to see the many introduced parrots and parakeets that have become naturalized in the Miami area.

Warblers pass through the park in large numbers during the spring and fall. Short-tailed, broad-winged, and other hawks are seen here. Spot-breasted orioles are found from March to October.

Herons come to roost in the mangroves at dusk. At sunrise, they'll be off again to their favorite feeding sites in nearby marshes. Yellow-crowned night herons and great blue herons nest in the spring.

In 1996, the staff removed the growing population of alligators from the park's waters. That year, the wading birds did not return. It is likely that the birds knew their fearsome bodyguards against predation from terrestrial predators (such as raccoons, opossums, and rat snakes) were absent.

Best Time of Year

March to April and October to November for warblers; year-round for birds.

Pets

Not allowed.

MATHESON HAMMOCK PARK— MIAMI-DADE COUNTY PARKS

When William J. Matheson donated 84 acres to Dade county in 1930, he stipulated that the hammock be used as a botanical park for the public's benefit, to be preserved in its natural state. The park currently covers 629 acres of land, much of which is left natural.

This Miami-Dade County park along Biscayne Bay has two sections, a water recreation–based fee area and a land-based non-fee area. The water recreation, which contains a full-facility marina and swimming areas, is frequently crowded. The land-based area has picnic areas, playing fields, and nature trails. If you happen to be in the area (to visit Fairchild Tropical Garden, for example), the West Hammock Trail is worth a short side trip.

The park was just outside Andrew's northern eye wall. It sustained heavy damage from wind and storm surge. Extensive damage to the hammock will be visible for years.

Location, Mailing Address and Phone

9610 Old Cutler Rd., Coral Gables, just north of Fairchild Tropical Garden.

9610 Old Cutler Rd., Miami 33156; 305-665-5475

Facilities and Activities

Fee area: boat ramp, snack bar, wading and swimming beaches, large marina. Non-fee area: nature trails, bicycle path, picnic tables with grills. Bathrooms handicapped-accessible.

Trails

The water sports area has little to offer an exploring naturalist. Go instead to the non-fee picnic area where there are a few foot trails for getting off the beaten path. The parking lot is a few hundred yards north of Fairchild Tropical Garden.

In the vicinity of the parking lot are the picnic tables around which spot-breasted orioles and hill mynas may be seen. There are several small ponds surrounded by red mangroves that occasionally harbor alligators and wading birds. The East Hammock Trail is a short, paved trail with educational signs.

The better trail is on the west side of Old Cutler Road in a remnant West Indian hardwood hammock. The West Hammock Trail passes through mostly native vegetation. The trail was rebuilt and improved after Hurricane Andrew. Much exotic plant removal has been accomplished and a new trail guide identifies hammock plants. The trail is rocky and solution holes are common.

Best Time of Year

September, October, March, and April for migrating warblers and small land birds in the hammock.

Pets

Not allowed.

NAVY WELLS PINELAND PRESERVE— MIAMI-DADE COUNTY PARKS

Scattered throughout Miami-Dade County are remnant patches of pinelands. The largest outside of Everglades National Park survived because it happened to be perched atop a very important wellfield. In 1940, the U.S. Navy built an 18-inch diameter pipeline to supply the naval station on Boca Chica, near Key West. The source of the water was a well in Florida City on the mainland 130 miles away. The Florida Keys Aqueduct Authority bought water from the Navy to sell to civilian Keys residents. The 310-acre slash pine preserve surrounds the original wellfield compound. The aqueduct has since been purchased by the Aqueduct Authority and enlarged to meet the growing need for water in the Keys. The Miami-Dade County Park and Recreation Department now owns most of the land around the wellfield.

The mature pines were almost entirely destroyed in some areas by Hurricane Andrew. Many trees snapped off and many were uprooted, but many also survived. The problem may be that the trees were stressed before the storm by the lowering of the water table, caused by human usage. The taproots could no longer reach the water table, and the trees lived from rainfall to rainfall. The additional loss of limbs and needles was too much. Some weakened stands were also attacked by a pine bark beetle. The results were devastating. If not for a lucky twist of fate, there would be slow regeneration of pines in this stand. However, just prior to the storm, the Florida Department of Forestry decided to spread some leftover pine seeds where a prescribed burn had

The skeletons of slash pines are a silent reminder of the fury of Hurricane Andrew compounded by the human-created stress that prevented their regrowth (photo taken 4 years after hurricane).

occurred. These seeds thrived, and the resulting young pines are visible on the north side. Since then, the county has planted more seedlings, and some sprouted on their own. Be careful of falling dead trees.

Location, Mailing Address and Phone

192nd Ave./Tower Rd. in Florida City. From Krome Ave. or US 1 in Florida City, turn west onto SW 344th St./Palm Drive. Turn left at 192nd Ave. (at "Robert Is Here" Fruit Stand), and drive 0.6 miles. The Preserve is on the right, at the sign "Well Field and Treatment Facility". Call Castellow Hammock: 305-242-7688

Facilities and Activities

Hiking trail. No visitor facilities. No admission fee.

There are several grassy firebreak roads through the preserve. Walk through the gate to the left of the parking area. The surficial limestone bedrock makes this a rough area to walk around, complete with frequent poisonwood trees.

Swallow-tailed kites may be seen from March to August. Look for coontie, the ancient cycad. The starchy root of the coontie was a staple food of the Seminoles and Miccosukees. The larvae of the Florida atala (*Eumaeus atala*), a threatened tropical butterfly, depends on the coontie for food as well. The adult butterflies feed on the nectar of palmettos and other flowers.

Other plants of special interest include silver palm, tetrazygia, pineland jacquemontia, and pineland croton. The croton is the host plant of the Florida leafwing (*Anaea troglodyta floridalis*) larvae. This rare butterfly is endemic to the pinelands of southern Florida. Forty-six species of grasses sprout beneath the pines in this preserve. One of them, Florida gamagrass, is endemic to southern Florida.

Best Time of Year

November to May (the nonmosquito season).

Pets

Not allowed.

REDLAND FRUIT AND SPICE PARK—
MIAMI-DADE COUNTY PARKS

This 32-acre park in the Redland Historic District of Miami-Dade County is a unique component of the county's Park and Recreation Department—there are no other such parks in the United States. Since 1944, the park has cultivated and displayed over 500 varieties of tropical and subtropical fruit, herb, spice, and nut trees from all over the world. Some examples are lychee, carambola, durian, jackfruit, longan, tamarind, cinnamon, cocoa, jujube, loofah, and allspice. They thrive in this climate. The park's primary functions are education and agricultural research.

This park is included in this book because it adds a little "spice" to the total enjoyment of exploring tropical Florida. Few of the trees are native, but you'll see many of the same trees growing along roadsides in the Homestead area. Many species of birds are attracted to feed on the variety of fruits ripening year-round. Considering the proximity to other natural areas in Homestead, the very reasonable admission fee, and all you can learn, this is a worthwhile side trip. Plan to spend two to three hours.

Since this park was directly in the worst part of Hurricane Andrew, it sustained severe damage in 1992. Some magnificent old trees were destroyed. Workers spent three weeks after the storm propping up windthrown trees. Seven hundred trees were lost and 300 were replanted. The park is making improvements as they continue to replant by making sections for the Pacific, Asia, and so on.

Location, Mailing Address and Phone

24801 SW 187th Ave., Homestead 33031, on the corner of Redland Rd. (SW 187th Ave.) and Coconut Palm Drive (SW 248th St.); 305-247-5717

Facilities and Activities

Tours of the groves and gardens, Gourmet & Fruit Store, picnic tables, weekly plant workshops. Open 10 AM to 5 PM daily. Admission fee for groves; fees for programs.

Groves and Gardens

Daily tours last about an hour. The guide will gather ripe fruits for you to taste. You may also walk around on your own. You can buy or borrow a guide book that describes area of origin, uses, propagation techniques, flowering season, and so on of the trees found here, as well as recipes and some natural history. It also contains the park's list of the 81 species of birds that have been seen here. You may eat any fruit you find on the ground.

Gourmet and Fruit Store

The Gourmet and Fruit Store has a wonderful selection of dried and canned exotic fruits and vegetables from all over the tropics. Herbs and spices, jams and jellies, teas, chips, and many other unusual foods are sold here. Cold natural fruit juices and soft drinks are available. Try something new! Also for sale are books on tropical fruits, gardening, cookbooks, and local natural history.

The store, groves, and restrooms are handicapped accessible. No admission fee is charged if you just wish to visit the store.

Special Events

Several special events draw large crowds each year. At the Natural Arts Festival in January, you will be treated to dozens of exhibits and demonstrations of natural foods, crafts, plants, gardening, and horticulture. The Asian Festival is in March. Food booths sell tasty exotic foods for lunch. Plants and gifts are for sale.

Local residents may wish to inquire about the park's workshops, classes, and off-site tours on tropical fruit cooking and growing.

Best Time of Year

There is always something in fruit. In summer more things ripen, but heat and mosquitoes are intense. Winter is a delightful time to visit.

Pets

Not allowed.

GUMBO LIMBO NATURE CENTER AND RED REEF PARK

The nature center is part of the Gumbo Limbo Environmental Complex at Red Reef Park, which is operated by the City of Boca Raton. The 20-acre complex also includes classrooms, biology laboratory, amphitheater, marine observation tanks, and marine research facility. Its location between the Intracoastal Waterway and the Atlantic Ocean affords the opportunity for studies of tropical hammocks, coastal dunes, mangroves, sea turtles, and manatees. Florida Atlantic University runs the marine research, which includes large tanks into which fresh sea water is pumped.

The 67-acre Red Reef Park includes oceanside swimming, snorkeling, dunes, and hammocks. Loggerhead sea turtles nest on the ¾-mile-long beach in the summer.

The nature center's name was borrowed from a tropical tree called the gumbo-limbo, which grows commonly here. The wood is easily carved and was used in bygone years to make carousel horses. A remarkable feature of the wood is that a branch stuck in the ground will sprout roots and leaves and become a whole tree.

Location, Mailing Address and Phone

From northern Boca area, take NW 40th Street east to SR A1A/ Ocean Blvd., turn south and go about 1.5 miles to Nature Center. From southern Boca area, take Palmetto Park Road east to SR A1A, turn north and go 1.1 miles to Nature Center.

1801 N. Ocean Blvd., Boca Raton 33432; 561-338-1473; www.fau.edu/gumbo

Red Reef Park, 1400 N. Ocean Blvd., Boca Raton 33432; 561-393-7820

Facilities and Activities

Nature center, boardwalk, nature trail, observation tower, butterfly garden, educational programs, swimming, snorkeling. Open Monday through Saturday 9 AM to 4 PM, Sunday 12 to 4 PM; closed Thanksgiving, December 25, January 1. Free admission. Red Reef Park is open sunrise to sunset daily.

Nature Center

The forte of this educational center is the marine aquaria containing local fish and invertebrates. Other live exhibits include gopher tortoises, snakes, and lizards. Other displays include sea turtles, local birds, reptiles, fish, and a comparison of the wood from native trees. The gift shop sells books (mostly for children), tee shirts, jewelry, and posters. Outside are a butterfly garden and live sea turtle tanks. Sea turtle nesting programs are conducted from May to July (call for reservations).

Boardwalk, Observation Tower, and Trail

The 0.3-mile-long boardwalk rambles through high and low hammocks and mangroves along the Intracoastal Waterway. It also leads to the 50-foot observation tower, which affords a view above the tree tops. The walk is handicapped-accessible. Some native trees you'll see are paradise-tree, pigeon-plum, tallowwood, mastic, guiana-plum, white indigo-berry, lancewood, Spanish stopper, and Jamaica caper. Most of the exotic plants were removed when the boardwalk was built. A small oyster shell midden is along the way.

The North Trail is shorter than the boardwalk and not handi-capped-accessible. It also passes by the Intracoastal Waterway, where the white mangroves grow.

Best Time of Year

No preference.

Pets

Not allowed.

LEE COUNTY PARKS
SIX MILE CYPRESS SLOUGH PRESERVE—
LEE COUNTY PARKS

Part of the preserve was purchased by the South Florida Water Management District under Save Our Rivers Program. The preserve is managed by Lee County. It is 2,200 acres of a long, narrow cypress strand—about 9 miles long and ¾-mile wide. It drains a 57-square-mile watershed and empties into Estero Bay. The county has built a 1.2-mile handicapped-accessible board-walk, an amphitheater, picnic area, restrooms, and observation decks.

Location, Mailing Address and Phone

At 7751 Penzance Crossing, off of Six Mile Cypress Parkway in southeastern Ft. Myers, 3 miles south of Colonial Boulevard (Exit 22 from I-75) and 2 miles north of Daniels Parkway (Exit 21).

Mailing address: Lee Co. Parks and Recreation Department, 3410 Palm Beach Blvd., Ft. Myers 33916; 239-461-7400

Facilities and Activities

Interpretive boardwalk, amphitheater, picnicking, observation decks, guided walks every Wednesday and Saturday at 9:30 AM (in winter). Open 8:00 AM to 5:00 PM October to March, 8:00 AM to 8:00 PM April to September. Parking fee.

Best Time of Year

Winter for more bird activity.

Pets

Not allowed.

LOXAHATCHEE PRESERVE NATURE CENTER

Once upon a time the Everglades overflowed into the Loxahatchee Slough then out to the ocean during the wet season. During the dry season, however, water from the coastal ridge sometimes flowed the other way from the Slough into the Everglades! The Loxahatchee Preserve is contained within the now-fragmented Loxahatchee Slough. The Slough was once connected at the south end to the area that is now A.R.M. Loxahatchee National Wildlife Refuge (see separate entry) and at the north end to the Loxahatchee River. The Preserve is part of the 20-square-mile Water Catchment Area that is owned by the City of West Palm Beach.

The City purchased the Water Catchment Area in 1955 to supply water to its residents. Since water usage has become such a hot issue in south Florida, the City has proposed some innovative techniques for conserving and purifying water. It goes like this: Wastewater gets treated at a conventional treatment plant and then discharged into man-made and existing wetlands for natural purification. From the wetlands, the water seeps underground into the aquifer next to a wellfield. It gets recovered by pumping from the wellfield and sent to the M-2 Canal. The last step is another water treatment plant. Then the water is ready to be reused. Without this elaborate system, the City would continue to dispose of its wastewater by deep well injection (deep underground) . . . bye-bye water!

The City has opened a nature center and a boardwalk within the Preserve. Good vistas of sawgrass marshes, cypress strands and domes, and some pinelands are visible. Snail kites nest on an adjacent site and are occasionally seen. Bald eagles, limpkins, and otters may also be seen.

Location, Mailing Address and Phone

8264 Northlake Blvd., West Palm Beach. Take Northlake Boulevard west, passing the Turnpike. Go 1 mile west of Beeline Highway/SR 710, south entrance on left, north entrance on right. P.O. Box 3506, West Palm Beach 33402-3506; 561-627-8831

Facilities and Activities

Nature Center, boardwalk, nature trails, canoeing, guided walks.
Southside—The Southside Mini Nature Center opened in 1995 and contains classrooms, meeting halls, exhibits, and a 10-minute video on the water supply plan. The 1500-foot boardwalk is at the nature center. Canoe trips can be arranged by calling in advance.

Northside—There are two ½-mile trails through the oak-palmetto hammock and a small area for canoeing.

Best Time of Year

No preference.

Pets

Allowed on leash on north side, not allowed on south side.

MICCOSUKEE INDIAN VILLAGE

The tiny reservation set aside for the Miccosukee Tribe is squeezed between Everglades National Park and Big Cypress National Preserve. The Miccosukees are Native Americans whose ancestors, the Creeks, lived in Alabama, Georgia, and northern Florida. Many Miccosukees were killed during the 1600s and 1700s by disease, probably introduced by the Spanish and British. During the Indian Wars of the 1800s, most of the survivors were killed by the colonists or sent to a reservation in Oklahoma.

The remaining few hundred Miccosukees were pushed south and hid in the Everglades in family-sized groups that could escape detection by soldiers. Besides farming small patches of upland on the hammocks, they fished and hunted in the marshes and hammocks. Game animals were plentiful until the newly dug canals of 1906 and 1913 began draining the Everglades. In 1928, the completion of the Tamiami Trail cut the tribe in two, literally and figuratively. Not only did the road bisect their territory, but it also caused many tribal people to be drawn into the encroaching white civilization. Through all the broken treaties, encroachment on their land, and destruction of their hunting grounds, the Miccosukees never surrendered to the American government.

In 1962, the Miccosukees were recognized by the U.S. government as an Indian tribe, separate from the Seminoles. Their reservation is small, only a 500-foot-wide strip of land between Everglades National Park and the Tamiami Trail. Not all of the approximately 450 Miccosukees live on the reservation; some live elsewhere in Florida. The Miccosukee clans maintain their original ways of life as best they can in our modern world. Some still live on tree islands in the Everglades that are not accessible by road.

Unlike the Indians of the Great Plains, who lived in large multi-family villages, the Miccosukees lived in small extended family clans. Each family lived on a separate tree island, and they visited each other by cypress dugout canoes. The village that now is set up for the guided tours originally was a one-family village.

These native people currently make their living through the tourist industry (craft-making, village tours, and airboat tours of the Everglades). They cannot support themselves "off the land" because the reservation is surrounded by land protected by white people's laws. Their alternative would be to go to the city and assimilate into white people's jobs. The tourist industry gives the natives a chance to maintain their ways of life and teach outsiders about their culture.

Although the village is not distinguished as a natural area, the value in visiting it is to learn how these people lived off the land naturally. For example, logging cypress trees is one of their livelihoods. Before felling a cypress, they first determine how high above the waterline on the trunk to cut so the stump will later sprout. The resulting tree will not be good for lumber, but it will replace the one they removed. Since cypress trees normally only regenerate from seed under certain water conditions (which may not occur in an area for many years), this is an important method for maintaining cypress stands. Also, when the Miccosukees cut palmetto fronds for thatched roofs, they leave enough for the tree to stay healthy. Your tour guide will be able to speak on such subjects, so ask questions.

The Indian creed is worth mentioning, since it should apply to all people, including non-Indians. The Miccosukees feel that the land and its resources are sacred gifts to them, and it is their privilege (not their *right*) to use them. Since the trees, animals, rivers, and so on are gifts, they must all be treated with respect. If they abuse these gifts, they will be taken away. Haven't our higher spirits already started doing that to us?

Allow about a half day to see the village and airboat tour. A good plan would be to combine this with a visit to the Shark Valley section of Everglades National Park for a whole day trip.

Location, Mailing Address and Phone

On Tamiami Trail, 18.5 miles west of Krome Avenue or 0.5 miles west of the Shark Valley entrance to Everglades National Park.

P.O. Box 440021, Tamiami Station, Miami 33144; 305-223-8380; www.miccosukeetribe.com

Facilities and Activities

Village (with museum and gift shop), restaurant, airboat tours. Admission fee for village (9:30 AM to 5:00 PM); fee for airboat tour.

An aerial view shows the Miccosukee Indian Village in the Everglades.

Village

The focal point of the reservation is the Indian Village. Guided tours leave every one or two hours from 10:00 AM. For a self-guided tour, ask for the village map and the schedule of alligator shows. The village consists of a family living chickee, a cooking chickee, displays of basketry, a crafts area (bows, arrows, canoes, etc.), a nature walk, a museum, an alligator arena, and a bow-shooting range. Authentic cypress dugout canoes are on display.

"Chickee" is the Miccosukee word for house. A traditional chickee was about 16 feet long and 9 feet wide and was made from cypress logs. It had a platform floor raised about three feet off the ground to keep water out during the wet season, to discourage snakes, and to catch the cooling breezes. The roof was thatched with cabbage palm fronds and there were no walls. Today many Miccosukees still live in chickees. The term "chickee" is now widely used in Florida for similar structures that non-natives have, such as backyard pavilions and picnic shelters. Very often it is the expert Miccosukees and Seminoles who are hired to build these backyard chickees, providing them with a source of income.

The museum has displays of cooking utensils, clothing,

games, local wildlife, and village life. There is a 10-minute film on Miccosukee history and paintings by local Miccosukee artist, Stephen Tiger.

The nature walk is a short boardwalk into the Everglades, with a vista across the sawgrass and tree islands on the horizon. Watch for wading birds, limpkins, and rails.

The alligator arena is an outdoor pit that houses some hefty alligators for cultural demonstrations. These demonstrations don't really resemble a traditional method of gator handling, but they do attract a lot of thrill-seeking tourists. There are shows periodically throughout the day.

The gift shop sells Miccosukee and Seminole patchwork clothing, crafts from other Native Americans, local guide books, and Florida souvenirs. You can get Miccosukee and American food at the snack chickee.

After leaving the village, try driving west on the small dead-end road paralleling Tamiami Trail on the south side. This is the original Tamiami Trail and the road that many Miccosukees live on now. It passes the tribal headquarters, school, and health clinic. The men who specialize in making chickees for a living can be seen shaving cypress poles and piling thatch by the roadside.

Airboat Tours

The 30-minute airboat tours begin across the street and leave whenever there are enough people. If you plan to take an airboat ride during your visit in South Florida, the Miccosukee tour would be a good choice. The guide will take you to an isolated hammock to see how a family would live the traditional way.

For those readers unfamiliar with airboats, a short explanation is offered here. Airboats are shallow, flat-bottomed boats that skim over the surface of the water. Propulsion comes from an airplane propeller mounted on the back of the boat, high above the water. In effect, the propeller pushes the boat through air rather than water, as in a typical motorboat. Airboats are able to cross vast expanses of sawgrass-covered marsh that may have only two inches of water.

The first airboat was designed by Glenn Curtiss in 1920 for gliding over the Everglades. The idea didn't catch on until Johnny Lamb and Russell Howard built a similar boat for frog hunting in 1933. Other "froggers" copied their design. Now the Miccosukees use them regularly; in fact, many depend on them for logging and transportation to their chickees. Airboats are very noisy and disruptive to wildlife, but the alternative forms of transportation (such as swamp buggies and all-terrain-vehicles, which cause serious permanent damage to the ecosystem) are worse. Park rangers, biologists, and wildlife managers in the Everglades use airboats regularly.

Restaurant

The two restaurants near the village are run by Miccosukees and offer both Miccosukee and American meals. Miccosukee specialties include pan-fried bread, frog legs, and catfish.

Best Time of Year

Winter is best for the village. Airboat tours may not be possible during the dry months (January–May). There is a major Indian Arts Festival (annually from December 26 to January 1) that features authentic Indian arts, crafts, dancing, and music from over 40 tribes across North America, including local Miccosukees and Seminoles, and another week-long festival in late July.

Pets

Allowed in the village, not allowed on the airboats.

MOUNTS BOTANICAL GARDEN

The 13 acres of this botanical garden are a pleasant haven in this fast-paced region. The plantings were initiated in 1954 as an Extension Service project by Marvin Mounts, the county extension agent. There are special collections of rare trees, cacti, roses, herbs, poisonous plants, and palms, as well as habitat groupings for native plants, rain forests, wetlands, and more. The garden supports botanical research and education. Allow about two hours.

Location, Mailing Address and Phone

Located on Military Trail directly west of Palm Beach International Airport, between Belvedere Road and Southern Blvd.

531 North Military Trail, West Palm Beach 33415-1358; 561-233-1757

Facilities and Activities

Botanical garden, guided tours, lectures, gift and book shop. Open 8:30 AM to 4:30 PM Monday through Saturday and 1 to 5 PM Sunday; closed Thanksgiving, December 24-25, January 1. Gift shop has limited hours; closed Mondays. Donation appreciated.

Short trails lead visitors through the well-manicured garden areas. Almost all the plants are labeled. People seem to enjoy just walking in the lovely surroundings to relax. Indeed, the only thing marring this tranquil garden is the occasional jet departing the adjacent airport. Volunteers give free guided tours on weekends and operate the gift shop. The shop has a superb selection of plant books, as well as other natural history books and nature-related gifts. Once a month there is an evening lecture on various natural history subjects. The county extension service office is on this property.

Best Time of Year

Always something in flower and fruit at any time of year.

Pets

Not allowed.

NAPLES NATURE CENTER

In the heart of Naples lies a quiet refreshing break from city life. The Naples Nature Center, located on a 14-acre sanctuary, is owned and operated by The Conservancy of Southwest Florida, a private nonprofit conservation organization active in the Naples area (see BRIGGS NATURE CENTER for background on The Conservancy). The Naples Nature Center was completed in 1981 and has since been serving Collier County with educational programs. The Conservancy's extensive schedule of quality programs is enhanced by the dedication of several hundred well-trained volunteers.

The Nature Center Complex contains the Nature Discovery Center museum, auditorium, nature store, wildlife rehabilitation center, classrooms, and nature trails. Altogether, it is one of the best examples in south Florida of a complete environmental education and conservation center. Because their programs encompass all ecosystems of south Florida, The Conservancy encourages people to visit the Nature Center before exploring natural areas such as the ones described in this book. Then they will have a good understanding of all they are seeing.

Location, Mailing Address and Phone

From the south: from the intersection of SR 29 and Tamiami Trail, go west on Tamiami Trail about 23 miles to SR 851/Goodlette Rd. Turn right and go north on Goodlette about 2 miles. Turn right onto 14th Ave. North and go short distance to end of street. From the north: Get onto SR 851 either from SR 886/Golden Gate Parkway or Tamiami Trail. Go south on Goodlette to 14th Ave. North. Turn left and go short distance to end.

1450 Merrihue Dr., Naples 34102; 239-262-0304

Facilities and Activities

Nature Discovery Center Museum, nature trails, boat tour, canoe and kayak rentals, self-guided canoe trail, wildlife rehabilitation center and aviary, nature store, and environmental education programs. Open Monday to Saturday from 9 AM to 4:30 PM year-round; Sundays from 1 to 5 PM January to March only. Admission fee (also good for same day admission to Briggs Nature Center).

Around the Nature Center complex are special conservation plantings. A xeriscape demonstration plot shows what plants to add to your garden that don't require watering. A screened-in butterfly garden has both the plants that attract butterflies and the live butterflies that feed on them. The aviary, which houses injured birds, can be seen from the outside. There is much to see and do in the small area of the Nature Center. School groups and children's summer camps are Nature Center specialties. Call ahead for a schedule of tours and programs.

Nature Discovery Center

This 5,000-square foot interactive museum, opened in 1986, has been hosting thousands of visitors a month. Just about every aspect of south Florida natural history is represented in the exhibits: hydrology, habitats, wildlife, early Indians, and so on. Exhibits include a life-sized diorama of part of a cypress swamp and its bird life, a rare shell collection, and a 2,300-gallon marine aquarium. The live serpentarium houses virtually every species of non-venomous snake found locally. You will want to spend at least an hour looking around.

Trails

Three self-guided interpretive trails radiate from the Nature Center complex. All three are short (about 10 minutes). The wide, wood-chipped trails are carefully maintained. The numbered markers correspond to the guide booklet available at the Nature Store. Characteristic of everything The Conservancy does, the booklet is thorough and excellently prepared. Guided walks are also available.

The Hammock Trail goes through a typical hardwood hammock. Bromeliads and ferns are abundant in the live oaks. The Arboretum Trail displays a variety of native plants, including those suitable for xeriscaping. The Peninsula Trail takes you to the edge of a tidal lagoon, where you may see an alligator or a manatee.

Boat Tour

The Conservancy offers boat tours from the Nature Center every morning except Sundays (included with admission). Reservations must be made in person on the day of the tour. The boat seats five to six people. The trip lasts 45 minutes and cruises through a tidal lagoon to the Gordon River. Mangroves line the water. There is even a mangrove planting along the way, the result of a mitigation agreement by a developer who destroyed mangroves and was required to replace them. Mangroves are protected by state law; for every one destroyed, five must be planted. Wading birds, like yellow-crowned night-herons, can be viewed along the way. It's hard to believe you're still in the middle of Naples when you take this tour.

Nature Store

If you're looking to buy nature-related items, this store has an exceptional selection. Get those birthday lists ready! Among the thousands of items for sale are jewelry, tee-shirts, nature art prints, children's educational toys, and bird feeders. There is an excellent selection of field guides, children's books, hard-to-find regional books, and other natural history books.

Best Time of Year

Year-round. Although naturalist programs are reduced in the summer, there are still boat tours and other programs. The museum, trails, and gardens are worth a visit any time.

Pets

Not allowed.

PALM BEACH COUNTY PARKS
JOHN PRINCE PARK—
PALM BEACH COUNTY PARKS

Lake Osborne (338 acres)is the focus of the activities in this park. The long, narrow lake (about 3 miles long) is a mecca for water birds, such as limpkins, anhingas, moorhens, herons, and egrets. The limpkins are residents and have become accustomed to humans, so it is almost guaranteed that you'll see one if you walk around the shore.

Location, Mailing Address and Phone

From I-95, take Exit 47 (6th Ave. S) and go west less than a mile. Entrances also on Lake Worth Road and Congress Ave.
   2700 6th Ave. South, Lake Worth 33461; 561-582-7992

Facilities and Activities

Nature trails, 5-mile bicycle/jogging path, birding, boating, campground, picnicking.

Nature Trails

The several short trails at the south end of the 726-acre park have been restored by removal of exotics and planting of native species. It was a massive effort because numerous mature Australian-pines were felled. The endeavor was greatly aided by volunteer help from the local Audubon Society. Native plants that you may see are coreopsis, wax myrtle, coco-plum, cypress, red maple, wild-tamarind, pond-apple, and paradise-tree.

Campground

Situated on an isolated spit of land mostly surrounded by water and accessible only through the campground gate, this camping area is relatively quiet, especially for suburbia. It contains 266 sites, all with water and electric hookups and nearby showers. Some are on the waterfront. Reservations are accepted.

Best Time of Year

No preference. Limpkins are there year-round.

Pets

Allowed on leash.

MARINELIFE CENTER OF JUNO BEACH AND LOGGERHEAD PARK— PALM BEACH COUNTY PARKS

Marinelife Center is a non-profit educational and conservation facility dedicated to protecting marine creatures, particularly sea turtles. The center maintains large outdoor rehabilitation tanks to care for injured turtles. Indoor museum exhibits highlight different types of marine (as well as non-marine) life. There are many hands-on activities for children, making this a great afternoon outing for young families. Special school group tours can be arranged. The center is operated almost entirely by volunteers.

Loggerhead Park (17 acres) is named for the loggerhead sea turtles that come ashore every summer to lay their eggs on the beach. In 1993, 3778 loggerhead nests were found, as well as 16 green and 16 leatherback nests. This Palm Beach County park has a 2-acre coastal scrub area preserved as relatively natural.

This is a good destination for anyone interested in marine life. Allow a few hours for the center and park.

Location, Mailing Address and Phone

The Marinelife Center is in Loggerhead Park: take US 1 (Federal Highway) to Juno Beach. The park is 0.3 miles north of Donald Ross Road on the east side.

14200 US 1, Juno Beach 33408; 561- 627-8280

Facilities and Activities

Marinelife Center: museum, turtle nesting walks, rehabilitation displays, gift shop. Open Tuesday through Saturday 10 AM to 4 PM, Sunday 12 noon to 3 PM, closed Mondays and major holidays. Donation requested. Loggerhead Park: short hiking trails, overlook tower, picnicking. Open sunrise to sunset and admission is free. Juno Beach: swimming.

The center is small but packed with exhibits in every corner. The live tanks have small sharks and turtles, crabs, sea urchins, and other local marine creatures. Kids do much of the volunteer work of caring for the rehabilitating animals. From April to October each year, the volunteer staff conducts counts of sea turtle nests on the adjacent 5-mile stretch of beach. Turtle nesting watches for the public are held four nights a week during June and July; call for reservations. Lectures are held in winter for adults. The gift shop has books, tee-shirts, jewelry, and games on sea life, mostly for children.

Loggerhead Park is has a network of loose sandy trails leading through this small patch of coastal scrub. The overlook tower allows a beautiful 360-degree view. Some of the plants you should see are coral bean, prickly-pear cactus, saw palmetto, and poisonwood. Look for land crab holes and gopher tortoise burrows. Look for shorebirds and turtle tracks on the beach.

Best Time of Year

June and July when the sea turtles nest, if you can arrange to go on a night walk. Otherwise, no preference.

Pets

Not allowed in Marinelife Center; allowed in the park on a leash.

MORIKAMI MUSEUM AND JAPANESE GARDENS—PALM BEACH COUNTY PARKS

In the early 1900s, a Japanese entrepreneur attempted to establish an agricultural community in Boca with fellow countrymen. It failed. But one farmer, George Sukeji Morikami, remained. In the mid-1970s, Morikami donated 200 acres of his land to Palm Beach County. The gardens are maintained in Japanese style, with small pools and native Florida bonsai. The mile-long nature trail is left in its natural state and goes through pine flatwoods and cypress.

Location, Mailing Address and Phone

Morikami Park Road is off of Carter-Jog Road, about 1 mile north of Clint Moore and 2 miles south of Linton Blvd.
16869 Jog Road, Delray Beach 33446; 561-495-0233

Facilities and Activities

Japanese museum and gift shop, gardens, nature trails, Asian cafe. Admission fee for museum. Trails open sunrise to sunset. Museum open 10 AM to 5 PM, closed Mondays.

The facility concentrates on Japanese culture, history, and art. However, the woodland around the museum is a quiet place for birding or botanizing. Over 250 species of birds have been observed, including 31 warblers.

Best Time of Year

No preference.

Pets

Allowed on leash in park area.

OKEEHEELEE PARK AND NATURE CENTER— PALM BEACH COUNTY PARKS

Most of the 900-acre park is reclaimed from a shellrock quarry. A hundred acres was set aside as a natural area and has been managed with prescribed burns and exotic plant control. It has grown into a lovely setting of native pines and wetlands. Several miles of trails and a nature center attract visitors to share it.

Location, Mailing Address and Phone

Take I-95 Exit 49 (Forest Hill Blvd.) west about 5 miles.
7715 Forest Hill Boulevard, West Palm Beach 34413; 561-233-1400

Facilities and Activities

Nature Center, nature trails, bicycle/jogging path, birding, picnicking. Nature Center closed mornings and Mondays; also closed Sundays from Memorial Day to Labor Day. Trails open sunrise to sunset daily.

The Nature Center has a few natural history displays and live animal exhibits. It also provides programs for kids and adults. On Saturdays at 10 AM and 3 PM, a naturalist leads a walk through the trails. The 2.5 miles of trails twist through upland and wetland habitats. The Pine Trail and Cypress Trails (totalling one mile) are paved and the others are shellrock.

Best Time of Year

No preference.

Pets

Not allowed on trails or in Nature Center; allowed elsewhere in the park.

RIVERBEND PARK—
PALM BEACH COUNTY PARKS

The park is situated on the Loxahatchee River and it exists to provide recreational access to it. The park concession provides complete canoeing service for the trip downstream to Jonathan Dickinson State Park, including the return bus. Allow six hours for the whole trip. Independent souls can rent canoes and go later in the day or return via the river, ignoring the bus. The trip downstream is approximately 8 miles and of moderate difficulty. Two water control structures necessitate minor pull-throughs, depending on water levels.

The Loxahatchee River is a nationally-designated Wild and Scenic River that winds through subtropical cypress and mangrove swamps. Pond-apple trees, orchids, and ferns also line the tannin-stained waters. The skeletal ghosts of the cypress trees and cabbage palms are evidence of the increase in the river's salinity. Red mangroves encroach farther upstream each year as the line of fresh water recedes and the salt water intrudes. The cause is channelization and diversion of fresh water upstream for drainage.

Otters, raccoons, bobcats, ospreys, wading birds, and alligators live along the river. Turtles frequently bask on fallen logs in midstream, alluding to the source of the river's name "Loxahatchee," which means River of Turtles in the native tongue. Peninsula cooters, softshells, and Florida snapping turtles are common.

About four miles between Riverbend County Park and Jonathan Dickinson State Park is the landmark destination of Trapper Nelson's cabin. Before he died in 1968, Trapper Nelson, known as the "Wild Man of Loxahatchee," lived off the land without electricity in his self-built cabin. The cabin is on the highest land along the river. He trapped otters and raccoons for pelts. He planted fruit trees and kept penned gopher tortoises for food. He earned money by housing and feeding river-going travelers. His homestead is now maintained by the state park and is a popular stop by canoeists. A ranger is often present to give short tours.

Location, Mailing Address and Phone

Take SR 706/Indiantown Road for 1.5 miles west of the Turnpike (Exit 116) or I-95 (Exit 59).

8900 W. Indiantown Road, Jupiter, FL 33478; Canoe Outfitters (concession): 561-746-7053 or toll-free 888-272-1257

Facilities and Activities

Canoeing and rentals. Round-trip canoeists with bus return must enter the water between 8 and 11:30 AM.

Best Time of Year

Water level is higher in summer, which is better for paddling, but weather is cooler in winter.

Pets

No pets allowed on the river.

SOUTH COUNTY REGIONAL PARK— PALM BEACH COUNTY PARKS

The newest addition to the county park system is this 856-acre recreation area. Phase I opened in late 1996 with numerous ball fields and a nature center complex. The 3,000-square-foot nature center contains an exhibit area, classrooms, and amphitheater. A 2,000-foot boardwalk penetrates a cypress forest. Special group programs are available. Later phases will include an RV and tent campground, equestrian facilities, and an aquatic complex.

Location, Mailing Address and Phone

Nature Center Complex: From US 441/SR 7, go west on Yamato Road 0.4 miles to Cain Blvd., then left 0.8 miles to Old Pump House Road; right turn, then 0.4 miles to entrance on left.

11200 Park Access Road, West Boca Raton 33498; 561-488-9953

Facilities and Activities

Nature center, boardwalk and observation tower, butterfly garden, guided walks, and programs. Open afternoons only, except 8 AM to 4:45 PM Saturdays (9 AM to 4:30 PM in summer); closed Mondays all year and Sundays in summer.

The Dagger Wing Nature Center has a few live native reptile displays and an auditorium. The boardwalk winds through a hardwood hammock, with red maples, strangler figs, pond-apples, and wild coffee. The ferns are prolific, including strap, resurrection, leather, sword, and giant sword ferns. The 40-foot observation tower overlooks part of the hammock and some playing fields. There are two cypress trees by the tower; the rest of the cypress is in another part of the park, where there are two 50-acre stands. The name of the nature center comes from the dagger wing butterfly (*Marpesia petreus*) that is found in the hammock along the boardwalk. This orange butterfly with long dagger-like extensions on its wings is found in hardwood hammocks of the southern mainland. The larvae feed on strangler fig leaves and the adults feed on sea-grape nectar.

Best Time of Year

No preference.

Pets

Allowed on leash.

SANIBEL-CAPTIVA CONSERVATION FOUNDATION

The Sanibel-Captiva Conservation Foundation (SCCF) was founded in 1967 to protect the sand dunes, lush hammocks, and wildlife on and around Sanibel and Captiva Islands. This not-for-profit group owns and protects almost 1,800 acres in several parcels. SCCF's primary function is the acquisition, restoration, and management of wildlife habitat. It is active in environmental research, education, sea turtle nest protection, native plant propagation, and removal of exotic plants. The Barrier Island Research Laboratory at Tarpon Bay is operated by SCCF under a cooperative agreement with the U.S. Fish and Wildlife Service and Iowa State University.

Location, Mailing Address and Phone

At 3333 Sanibel-Captiva Road, one mile west of Tarpon Bay Road. P.O. Box 839, Sanibel 33957-0839; 239-472-2329; www.sccf.org; sccf@sccf.org

Facilities and Activities

Nature center, educational programs, hiking, native plant sales, butterfly house. Admission fee. Open 8:30 AM to 3:00 PM Monday through Friday in summer; 8:30 AM to 4:00 PM Monday through Saturday in winter.

Nature Center Complex

The Nature Center houses excellent exhibits of local natural history. Guided programs are provided for exploring the beaches and trails. The staff also narrates the boat tours that are run by an independent operator (Captiva Cruises at 239-472-5100). In the butterfly house, SCCF raises butterflies to be released into the wild, similar to a fish hatchery. However, special arrangements must be made in advance for a tour of the butterfly house.

The Nature Shop carries about 150 book titles for adults and 65 for children, including field guides and guide books. A large selection of nature gifts and handicrafts is available. It is open Monday through Saturday from 8:30 AM to 3 PM. The native plant nursery specializes in the retail selling of hard-to-find south Florida plants.

Hiking

Four and a half miles of short loop trails lace the 250-acre area around the Nature Center. They span hammocks and wetlands along the Sanibel River. Many of the native plants are labeled, making this an excellent destination for botanists. Ask for the "Walk in the Wetlands" trail guide. Some plants you can see are Jamaica dogwood, snowberry, Christmas berry, paurotis palm, coontie, shoestring fern, mastic, sawgrass, myrsine, and white indigo-berry. Gopher tortoise burrows are evident. Short 15-minute loops can be taken or longer hikes of several miles.

A quarter-mile hike on the Center Road trail leads to a 40-foot high observation tower overlooking the Sanibel River, an excellent place for observing wildlife. Along this trail is evidence of the battle SCCF wages with Brazilian pepper and other exotic plants, which they have treated with herbicides, flooding, and fire. From the tower an artificial nesting platform for ospreys is visible and usually occupied.

Best Time of Year

Spring and fall for warbler migrations. Summer is hot, but many plants in flower and fruit, attracting birds.

Pets

Not allowed.

VIII
ADDITIONAL
INFORMATION

WILDLIFE CHECKLISTS

The following checklists are intended to include all the known native and some of the more common, naturalized vertebrates (except fish) found in south Florida. Species of unknown status, accidentals, or those numbering only a few individuals may not be included. Obscure subspecies, particularly in the Florida Keys, may be excluded.

Population status is given in relative terms as follows:

abundant—likely to be seen in the right habitat, population dense

common—often seen in the right habitat, population numerous

uncommon—infrequently seen, population low

rare—not likely to be seen, population very small or endangered

Geographic areas may be defined as follows:

Mainland—Florida mainland, excluding the Florida Keys

Keys—the developed islands of the Florida Keys

Everglades—the freshwater marsh system from Lake Okeechobee to Florida Bay

+ = known breeder in south Florida (bird checklist only)
* = exotic species (breeds locally)
E = federally endangered
T = federally threatened

BIRD CHECKLIST

The following list of 328 bird species includes some which have occurred rarely in the south Florida region but which may be expected to occur in the future. At least 75 other naturally-occurring species reported in the region are less likely to be found in the future and have been omitted. More than 100 exotic species having uncertain reproductive success in southern Florida have been omitted. Readers who desire detailed information should refer to *Florida Bird Species: An Annotated List* by William B. Robertson Jr. and Glen E. Woolfenden (published in 1992 by the Florida Ornithological Society; for ordering information write to Glen Woolfenden, Editor of Special Publications, Archbold Biological Station, Venus, FL 33960). Another excellent resource is *Florida's Birds: A Handbook And Reference*, by Herbert W. Kale and David S. Maehr, available through Pineapple Press, Inc., P.O. Box 3899, Sarasota, FL 34230. The following list has been compiled predominantly by the late William B. Robertson Jr. and P. William Smith.

Loons and Grebes

- [ ] **Common loon** (*Gavia immer*)—variably common migrant and winter visitor; ocean and bays
- [ ] **+Pied-billed grebe** (*Podilymbus podiceps*)—common migrant and winter visitor, some resident; fresh water
- [ ] **Horned grebe** (*Podiceps auritus*)—uncommon winter visitor; bays

Shearwaters and Storm-petrels

- [ ] **Cory's shearwater** (*Calonectris diomedea*)—uncommon summer and fall migrant; pelagic
- [ ] **Greater shearwater** (*Puffinus gravis*)—uncommon late spring and summer migrant; pelagic
- [ ] **Sooty shearwater** (*Puffinus griseus*)—rare, chiefly spring migrant; pelagic
- [ ] **Audubon's shearwater** (*Puffinus lherminieri*)—fairly common; pelagic
- [ ] **Wilson's storm-petrel** (*Oceanites oceanicus*)—uncommon late spring and summer migrant; pelagic

Pelicans and Allies

- [ ] **White-tailed tropicbird** (*Phaethon lepturus*)—rare, chiefly spring and summer visitor; Dry Tortugas and pelagic

- ☐ **+Masked booby** (*Sula dactylatra*)—uncommon resident at Dry Tortugas, rare elsewhere; pelagic
- ☐ **Brown booby** (*Sula leucogaster*)—uncommon visitor; pelagic and Dry Tortugas
- ☐ **Red-footed booby** (*Sula sula*)—rare spring and summer visitor; Dry Tortugas
- ☐ **Northern gannet** (*Morus bassanus*)—common migrant and winter visitor; chiefly pelagic
- ☐ **American white pelican** (*Pelecanus erythrorhynchos*)—common in winter, some in summer; bays, rare in Keys
- ☐ **+Brown pelican** (*Pelecanus occidentalis*)—abundant resident; coasts and bays

Cormorants and Anhingas

- ☐ **+Double-crested cormorant** (*Phalacrocorax auritus*)—abundant resident; coasts, bays, and deeper inland waters
- ☐ **+Anhinga** (*Anhinga anhinga*)—common resident; fresh water, mainland

Frigatebirds

- ☐ **+Magnificent frigatebird** (*Fregata magnificens*)—variably common resident, breeds Dry Tortugas; coast and bays

Herons, Egrets, and Other Waders

- ☐ **American bittern** (*Botaurus lentiginosus*)—fairly rare migrant and winter visitor; fresh water marshes
- ☐ **+Least bittern** (*Ixobrychus exilis*)—uncommon resident; fresh water marshes
- ☐ **+Great blue heron** (*Ardea herodias*)—common resident; shallow fresh and salt water
- ☐ **+Great white heron** (*Ardea herodias occidentalis*)—common resident; usually shallow salt water, mainly Florida Bay and Keys
- ☐ **+Great egret** (*Casmerodius albus*)—common resident; shallow fresh and salt water
- ☐ **+Snowy egret** (*Egretta thula*)—common resident; shallow fresh and salt water
- ☐ **+Little blue heron** (*Egretta caerulea*)—common resident; shallow fresh and salt water

☐ **+Tricolored heron** (*Egretta tricolor*)—common resident; shallow fresh and salt water

☐ **+Reddish egret** (*Egretta rufescens*)—uncommon resident; shallow salt water, mainly Keys and Florida Bay

☐ **+Cattle egret** (*Bubulcus ibis*)—abundant resident, less common in winter; agricultural fields and roadsides

☐ **+Green heron** (*Butorides virescens*)—fairly common resident; shaded shallow fresh and salt water shorelines

☐ **+Black-crowned night-heron** (*Nycticorax nycticorax*)—fairly common resident; shallow fresh and salt water, scarce in Keys

☐ **+Yellow-crowned night-heron** (*Nyctanassa violacea*)—common resident (less common in east); shallow salt and fresh water

☐ **+White ibis** (*Eudocimus albus*)—common resident; shallow fresh and salt water, agricultural fields and lawns

☐ ***Scarlet ibis** (*Eudocimus ruber*)—occasional escapees or hybrids from past introduction; shallow fresh and salt water

☐ **+Glossy ibis** (*Plegadis falcinellus*)—uncommon resident; shallow fresh water, mainland

☐ **+Roseate spoonbill** (*Ajaia ajaja*)—locally common resident; shallow salt water, Florida Bay and Ten Thousand Islands

☐ **+Wood stork** (*Mycteria americana*)—common resident; fresh water margins and swamps, mainland **E**

☐ **Greater flamingo** (*Phoenicopterus ruber*)—rare visitor or escapee (mainly fall and winter); bays (particularly northern Florida Bay)

Ducks

☐ **Fulvous whistling-duck** (*Dendrocygna bicolor*)—rare visitor; fresh water marshes; breeds L. Okeechobee area

☐ ***Muscovy duck** (*Cairina moschata*)—locally common resident; urban ponds

☐ **+Wood duck** (*Aix sponsa*)—rare resident; wooded swamps

☐ **Green-winged teal** (*Anas crecca*)—variably uncommon winter visitor; ponds and bays

☐ **+Mottled duck** (*Anas fulvigula*)—uncommon resident; ponds and marshes, chiefly mainland

☐ ***Mallard** (*Anas platyrhynchos*)—fairly common resident; urban ponds

☐ **White-cheeked pintail** (*Anas bahamensis*)—rare winter and spring visitor, also some escapees; mangrove ponds

☐ **Northern pintail** (*Anas acuta*)—variably uncommon migrant and winter visitor; ponds and bays

☐ **Blue-winged teal** (*Anas discors*)—common migrant and winter visitor, some summer; ponds and bays

☐ **Northern shoveler** (*Anas clypeata*)—variably uncommon migrant and winter visitor; ponds and bays

☐ **Gadwall** (*Anas strepera*)—rare migrant and winter visitor; ponds and bays

☐ **American wigeon** (*Anas americana*)—fairly common migrant and winter visitor; ponds and bays

☐ **Ring-necked duck** (*Aythya collaris*)—fairly common migrant and winter visitor; mainly ponds

☐ **Lesser scaup** (*Aythya affinis*)—variably uncommon migrant and winter visitor; mainly bays, rare in east

☐ **Black scoter** (*Melanitta nigra*)—rare to uncommon migrant and winter visitor; ocean and bays

☐ **Hooded merganser** (*Lophodytes cucullatus*)—fairly rare migrant and winter visitor; ponds

☐ **Red-breasted merganser** (*Mergus serrator*)—common migrant and winter visitor, some summer; ocean and bays

☐ **Ruddy duck** (*Oxyura jamaicensis*)—variably uncommon migrant and winter visitor; ponds and bays

Hawks, Falcons, Kites, and Other Raptors

☐ +**Black vulture** (*Coragyps atratus*)—locally common resident; mainland

☐ +**Turkey vulture** (*Cathartes aura*)—abundant winter visitor, fewer resident; mainland and Keys

☐ +**Osprey** (*Pandion haliaetus*)—common resident; bays, canals, and ponds

☐ +**American swallow-tailed kite** (*Elanoides forficatus*)—common spring and summer visiting breeder; wet and dry woodlands

☐ +**White-tailed kite** (formerly black-shouldered) (*Elanus leucurus*)—rare resident; former sawgrass prairies that have dried out, mainland

☐ +**Snail kite** (*Rostrhamus sociabilis plumbeus*)—variably uncommon resident; freshwater marshes **E**

☐ **Mississippi kite** (*Ictinia mississippiensis*)—rare migrant

☐ **+Bald eagle** (*Haliaeetus leucocephalus*)—fairly common resident; mainly bays **T**

☐ **Northern harrier** (*Circus cyaneus*)—common migrant and winter visitor; agricultural fields and marshes

☐ **Sharp-shinned hawk** (*Accipiter striatus*)—common migrant, uncommon winter visitor

☐ **Cooper's hawk** (*Accipiter cooperii*)—fairly rare migrant and winter visitor

☐ **+Red-shouldered hawk** (*Buteo lineatus*)—common resident; woodlands and edges

☐ **Broad-winged hawk** (*Buteo platypterus*)—common migrant and variably uncommon winter visitor

☐ **+Short-tailed hawk** (*Buteo brachyurus*)—uncommon fall and winter visitor, rare in spring and summer; woodlands, usually near creeks

☐ **Swainson's hawk** (*Buteo swainsoni*)—variably uncommon migrant and rare winter visitor

☐ **+Red-tailed hawk** (*Buteo jamaicensis*)—uncommon migrant and winter visitor, rare in summer

☐ **+Audubon's crested caracara** (*Caracara plancus audubonii*)—uncommon resident; prairies and cattle ranches north and west of Lake Okeechobee **T**

☐ **+American kestrel** (*Falco sparverius*)—common migrant and winter visitor (throughout), also former or rare breeder (northern mainland); fields and edges. *F.s. paulus* is resident

☐ **Merlin** (*Falco columbarius*)—fairly common migrant and uncommon winter visitor

☐ **Peregrine falcon** (*Falco peregrinus*)—fairly common migrant and uncommon winter visitor

Turkeys and Quails

☐ **+Wild turkey** (*Meleagris gallopavo*)—rare resident; undisturbed woodlands, mainland (except extreme southern)

☐ **+Northern bobwhite** (*Colinus virginianus*)—uncommon resident; mainly old fields, groves, and pine woods, mainland

Rails, Limpkins, and Cranes

☐ **Black rail** (*Laterallus jamaicensis*)—variably rare migrant and possible resident; extensive damp marshes

☐ **+Clapper rail** (*Rallus longirostris*)—uncommon resident; mangroves and salt marshes

☐ **+King rail** (*Rallus elegans*)—fairly common resident; fresh water marshes

☐ **Virginia rail** (*Rallus limicola*)—rare winter visitor; fresh water marshes

☐ **Sora** (*Porzana carolina*)—common migrant and uncommon winter visitor; fresh water marshes and concealed margins

☐ **+Purple gallinule** (*Porphyrula martinica*)—variably uncommon migrant and local resident; fresh water marshes

☐ **+Common moorhen** (*Gallinula chloropus*)—common resident; fresh water ponds and marshes

☐ **+American coot** (*Fulica americana*)—variably common migrant and winter visitor, uncommon in summer; bays, ponds, and marshes

☐ **+Limpkin** (*Aramus guarauna*)—locally uncommon resident; fresh water swamps and marshes, chiefly northern mainland

☐ **+Sandhill crane** (*Grus canadensis*)—uncommon resident; prairies, chiefly northern mainland

☐ **+Whooping crane** (*Grus americana*)—extremely rare; introduced into prairies of central Florida; occasionally wanders south **E**

Plovers, Sandpipers, and Other Shorebirds

☐ **Black-bellied plover** (*Pluvialis squatarola*)—common migrant and winter visitor, some summer; coastal and interior shallow water and fields

☐ **Lesser golden-plover** (*Pluvialis dominica*)—rare migrant, chiefly fall; usually interior fields

☐ **+Snowy plover** (*Charadrius alexandrinus*)—rare winter visitor (Gulf coast and Keys), also former or rare breeder (Gulf coast); undisturbed sandy beaches

☐ **+Wilson's plover** (*Charadrius wilsonia*)—locally common resident; spoil banks, especially Florida Bay and Keys

☐ **Semipalmated plover** (*Charadrius semipalmatus*)—common migrant and winter visitor; coastal flats, sometimes inland

☐ **Piping plover** (*Charadrius melodus*)—uncommon migrant and winter visitor; salt water banks and pond edges, mainly Florida Bay and Keys **T**

☐ **+Killdeer** (*Charadrius vociferus*)—common resident; fields and fresh water margins, chiefly mainland

☐ **American oystercatcher** (*Haematopus palliatus*)—rare visitor (mostly winter); salt water flats, chiefly Gulf coast

☐ **+Black-necked stilt** (*Himantopus mexicanus*)—common resident, except uncommon and local in winter; mainly fresh water ponds and margins

☐ **American avocet** (*Recurvirostra americana*)—rare migrant and winter visitor; usually salt water ponds and flats

☐ **Greater yellowlegs** (*Tringa melanoleuca*)—common migrant, less common winter visitor; flats and margins

☐ **Lesser yellowlegs** (*Tringa flavipes*)—common migrant, less common winter visitor; flats and margins

☐ **Solitary sandpiper** (*Tringa solitaria*)—uncommon migrant, rare winter visitor; fresh water margins

☐ **+Willet** (*Catoptrophorus semipalmatus*)—common migrant and winter visitor, less common in summer; chiefly salt marshes and flats

☐ **Spotted sandpiper** (*Actitis macularia*)—fairly common migrant and winter visitor; margins, usually fresh water

☐ **Upland sandpiper** (*Bartramia longicauda*)—uncommon migrant; chiefly fields

☐ **Whimbrel** (*Numenius phaeopus*)—uncommon migrant and winter visitor; salt water flats

☐ **Long-billed curlew** (*Numenius americanus*)—rare winter visitor; salt water flats, chiefly Gulf coast

☐ **Marbled godwit** (*Limosa fedoa*)—abundant migrant and winter visitor; salt water flats, mainly Gulf coast and Florida Bay

☐ **Ruddy turnstone** (*Arenaria interpres*)—common migrant and winter visitor; beaches and rocky areas

☐ **Red knot** (*Calidris canutus*)—locally common migrant and winter visitor; salt ponds and flats, mainly Gulf coast

☐ **Sanderling** (*Calidris alba*)—common migrant and winter visitor; beaches

☐ **Semipalmated sandpiper** (*Calidris pusilla*)—common migrant, rare in winter; flats and margins

☐ **Western sandpiper** (*Calidris mauri*)—abundant migrant and winter visitor; flats and margins, chiefly salt water

☐ **Least sandpiper** (*Calidris minutilla*)—common migrant and winter visitor; flats and margins, chiefly fresh water

☐ **White-rumped sandpiper** (*Calidris fuscicollis*)—uncommon (especially in spring) migrant; beaches, flats, and margins

☐ **Baird's sandpiper** (*Calidris bairdii*)—rare migrant; usually fields and fresh water margins

☐ **Pectoral sandpiper** (*Calidris melanotos*)—common migrant; fields, flats, and margins (usually fresh water)

☐ **Purple sandpiper** (*Calidris maritima*)—rare winter visitor; rock jetties

☐ **Dunlin** (*Calidris alpina*)—abundant migrant and winter visitor; flats and margins (usually salt water)

☐ **Stilt sandpiper** (*Calidris himantopus*)—uncommon migrant, usually rare in winter; flats and shallow ponds (often fresh water)

☐ **Buff-breasted sandpiper** (*Tryngites subruficollis*)—rare migrant, chiefly fall; usually interior fields

☐ **Short-billed dowitcher** (*Limnodromus griseus*)—abundant migrant and winter visitor; chiefly flats and shallow salt ponds

☐ **Long-billed dowitcher** (*Limnodromus scolopaceus*)—variably common migrant and winter visitor; usually shallow fresh water ponds

☐ **Common snipe** (*Gallinago gallinago*)—fairly common migrant, less common in winter; fresh water margins, chiefly mainland

☐ **+American woodcock** (*Scolopax minor*)—uncommon winter visitor, rarely breeds; old fields, mainland

☐ **Wilson's phalarope** (*Phalaropus tricolor*)—rare migrant; fresh water margins

☐ **Red-necked phalarope** (*Phalaropus lobatus*)—rare migrant or winter visitor; usually pelagic, sometimes ashore

☐ **Red phalarope** (*Phalaropus fulicaria*)—rare migrant, may winter; usually pelagic, rarely ashore

Gulls and Terns

☐ **Pomarine jaeger** (*Stercorarius pomarinus*)—fairly common migrant, less common in winter; usually pelagic

☐ **Parasitic jaeger** (*Stercorarius parasiticus*)—fairly common migrant, some may winter; usually pelagic, sometimes coastal

- ☐ +**Laughing gull** (*Larus atricilla*)—abundant resident; chiefly coasts and bays, sometimes inland
- ☐ **Bonaparte's gull** (*Larus philadelphia*)—variably uncommon migrant and winter visitor; usually coasts and bays
- ☐ **Ring-billed gull** (*Larus delawarensis*)—abundant migrant and winter visitor, some summer; coasts, bays, and inland ponds and fields
- ☐ **Herring gull** (*Larus argentatus*)—uncommon winter visitor; coasts, bays, and ponds
- ☐ **Lesser black-backed gull** (*Larus fuscus*)—rare winter visitor; coasts, bays, and ponds
- ☐ **Glaucous gull** (*Larus hyperboreus*)—rare winter visitor; coasts, bays, and ponds
- ☐ **Great black-backed gull** (*Larus marinus*)—rare winter visitor; coasts, bays, and ponds
- ☐ +**Gull-billed tern** (*Sterna nilotica*)—local and uncommon resident and uncertain breeder; salt marshes and flats, chiefly mainland
- ☐ **Caspian tern** (*Sterna caspia*)—common migrant and winter visitor, some summer; coasts and bays, less common in east
- ☐ **Royal tern** (*Sterna maxima*)—abundant migrant and winter visitor, many summer; coasts and bays
- ☐ **Sandwich tern** (*Sterna sandvicensis*)—fairly common migrant and winter visitor, some summer; coasts and bays, less common in east
- ☐ +**Roseate tern** (*Sterna dougallii*)—variably common late spring and summer breeding visitor, rare at other seasons; coastal, chiefly lower Keys and Dry Tortugas **T**
- ☐ **Common tern** (*Sterna hirundo*)—fairly common migrant, rare in winter; coasts and bays, less common in east
- ☐ **Arctic tern** (*Sterna paradisaea*)—rare migrant (stops over during transcontinental migrations); coastal
- ☐ **Forster's tern** (*Sterna forsteri*)—common migrant and winter visitor, some summer; bays and ponds
- ☐ +**Least tern** (*Sterna antillarum*)—fairly common spring and summer visitor; bays, ponds, and urban rooftops
- ☐ +**Bridled tern** (*Sterna anaethetus*)—uncommon, probably resident, rare breeder; offshore, lower Keys

☐ +**Sooty tern** (*Sterna fuscata*)—abundant spring and summer visitor and breeder, common offshore except absent in late fall and winter; Dry Tortugas, pelagic when not breeding

☐ **Black tern** (*Chlidonias niger*)—locally common migrant, chiefly summer and fall; fresh water ponds and offshore

☐ +**Brown noddy** (*Anous stolidus*)—common spring and summer visitor and breeder, uncommon offshore except absent in late fall and winter; Dry Tortugas, pelagic

☐ **Black noddy** (*Anous minutus*)—rare spring visitor; Dry Tortugas

☐ +**Black skimmer** (*Rynchops nigra*)—locally common resident; flats, spoil islands

Doves and Pigeons

☐ *****Rock dove** (*Columba livia*)—common resident; urban areas

☐ +**White-crowned pigeon** (*Columba leucocephala*)—common resident, fewer in winter; tropical hardwood hammocks and mangroves, Keys and extreme southern mainland

☐ *****Eurasian collared-dove** (*Streptopelia decaocto*)—locally abundant resident; southern suburban areas, including Keys

☐ +**White-winged dove** (*Zenaida asiatica*)—locally common resident; groves and suburban areas

☐ +**Mourning dove** (*Zenaida macroura*)—common resident; open areas

☐ +**Common ground-dove** (*Columbina passerina*)—uncommon resident; fields

Parakeets

☐ *****Monk parakeet** (*Myiopsitta monachus*)—locally common resident; suburban areas

☐ *****Canary-winged parakeet** (*Brotogeris versicolurus*)—uncommon resident; Coconut Grove area of Miami

Cuckoos and Anis

☐ **Black-billed cuckoo** (*Coccyzus erythropthalmus*)—rare migrant; woodlands

☐ +**Yellow-billed cuckoo** (*Coccyzus americanus*)—common migrant and uncommon summer visitor and breeder; woodlands

☐ +**Mangrove cuckoo** (*Coccyzus minor*)—uncommon resident, seldom seen in fall and winter; tropical hammocks and mangroves, Keys and southern mainland

☐ +**Smooth-billed ani** (*Crotophaga ani*)—local and decreasing resident; brushy areas

Owls

☐ +**Barn owl** (*Tyto alba*)—uncommon permanent resident; chiefly mainland

☐ +**Eastern screech-owl** (*Otus asio*)—common resident; suburbs and woodlands, mainland and upper Keys

☐ +**Great horned owl** (*Bubo virginianus*)—uncommon resident; chiefly pine woodlands, mainland

☐ +**Burrowing owl** (*Speotyto cunicularia*)—locally common resident; airports, campuses, and other open grassy areas

☐ +**Barred owl** (*Strix varia*)—common resident; mesic woodlands, mainland

☐ **Short-eared owl** (*Asio flammeus*)—rare winter and spring visitor; chiefly Keys, Dry Tortugas; also grassy marshes and fields on mainland

Goatsuckers

☐ **Lesser nighthawk** (*Chordeiles acutipennis*)—rare spring migrant; chiefly Dry Tortugas

☐ +**Common nighthawk** (*Chordeiles minor*)—common migrant and summer breeding visitor; open areas and urban rooftops, chiefly mainland and upper Keys

☐ +**Antillean nighthawk** (*Chordeiles gundlachii*)—uncommon spring and summer breeding visitor; open areas and urban rooftops, chiefly lower Keys

☐ +**Chuck-will's-widow** (*Caprimulgus carolinensis*)—common migrant and uncommon winter visitor throughout, fairly common summer breeder; woodlands, mainland and upper Keys

☐ **Whip-poor-will** (*Caprimulgus vociferus*)—common fall and winter visitor; woodlands, chiefly mainland

Swifts

☐ **+Chimney swift** (*Chaetura pelagica*)—fairly common migrant throughout and uncommon summer breeder on suburban mainland

Hummingbirds

☐ **+Ruby-throated hummingbird** (*Archilochus colubris*)—common migrant and winter visitor throughout, rare breeding visitor on northern mainland; around flowering plants

☐ **Rufous hummingbird** (*Selasphorus rufus*)—rare migrant and winter visitor; around flowering plants

Kingfishers

☐ **Belted kingfisher** (*Ceryle alcyon*)—common visitor from late summer through early spring; canals and ponds

Woodpeckers

☐ **+Red-headed woodpecker** (*Melanerpes erythrocephalus*)—rare migrant throughout, resident in pine-oak woodlands, northern mainland

☐ **+Red-bellied woodpecker** (*Melanerpes carolinus*)—common resident; suburban and wooded areas

☐ **Yellow-bellied sapsucker** (*Sphyrapicus varius*)—fairly common migrant and uncommon winter visitor; suburban and wooded areas

☐ **+Downy woodpecker** (*Picoides pubescens*)—fairly common resident; suburban and wooded areas, mainland

☐ **+Hairy woodpecker** (*Picoides villosus*)—rare resident; pine woodlands, mainland

☐ **+Red-cockaded woodpecker** (*Picoides borealis*)—rare resident; pine woodlands, northern mainland **E**

☐ **+Northern flicker** (*Colaptes auratus*)—fairly common resident; suburban and wooded areas

☐ **+Pileated woodpecker** (*Dryocopus pileatus*)—uncommon resident; suburban and wooded areas, chiefly mainland

Flycatchers

☐ **Olive-sided flycatcher** (*Contopus borealis*)—rare migrant, chiefly fall

- [ ] **Eastern wood-pewee** (*Contopus virens*)—uncommon migrant, chiefly fall
- [ ] **Yellow-bellied flycatcher** (*Empidonax flaviventris*)—rare migrant, chiefly fall
- [ ] **Acadian flycatcher** (*Empidonax virescens*)—rare migrant, chiefly fall
- [ ] **Willow flycatcher** (*Empidonax traillii*)—rare migrant, chiefly fall
- [ ] **Least flycatcher** (*Empidonax minimus*)—uncommon migrant and winter visitor; second growth, edges
- [ ] **Eastern phoebe** (*Sayornis phoebe*)—common fall and winter visitor; suburban and wooded areas, chiefly mainland
- [ ] **+Great crested flycatcher** (*Myiarchus crinitus*)—common migrant and resident; suburban and wooded areas
- [ ] **Brown-crested flycatcher** (*Myiarchus tyrannulus*)—rare winter visitor; woodlands
- [ ] **La Sagra's flycatcher** (*Myiarchus sagrae*)—rare winter and spring visitor; coastal hammocks
- [ ] **Western kingbird** (*Tyrannus verticalis*)—locally uncommon migrant and winter visitor; open areas, fruiting trees
- [ ] **+Eastern kingbird** (*Tyrannus tyrannus*)—uncommon spring migrant and summer breeder, very common late summer migrant; woodland edges, only breeds on mainland
- [ ] **+Gray kingbird** (*Tyrannus dominicensis*)—uncommon migrant and summer breeder (local away from Keys); suburban and wooded areas
- [ ] **Scissor-tailed flycatcher** (*Tyrannus forficatus*)—locally uncommon migrant and winter visitor; open areas, around fruiting trees
- [ ] **Fork-tailed flycatcher** (*Tyrannus savana*)—rare visitor, chiefly summer; open areas, around fruiting trees

Swallows

- [ ] **+Purple martin** (*Progne subis*)—common winter and spring breeder, spring and fall migrant; open areas, only nests in man-made nesting structures on mainland
- [ ] **Tree swallow** (*Tachycineta bicolor*)—variably abundant visitor, late fall through early spring; marshy and open areas
- [ ] **Bahama swallow** (*Tachycineta cyaneoviridis*)—rare spring and summer migrant

☐ **+Northern rough-winged swallow** (*Stelgidopteryx serripennis*)— uncommon migrant throughout in open areas, rare summer breeder in holes near water on mainland

☐ **Bank swallow** (*Riparia riparia*)—uncommon spring, common late summer and fall migrant; open areas

☐ **Cliff swallow** (*Hirundo pyrrhonota*)—rare spring, uncommon late summer and fall migrant; open areas

☐ **+Cave swallow** (*Hirundo fulva*)—rare migrant throughout in open areas, locally uncommon breeder under highway bridges near water in southeast Miami area

☐ **+Barn swallow** (*Hirundo rustica*)—abundant migrant throughout in open areas, rare breeder under highway bridges in Keys

Jays and Crows

☐ **+Blue jay** (*Cyanocitta cristata*)—common resident; suburban and wooded areas, mainland and upper Keys

☐ **+Florida scrub jay** (*Aphelocoma coerulescens*)—uncommon resident; scrub areas **T**

☐ **+American crow** (*Corvus brachyrhynchos*)—common resident; wilder wooded areas, chiefly mainland

☐ **+Fish crow** (*Corvus ossifragus*)—common resident; suburban areas, chiefly mainland

Titmice, Nuthatches, and Bulbuls

☐ **+Tufted titmouse** (*Parus bicolor*)—uncommon resident; chiefly cypress woodlands, northern mainland

☐ **+Brown-headed nuthatch** (*Sitta pusilla*)—locally rare resident; pine woodlands, northern mainland

☐ ***Red-whiskered bulbul** (*Pycnonotus jocosus*)—uncommon resident; suburbs, Kendall area

Wrens

☐ **+Carolina wren** (*Thryothorus ludovicianus*)—common resident; woodlands, mainland and upper Keys

☐ **House wren** (*Troglodytes aedon*)—common migrant and winter visitor; suburban and brushy areas

☐ **Sedge wren** (*Cistothorus platensis*)—variably uncommon winter and spring visitor; damp grassy marshes, mainland

☐ **Marsh wren** (*Cistothorus palustris*)—variably uncommon winter and spring visitor; reedy marshes, mainland

Kinglets and Gnatcatchers

☐ **Ruby-crowned kinglet** (*Regulus calendula*)—uncommon winter visitor; woodlands, chiefly mainland

☐ **+Blue-gray gnatcatcher** (*Polioptila caerulea*)—common migrant and winter visitor throughout in suburbs and wooded areas, local breeder in wooded areas on northern mainland

Bluebirds and Thrushes

☐ **+Eastern bluebird** (*Sialia sialis*)—local, uncommon resident; pine-oak woodland edges, northern mainland

☐ **Veery** (*Catharus fuscescens*)—variably uncommon migrant

☐ **Gray-cheeked thrush** (*Catharus minimus*)—variably uncommon migrant

☐ **Swainson's thrush** (*Catharus ustulatus*)—variably uncommon migrant

☐ **Hermit thrush** (*Catharus guttatus*)—variably rare winter visitor; woodlands, chiefly mainland

☐ **Wood thrush** (*Hylocichla mustelina*)—variably uncommon migrant, rare in winter

☐ **American robin** (*Turdus migratorius*)—variably abundant winter visitor; suburban and wooded areas, chiefly mainland and upper Keys

☐ **Gray catbird** (*Dumetella carolinensis*)—abundant migrant and common winter visitor; brushy areas

Mockingbirds and Thrashers

☐ **+Northern mockingbird** (*Mimus polyglottos*)—abundant resident; suburban and open wooded areas

☐ **Bahama mockingbird** (*Mimus gundlachii*)—rare spring and summer visitor; coastal woodlands and brush

☐ **+Brown thrasher** (*Toxostoma rufum*)—uncommon resident; brushy wooded areas, chiefly mainland and upper Keys (has nested to Key West)

Pipits

☐ **American pipit** (*Anthus rubescens*)—variably rare winter visitor; fields

Waxwings

☐ **Cedar waxwing** (*Bombycilla cedrorum*)—variably uncommon winter and spring visitor; in fruiting trees

Shrikes

☐ **+Loggerhead shrike** (*Lanius ludovicianus*)—uncommon resident; open areas with brush, mainland

Starlings and Mynas

☐ ***European starling** (*Sturnus vulgaris*)—common resident; suburbs
☐ ***Common myna** (*Acridotheres tristis*)—locally uncommon resident; chiefly shopping centers, mainland
☐ ***Hill myna** (*Gracula religiosa*)—locally uncommon resident; suburban areas with trees, chiefly Coconut Grove area

Vireos

☐ **+White-eyed vireo** (*Vireo griseus*)—common migrant and somewhat local resident; brushy woodlands
☐ **Thick-billed vireo** (*Vireo crassirostris*)—rare migrant and winter visitor; brushy coastal woodlands
☐ **Bell's vireo** (*Vireo bellii*)—rare migrant and winter visitor; brushy woodlands
☐ **Solitary vireo** (*Vireo solitarius*)—uncommon migrant and winter visitor; woodlands
☐ **Yellow-throated vireo** (*Vireo flavifrons*)—uncommon migrant and rare winter visitor; woodlands
☐ **Warbling vireo** (*Vireo gilvus*)—rare migrant, chiefly fall
☐ **Philadelphia vireo** (*Vireo philadelphicus*)—rare migrant, chiefly fall
☐ **+Red-eyed vireo** (*Vireo olivaceus*)—common migrant throughout, local summer breeding visitor in mesic woodlands on northern mainland
☐ **+Black-whiskered vireo** (*Vireo altiloquus*)—common summer breeding visitor; tropical woodlands, chiefly Keys and coastal mainland

Warblers

☐ **Blue-winged warbler** (*Vermivora pinus*)—variably uncommon migrant and rare winter visitor; woodlands

☐ **Golden-winged warbler** (*Vermivora chrysoptera*)—rare migrant

☐ **Tennessee warbler** (*Vermivora peregrina*)—uncommon migrant, chiefly fall

☐ **Orange-crowned warbler** (*Vermivora celata*)—fairly common winter visitor; brushy woodlands

☐ **Nashville warbler** (*Vermivora ruficapilla*)—variably uncommon migrant and rare winter visitor; brushy woodlands

☐ **+Northern parula** (*Parula americana*)—common migrant and uncommon winter visitor throughout, local summer breeder in mesic woodlands on northern mainland

☐ **+Yellow warbler** (*Dendroica petechia*)—uncommon resident (mangroves, chiefly Keys) and uncommon migrant elsewhere

☐ **Chestnut-sided warbler** (*Dendroica pensylvanica*)—variably uncommon migrant

☐ **Magnolia warbler** (*Dendroica magnolia*)—variably common migrant and rare winter visitor; woodlands

☐ **Cape May warbler** (*Dendroica tigrina*)—common migrant and locally uncommon winter visitor; in flowering and fruiting trees

☐ **Black-throated blue warbler** (*Dendroica caerulescens*)—common migrant and rare winter visitor; woodlands

☐ **Yellow-rumped warbler** (*Dendroica coronata*)—variably abundant winter visitor; brushy and wooded areas

☐ **Black-throated gray warbler** (*Dendroica nigrescens*)—rare migrant and winter visitor

☐ **Black-throated green warbler** (*Dendroica virens*)—variably uncommon migrant and winter visitor; woodlands

☐ **Blackburnian warbler** (*Dendroica fusca*)—variably uncommon migrant

☐ **Yellow-throated warbler** (*Dendroica dominica*)—common migrant and winter visitor; woodlands and palms

☐ **+Pine warbler** (*Dendroica pinus*)—common resident; pine woodlands, mainland (also rare migrant elsewhere)

☐ **Kirtland's warbler** (*Denroica kirtlandii*)—accidental migrant; east coast **E**

☐ **+Prairie warbler** (*Dendroica discolor*)—common resident in man-groves, abundant migrant and uncommon winter visitor in brushy woodlands

☐ **Palm warbler** (*Dendroica palmarum*)—abundant migrant and winter visitor; brushy areas and lawns

☐ **Bay-breasted warbler** (*Dendroica castanea*)—variably uncommon migrant

☐ **Blackpoll warbler** (*Dendroica striata*)—variably common spring migrant and variably rare fall migrant

☐ **Cerulean warbler** (*Dendroica cerulea*)—rare migrant

☐ **Black-and-white warbler** (*Mniotilta varia*)—common migrant and fairly common winter visitor; woodlands

☐ **American redstart** (*Setophaga ruticilla*)—common migrant and fairly rare winter visitor; woodlands

☐ **+Prothonotary warbler** (*Protonotaria citrea*)—fairly common migrant and rare winter visitor throughout, local breeding visitor in cypress swamps, northern mainland

☐ **Worm-eating warbler** (*Helmitheros vermivorus*)—common migrant and fairly rare winter visitor; brushy woodlands

☐ **Swainson's warbler** (*Limnothlypis swainsonii*)—uncommon migrant; usually in woods on damp leaf litter

☐ **Ovenbird** (*Seiurus aurocapillus*)—common migrant and uncommon winter visitor; woodlands

☐ **Northern waterthrush** (*Seiurus noveboracensis*)—common migrant and uncommon winter visitor; damp margins, often in mangroves

☐ **Louisiana waterthrush** (*Seiurus motacilla*)—uncommon migrant and fairly rare winter visitor; slightly damp margins, usually fresh water

☐ **Kentucky warbler** (*Oporornis formosus*)—rare migrant

☐ **Connecticut warbler** (*Oporornis agilis*)—uncommon spring and fairly rare fall migrant; brushy leaf litter

☐ **Mourning warbler** (*Oporornis philadelphia*)—rare migrant, chiefly fall; brushy areas

☐ **+Common yellowthroat** (*Geothlypis trichas*)—common migrant and winter visitor throughout, fairly common resident in swampy brush on mainland

☐ **Hooded warbler** (*Wilsonia citrina*)—uncommon migrant and rare winter visitor; woodlands

☐ **Wilson's warbler** (*Wilsonia pusilla*)—variably uncommon migrant and rare winter visitor; brushy areas

☐ **Canada warbler** (*Wilsonia canadensis*)—variably uncommon migrant

☐ **Yellow-breasted chat** (*Icteria virens*)—variably uncommon migrant and rare winter visitor; brushy areas

Bananaquits and Tanagers

☐ **Bananaquit** (*Coereba flaveola*)—rare visitor, chiefly winter; flowering trees usually near coast

☐ **Stripe-headed tanager** (*Spindalis zena*)—rare winter and spring visitor; fruiting trees

☐ **+Summer tanager** (*Piranga rubra*)—uncommon migrant and rare winter visitor throughout; local breeding visitor in pine-oak woodlands on northern mainland

☐ **Scarlet tanager** (*Piranga olivacea*)—variably uncommon migrant

☐ **Western tanager** (*Piranga ludoviciana*)—rare winter visitor; fruiting trees

Cardinals, Grosbeaks, and Buntings

☐ **+Northern cardinal** (*Cardinalis cardinalis*)—common resident (rare near Key West); suburban and wooded areas

☐ **Rose-breasted grosbeak** (*Pheucticus ludovicianus*)—variably uncommon migrant and rare winter visitor; woodlands

☐ **Blue grosbeak** (*Guiraca caerulea*)—variably uncommon migrant and rare winter visitor; brushy areas

☐ **Indigo bunting** (*Passerina cyanea*)—common migrant and uncommon winter visitor; brushy areas

☐ **Painted bunting** (*Passerina ciris*)—common migrant and winter visitor; brushy areas

☐ **Dickcissel** (*Spiza americana*)—variably uncommon migrant and rare winter visitor; brushy areas

Towhees and Sparrows

☐ **+Eastern towhee** (*Pipilo erythrophthalmus*)—common resident; chiefly pine woodlands, mainland

☐ **+Bachman's sparrow** (*Aimophila aestivalis*)—uncommon resident; pinelands, palmettos, and scrub south to Palm Beach County, wanders occasionally to Dade Co.

☐ **Chipping sparrow** (*Spizella passerina*)—variably uncommon migrant and winter visitor; brushy areas and lawns

☐ **Clay-colored sparrow** (*Spizella pallida*)—variably rare migrant and winter visitor; brushy areas

☐ **Field sparrow** (*Spizella pusilla*)—rare migrant and winter visitor; brushy areas, mainland

☐ **Vesper sparrow** (*Pooecetes gramineus*)—rare migrant and winter visitor; fallow fields with brush, mainland

☐ **Lark sparrow** (*Chondestes grammacus*)—variably rare migrant and winter visitor; brushy areas

☐ **Savannah sparrow** (*Passerculus sandwichensis*)—common migrant and winter visitor; open areas, chiefly mainland

☐ **+Grasshopper sparrow** (*Ammodramus savannarum*)—uncommon migrant and winter visitor; fallow fields with brush, chiefly mainland; Florida grasshopper sparrow (*A.s. floridanus*) is resident, breeds central Florida to Glades Co. **E**

☐ **Sharp-tailed sparrow** (*Ammodramus caudacutus*)—uncommon winter visitor; salt marsh prairie

☐ **+Cape Sable seaside sparrow** (*Ammodramus maritimus mirabilis*)—rare resident; fresh-to-brackish sloughs, mostly Everglades NP **E**

☐ **Lincoln's sparrow** (*Melospiza lincolnii*)—rare winter visitor; brushy areas

☐ **Swamp sparrow** (*Melospiza georgiana*)—variably uncommon migrant and winter visitor; swampy areas, chiefly mainland

☐ **White-throated sparrow** (*Zonotrichia albicollis*)—rare migrant and winter visitor; brushy areas

☐ **White-crowned sparrow** (*Zonotrichia leucophrys*)—locally uncommon winter and spring visitor; brushy areas

☐ **Bobolink** (*Dolichonyx oryzivorus*)—common migrant; fields and agricultural areas

Blackbirds and Orioles

☐ **+Red-winged blackbird** (*Agelaius phoeniceus*)—common resident; brushy fields and swamps

☐ **+Eastern meadowlark** (*Sturnella magna*)—common resident; fields, mainland

☐ **Yellow-headed blackbird** (*Xanthocephalus xanthocephalus*)—rare migrant and winter visitor; fields and swamps

☐ **+Boat-tailed grackle** (*Quiscalus major*)—abundant resident; swamps and fields, mainland

☐ **+Common grackle** (*Quiscalus quiscula*)—common resident; suburbs and fields, absent from Keys in winter

☐ **+Shiny cowbird** (*Molothrus bonariensis*)—variably uncommon spring migrant, chiefly Keys and Gulf coast; local resident throughout

☐ **Bronzed cowbird** (*Molothrus aeneus*)—variably rare winter visitor; mainland

☐ **+Brown-headed cowbird** (*Molothrus ater*)—common migrant and winter visitor, some breed; fields and edges, chiefly mainland

☐ **Orchard oriole** (*Icterus spurius*)—variably common migrant (rarer to the east); wooded areas

☐ ***Spot-breasted oriole** (*Icterus pectoralis*)—uncommon resident; suburbs with fruiting trees, Miami area

☐ **Northern oriole** (*Icterus galbula*)—common migrant, fairly rare winter visitor; wooded areas

Finches

☐ **Pine siskin** (*Carduelis pinus*)—variably rare winter and spring visitor; wooded edges

☐ **American goldfinch** (*Carduelis tristis*)—variably uncommon winter and spring visitor; wooded edges

Old World Sparrows

☐ ***House sparrow** (*Passer domesticus*)—common resident; urban areas, local in Keys

MAMMAL CHECKLIST

Marsupials

☐ **Opossum** (*Didelphis virginiana pigra*)—abundant; most habitats on mainland and Keys

Insectivores

☐ **Short-tailed shrew** (*Blarina brevicauda peninsulae*)—uncommon; mainland

☐ **Least shrew** (*Cryptotis parva floridana*)—common; mainland

☐ **Eastern mole** (*Scalopus aquaticus porteri*)—common; mainland

Bats

☐ **Eastern pipistrelle** (*Pipistrellus subflavus floridanus*)—uncommon; trees and crevices (in rocks, structures) on mainland and Keys

☐ **Big brown bat** (*Eptesicus fuscus osceola*)—rare; buildings and trees, range unconfirmed

☐ **Seminole bat** (*Nycteris seminola*)—rare; trees and Spanish moss, possibly south to Miami, not southwestern Florida or Keys

☐ **Northern yellow bat** (*Nycteris intermedia floridana*)—uncommon; trees around Big Cypress and Atlantic coastal ridge south to Miami

☐ **Evening bat** (*Nycticeius humeralis subtropicalis*)—common; trees and buildings on mainland

☐ **Brazilian free-tailed bat** (*Tadarida brasiliensis cynocephala*)—common; buildings, trees, and crevices (in rocks, structures) near coasts

☐ **Florida mastiff bat** (*Eumops glaucinus floridanus*)—rare; buildings and trees in South Miami (the most restricted range of any Florida mammal)

Edentates

☐ ***Nine-banded armadillo** (*Dasypus novemcinctus mexicanus*)—uncommon; drier areas of mainland

Lagomorphs

☐ **Marsh rabbit** (*Sylvilagus palustris paludicola*)—common; most habitats (prefers marshes) on mainland; Lower Keys rabbit (*S.p. hefneri*)—rare on Lower Keys **E**

☐ **Eastern cottontail** (*Sylvilagus floridanus floridanus* and *S. f. paulsoni*)—uncommon; in pinelands and hammocks on mainland

Rodents

☐ **Gray squirrel** (*Sciurus carolinensis extimus*)—common; hammocks on mainland and Keys

☐ **Mangrove fox squirrel** (*Scuirus niger avicennia*)—uncommon; mangroves, cypress, and pinelands on western mainland; extirpated elsewhere

☐ ***Red-bellied squirrel** (*Sciurus aureogaster*)—found only on Elliott Key and a few nearby keys

☐ **Southern flying squirrel** (*Glaucomys volans querceti*)—uncommon; pinelands on mainland

☐ **Marsh rice rat** (*Oryzomys palustris coloratus*)—common; fresh and salt water marshes on mainland; Lower Keys rice rat (*O.p. natator*) **E**

☐ **Oldfield (southeastern) beach mouse** (*Peromyscus polionotus niveiventris*)—rare (extirpated?); coastal dunes on eastern barrier islands **T**

☐ **Cotton mouse** (*Peromyscus gossypinus allapaticola* and *P. g. telmaphilus*)—common; hammocks on mainland and upper Keys; Key Largo cotton mouse (*P. g. allapaticola*) **E**

☐ **Florida mouse** (*Podomys floridanus*)—uncommon; along coastal uplands on mainland to Dade and Sarasota counties

☐ **Hispid cotton rat** (*Sigmodon hispidus exsputus, S. h. floridanus* and *S. h. spadicipygus*)—abundant; ubiquitous, mainland and Keys

☐ **Key Largo woodrat** (*Neotoma floridana smalli*)—rare (almost extirpated); hardwood hammocks on Key Largo **E**

☐ **Round-tailed muskrat** (*Neofiber alleni struix*)—uncommon; marshes and sloughs

☐ ***Black (Roof) rat** (*Rattus rattus*)—common; near development on mainland and Keys

☐ ***Norway rat** (*Rattus norvegicus*)—common; near development on mainland and Keys

☐ ***House mouse** (*Mus musculus*)—common; near development on mainland and Keys

Cetaceans

☐ **Atlantic bottle-nosed dolphin** (*Tursiops truncatus*)—common; shallow waters and estuaries of Atlantic Ocean, Gulf of Mexico, and Florida Bay

Carnivores

☐ **Gray fox** (*Urocyon cinereoargenteus floridanus*)—common; particularly eastern mainland near development

☐ **Red fox** (*Vulpes vulpes*)—status unknown, introduced into Florida?; local in interior mainland

☐ **Florida black bear** (*Ursus americanus floridanus*)—rare; uplands on mainland (mostly Big Cypress region in our area)

☐ **Raccoon** (*Procyon lotor auspicatus, P. l. elucus, P. l. incautus, P. l. inesperatus, P. l. marinus*)—abundant; all habitats on mainland and Keys

☐ **Long-tailed weasel** (*Mustela frenata peninsulae*)—status unknown; habitat generalist, Big Cypress region

☐ **Mink** (*Mustela vison evergladensis* and *M. v. lutensis*)—rare; freshwater wetlands of southern Everglades

☐ **Spotted skunk** (*Spilogale putorius ambarvalis*)—uncommon; palmetto scrub and hammocks on mainland

☐ **Striped skunk** (*Mephitis mephitis elongata*)—uncommon; uplands on mainland

☐ **River otter** (*Lutra canadensis lataxina*)—common; freshwater wetlands on mainland

☐ **Florida panther** (*Puma concolor coryi*)—rare (almost extirpated); pinelands, cypress, hammocks **E**

☐ **Bobcat** (*Lynx rufus floridanus*)—common; mainland and rarely to Key Largo

Artiodactyls

☐ **White-tailed deer** (*Odocoileus virginianus seminolus*)—common; many habitats on mainland

☐ **Key deer** (*Odocoileus virginianus clavium*)—locally common; primarily pinelands, only Big Pine Key and neighboring islands **E**

☐ ***Feral hog** (*Sus scrofa*)—common; many habitats in interior of mainland; nuisance

Sirenians

☐ **West Indian manatee** (*Trichechus manatus latirostris*)—locally common in shallow marine and estuary waters around mainland and Keys **E**

REPTILE CHECKLIST

Crocodilians

☐ **American crocodile** (*Crocodylus acutus*)—rare; coastal mangroves on mainland and Keys **E**

☐ **American alligator** (*Alligator mississippiensis*)—abundant; freshwater wetlands (occasionally on coasts) on mainland and fresh water on a few lower Keys **T** (by similarity of appearance to crocs)

☐ *****Spectacled caiman** (*Caiman crocodilus*)—rare; fresh water in Miami area

Turtles

☐ **Florida snapping turtle** (*Chelydra serpentina osceola*)—common; fresh water on mainland

☐ **Striped mud turtle** (*Kinosternon baurii*)—common; freshwater wetlands on mainland and Keys (**E** in Keys)

☐ **Florida mud turtle** (*Kinosternon subrubrum steindachneri*)—common; freshwater wetlands and salt marshes on mainland and Keys

☐ **Common musk turtle** (or stinkpot) (*Sternotherus odoratus*)—common; fresh water on mainland

☐ **Florida box turtle** (*Terrapene carolina bauri*)—common; pinelands and hammocks on mainland and some Keys (not middle Keys)

☐ **Diamondback terrapin** (*Malaclemys terrapin tequesta, M. t. rhizophorarum,* and *M. t. macrospilota*)—uncommon; mangroves and saltmarshes on coastal mainland and Keys

☐ **Peninsula cooter** (*Pseudemys floridana peninsularis*)—abundant; fresh water on mainland, except extreme southwest

☐ **Florida redbelly turtle** (*Pseudemys nelsoni*)—abundant; mostly freshwater wetlands, also mangrove borders on mainland

☐ *****Red-eared slider** (*Trachemys scripta elegans*)—established in canals in Dade County

☐ **Florida chicken turtle** (*Deirochelys reticularia chrysea*)—uncommon; freshwater marshes and ponds on mainland

☐ **Gopher tortoise** (*Gopherus polyphemus*)—uncommon and rapidly declining; pinelands and scrub of Atlantic coastal ridge, Long Pine Key (few), Middle Cape Sable, Big Cypress, and Naples **T**

☐ **Leatherback sea turtle** (*Dermochelys coriacea*)—rare; marine waters **E**

☐ **Green sea turtle** (*Chelonia mydas*)—rare; marine waters **E**

☐ **Hawksbill sea turtle** (*Eretmochelys imbricata imbricata*)—rare; marine waters **E**

☐ **Loggerhead sea turtle** (*Caretta caretta*)—uncommon in summer; marine waters near Cape Sable and other sandy beaches, and Florida Keys **T**

☐ **Kemp's Ridley sea turtle** (*Lepidochelys kempii*)—rare; marine waters **E**

☐ **Florida softshell turtle** (*Apalone ferox*)—common; freshwater marshes on mainland (introduced to Big Pine Key)

Lizards

☐ ***Tokay gecko** (*Gekko gekko*)—locally established near development; Miami and Ft. Lauderdale area

☐ ***Mediterranean gecko** (*Hemidactylus turcicus turcicus*)—locally established; near development on Atlantic coast of mainland and Upper and Lower Keys

☐ ***Indopacific gecko** (*Hemidactylus garnotii*)—locally common, nocturnal; near development on mainland and Upper Keys

☐ ***Ashy gecko** (*Sphaerodactylus elegans elegans*)—locally established, nocturnal; Lower Keys and Miami area

☐ **Florida reef gecko** (*Sphaerodactylus notatus*)—common; pinelands and hammocks on southeast mainland and Keys

☐ ***Ocellated gecko** (*Sphaerodactylus argus argus*)—locally established; Lower Keys

☐ ***Yellowhead gecko** (*Gonatodes albogularis fuscus*)—locally established; around Miami, Ft. Lauderdale, and Lower Keys

☐ **Green anole** (*Anolis carolinensis*)—common; many habitats on mainland and Keys

☐ ***Knight anole** (*Anolis equestris*)—locally common; near development on southeast mainland and Upper Keys

☐ ***Brown anole** (*Anolis sagrei*)—abundant and increasing; many habitats on mainland and Keys

☐ ***Jamaican giant anole** (*Anolis garmani*)—locally established; Miami and Ft. Lauderdale area

- ☐ **Puerto Rican crested anole* (*Anolis cristatellus cristatellus*)—locally established; Miami and Ft. Lauderdale area
- ☐ **Largehead anole* (*Anolis cybotes cybotes*)—locally established; Miami and Ft. Lauderdale area
- ☐ **Bark anole* (*Anolis distichus*)—locally common; Miami area
- ☐ **Brown basilisk* (*Basiliscus vittatus*)—locally established; Miami and Ft. Lauderdale area
- ☐ **Common* (or green) iguana (*Iguana iguana*)—uncommon; Miami and Ft. Lauderdale area
- ☐ **Spinytail iguana* (*Ctenosaura pectinata*)—locally established; South Miami near Biscayne Bay
- ☐ **Florida scrub lizard** (*Sceloporus woodi*)—rare; pinelands and scrub along coast north from Miami and Marco
- ☐ **Northern curlytail lizard* (*Leiocephalus carinatus armouri*)—locally established; around Miami and West Palm Beach
- ☐ **Red-sided curlytail lizard* (*Leiocephalus schreibersii schreibersii*)—locally established; Miami and Ft. Lauderdale area
- ☐ **Six-lined racerunner** (*Cnemidophorus sexlineatus*)—locally common; uplands on mainland and Keys
- ☐ **Giant ameiva* (*Ameiva ameiva*)—locally established; Miami area
- ☐ **Rainbow whiptail* (*Cnemidophorus lemniscatus*)—locally established; Miami area
- ☐ **Ground skink** (*Scincella lateralis*)—common; hammocks and pinelands on mainland (except Everglades) and Keys
- ☐ **Southeastern five-lined skink** (*Eumeces inexpectatus*)—common; often seen on trails on mainland and Keys
- ☐ **Florida Keys mole skink** (*Eumeces egregius egregius*)—rare, secretive; found under debris near shore on Keys and Dry Tortugas
- ☐ **Peninsula mole skink** (*Eumeces egregius onocrepis*)—uncommon; sandy scrub on mainland except Everglades
- ☐ **Eastern glass lizard** (*Ophisaurus ventralis*)—uncommon; pinelands and hammocks on mainland
- ☐ **Slender glass lizard** (*Ophisaurus attenuatus*)—uncommon; dry grasslands or woods on mainland except Everglades
- ☐ **Island glass lizard** (*Ophisaurus compressus*)—common; marshes and pinelands on eastern mainland

Snakes

- ☐ ***Brahminy blind snake** (*Ramphotyphlops braminus*)—worm-like burrower, locally common; east coast south to Homestead, also Upper and Lower Keys
- ☐ **Florida green water snake** (*Nerodia floridana*)—common; fresh or brackish marshes on mainland
- ☐ **Brown water snake** (*Nerodia taxispilota*)—common; clear, quiet waters on mainland
- ☐ **Florida water snake** (*Nerodia fasciata pictiventris*)—common; marshes and canals on mainland
- ☐ **Mangrove salt marsh snake** (*Nerodia clarkii compressicauda*)—common; mangrove swamps and salt marshes on coastal mainland and Keys
- ☐ **South Florida swamp snake** (*Seminatrix pygaea cyclas*)—common; freshwater wetlands on mainland
- ☐ **Florida brown snake** (*Storeria dekayi victa*)—common; pinelands, hammocks, and freshwater marshes on mainland and Lower Keys
- ☐ **Eastern garter snake** (*Thamnophis sirtalis sirtalis*)—common; many habitats on mainland
- ☐ **Peninsula ribbon snake** (*Thamnophis sauritus sackenii*)—common; many habitats on mainland and Lower Keys
- ☐ **Striped crayfish snake** (*Regina alleni*)—locally common; very aquatic, fresh water on mainland
- ☐ **Eastern hognose snake** (*Heterodon platyrhinos*)—rare; sandy areas of mainland
- ☐ **Southern ringneck snake** (*Diadophis punctatus punctatus* and *D. p. acricus*)—common; woodlands on mainland to Upper Keys (*D. p. punctatus*), pinelands and hammocks on Lower Keys (*D. p. acricus*, uncommon)
- ☐ **Pine woods snake** (*Rhadinaea flavilata*)—uncommon; moist pine flatwoods in northern and central Florida to Glades County
- ☐ **Eastern mud snake** (*Farancia abacura abacura*)—locally common; freshwater marshes, ponds, and canals on mainland
- ☐ **Southern black racer** (*Coluber constrictor priapus*)—abundant; many habitats on Lower Keys
- ☐ **Everglades racer** (*Coluber constrictor paludicola*)—abundant; many habitats on mainland and Upper Keys

- ☐ **Eastern coachwhip** (*Masticophis flagellum flagellum*)—locally common; many habitats on mainland
- ☐ **Rough green snake** (*Opheodrys aestivus*)—abundant; many habitats on mainland and Keys
- ☐ **Eastern indigo snake** (*Drymarchon corais couperi*)—rare; primarily dry areas on mainland and Lower Keys **T**
- ☐ **Corn snake or red rat snake** (*Elaphe guttata guttata*)—abundant; mostly around development on mainland and Keys
- ☐ **Everglades rat snake** (*Elaphe obsoleta rossalleni*)—locally common; freshwater marshes, hammocks, and pinelands in Everglades
- ☐ **Yellow rat snake** (*Elaphe obsoleta quadrivitatta*)—uncommon; many habitats on mainland (except Everglades) and upper Keys
- ☐ **Florida pine snake** (*Pituophis melanoleucus mugitis*)—uncommon; very dry oak-pine woodlands and scrub south to Lake Okeechobee and along Atlantic coastal ridge south to Broward County
- ☐ **Florida kingsnake** (*Lampropeltis getula florida*)—uncommon; freshwater marshes, hammocks, and pinelands on mainland
- ☐ **Scarlet kingsnake** (*Lampropeltis triangulum*)—rare; pinelands and hammocks on mainland and Keys (except middle Keys)
- ☐ **Florida scarlet snake** (*Cemophora c. coccinea*)—rare; pinelands and hammocks on mainland
- ☐ **Rim rock crowned snake** (*Tantilla oolitica*)—rare, secretive; limestone areas along Atlantic coast of mainland to Upper Keys
- ☐ **Coast dunes crowned snake** (*Tantilla relicta pamlica*)—uncommon; coastal dunes and scrub of central Atlantic coast to Palm Beach County
- ☐ **Eastern coral snake** (*Micrurus fulvius*)—locally common; pinelands and hammocks on mainland and Key Largo; venomous
- ☐ **Florida cottonmouth** (or water moccasin) (*Agkistrodon piscivorus conanti*)—common; freshwater marshes and mangroves on mainland and Keys (except lower Keys); venomous
- ☐ **Dusky pygmy rattlesnake** (*Sistrurus miliarius*)—common; pinelands and freshwater marshes on mainland; venomous
- ☐ **Eastern diamondback rattlesnake** (*Crotalus adamanteus*)—locally common; many habitats on mainland and Keys (including Florida Bay); venomous

AMPHIBIAN CHECKLIST
Salamanders

☐ **Two-toed amphiuma** (*Amphiuma means*)—common; freshwater marshes and sloughs on mainland

☐ **Greater siren** (*Siren lacertina*)—common; freshwater marshes, sloughs, and ponds on mainland

☐ **Everglades dwarf siren** (*Pseudobranchus striatus belli*)—common; freshwater marshes, sloughs, and ponds on mainland

☐ **Peninsula newt** (*Notophthalmus viridescens piaropicola*)—abundant; freshwater marshes and ponds on mainland

☐ **Dwarf salamander** (*Eurycea quadridigitata*)—secretive; wet hammocks and streams in Dade, Palm Beach, and Hendry counties

Toads and Frogs

☐ **Eastern spadefoot toad** (*Scaphiophus holbrookii holbrookii*)—uncommon, secretive; sandy, dry areas on Atlantic coastal ridge and Upper and Lower Keys

☐ **Southern toad** (*Bufo terrestris*)—abundant (uncommon in Everglades); hammocks, pinelands, and freshwater marshes on mainland and Lower Keys

☐ **Oak toad** (*Bufo quercicus*)—common; hammocks, pinelands, and freshwater marshes on mainland and Keys (except Lower Keys)

☐ ***Giant toad** (*Bufo marinus*)—common; breeds in fresh or brackish water around Miami area and Keys

☐ ***Greenhouse frog** (*Eleutherodactylus planirostris*)—may be immigrant; under leaf litter on mainland and Keys

☐ ***Puerto Rican coqui** (*Eleutherodactylus coqui*)—local, uncommon; Miami area

☐ **Florida cricket frog** (*Acris gryllus dorsalis*)—common; freshwater marshes on mainland

☐ **Green treefrog** (*Hyla cinerea*)—abundant; hammocks, pinelands, and freshwater marshes on mainland and Keys

☐ **Barking treefrog** (*Hyla gratiosa*)—uncommon; mainland except Everglades

☐ **Pine woods treefrog** (*Hyla femoralis*)—common; often around artificial lights on mainland

- [ ] **Squirrel treefrog** (*Hyla squirella*)—abundant; all habitats with fresh water on mainland and Keys
- [ ] **Cuban treefrog** (*Osteopilus septentrionalis*)—immigrant, locally abundant; often found around buildings on Atlantic coastal ridge, Keys, and Naples area
- [ ] **Florida chorus frog** (*Pseudacris nigrita verrucosa*)—common; fresh-water swamps and marshes on mainland
- [ ] **Little grass frog** (*Pseudacris ocularis*)—abundant; freshwater swamps and marshes on mainland
- [ ] **Eastern narrowmouth toad** (*Gastrophryne carolinensis*)—common, but a secretive burrower; under leaf litter in hammocks on mainland and Keys
- [ ] **Pig frog** (*Rana grylio*)—abundant, commercially exploited; all fresh water habitats on mainland
- [ ] **Southern leopard frog** (*Rana utricularia*)—abundant; all fresh water habitats on mainland and Lower Keys
- [ ] **Florida gopher frog** (*Rana capito aesopus*)—uncommon; found in gopher tortoise burrows on mainland

SCIENTIFIC NAMES OF PLANTS

This is a list of the scientific names of the plants mentioned in the text. All the plants are found in south Florida. However, it is not intended to be a complete list of plants found in the region covered by this book. There are too many to list comfortably.

* = exotic

TREES, SHRUBS, AND WOODY PLANTS

Gymnosperms:

CYCADACEAE—Cycad family
coontie (*Zamia pumila*)

PINACEAE—Pine family
slash pine (*Pinus elliottii var. densa*)

TAXODIACEAE—Redwood family
bald-cypress (*Taxodium distichum*)
pond-cypress (*Taxodium ascendens* or *T. distichum var. nutans*)

Angiosperms:

ACERACEAE—Maple family
red maple (*Acer rubrum*)

ANACARDIACEAE—Cashew family
Brazilian pepper (*Schinus terebinthifolius*)*
poison-ivy (*Toxicodendron radicans*)
poisonwood (*Metopium toxiferum*)

ANNONACEAE—Custard-apple family

pond-apple (*Annona glabra*)

AQUIFOLIACEAE—Holly family
dahoon (*Ilex cassine*)

ARECACEAE—Palm family
cabbage palm (or sabal palmetto) (*Sabal palmetto*)
coconut palm (*Cocos nucifera*)*
Florida (or Jamaica) thatch palm (*Thrinax radiata*)
Key (or brittle) thatch palm (*Thrinax morrisii*)
paurotis palm (*Acoelorrhaphe wrightii*)
royal palm (*Roystonea elata*)
saw palmetto (*Serenoa repens*)
scrub (or corkscrew) palmetto (*Sabal etonia*)
silver palm (*Coccothrinax argentata*)

AVICENNIACEAE—Black mangrove family
black mangrove (*Avicennia germinans*)

BORAGINACEAE—Forget-me-not family
Geiger-tree (*Cordia sebastena*)

BURSERACEAE—Torchwood family
gumbo-limbo (*Bursera simaruba*)

CAPPARACEAE—Caper family
Jamaica caper (*Capparis cynophallophora*)

CASUARINACEAE—Beefwood family
Australian-pine (*Casuarina litorea* and *C. glauca*)*

CHRYSOBALANACEAE—Coco-plum family
coco-plum (*Chrysobalanus icaco*)
gopher apple (*Licania michauxii*)

COMBRETACEAE—Combretum family
buttonwood (*Conocarpus erectus*)
white mangrove (*Laguncularia racemosa*)

ERICACEAE—Heath family

gallberry (*Ilex glabra*)
staggerbush (*Lyonia ferruginea*)

EUPHORBIACEAE—Spurge family
manchineel (*Hippomane mancinella*)

FABACEAE—Pea family
blackbead (*Pithecellobium guadalupense*)
catclaw (*Pithecellobium unguis-cati*)
coral bean (*Erythrina herbacea*)
Jamaica dogwood (*Piscidia piscipula*)
necklace pod (*Sophora tomentosa*)
sweet acacia (*Acacia farnesiana*)
wild-tamarind (*Lysiloma latisiliquum*)

FAGACEAE—Beech family
Chapman oak (*Quercus chapmanii*)
live oak (*Quercus virginiana*)
myrtle oak (*Quercus myrtifolia*)
sand live oak (*Quercus geminata*)

LAURACEAE—Laurel family
lancewood (*Ocotea coriacea*, formerly *Nectandra coriacea*)
redbay (*Persea borbonia*)

MAGNOLIACEAE—Magnolia family
sweet bay (*Magnolia virginiana*)

MALVACEAE—Mallow family
seaside mahoe (*Thespesia populnea*)

MELASTOMATACEAE—Melastoma family
tetrazygia (*Tetrazygia bicolor*)

MELIACEAE—Mahogany family
mahogany (*Swietenia mahagoni*)

MORACEAE—Mulberry family
fig, banyan (*Ficus* spp.)
strangler fig (*Ficus aurea*)

MYRICACEAE—Bayberry family
wax myrtle (*Myrica cerifera*)

MYRSINACEAE—Myrsine family
marlberry (*Ardisia escallonioides*)
myrsine (*Myrsine floridana*)

MYRTACEAE—Myrtle family
guava (*Psidium guajava*)*
melaleuca, cajeput (*Melaleuca quinquenervia*)*
Spanish stopper (*Eugenia foetida*)
white stopper (*Eugenia axillaris*)

POLYGONACEAE—Buckwheat family
pigeon-plum (*Coccoloba diversifolia*)
sea-grape (*Coccoloba uvifera*)

RHAMNACEAE—Buckthorn family
black ironwood (*Krugiodendron ferreum*)

RHIZOPHORACEAE—Mangrove family
red mangrove (*Rhizophora mangle*)

ROSACEAE—Rose family
West-Indian cherry (*Prunus myrtifolia*)

RUBIACEAE—Madder family
black-torch (*Erithalis fruticosa*)
firebush (*Hamelia patens*)
indigo-berry (*Randia aculeata*)
rough velvetseed (*Guettarda scabra*)
seven-year-apple (*Casasia clusiifolia*)
snowberry (*Chiococca alba*)
white indigo-berry (*Randia aculeata*)
wild coffee (*Psychotria nervosa*)

RUTACEAE—Citrus family
satinwood (*Zanthoxylum flavum*)
torchwood (*Amyris elemifera*)
wild-lime (*Zanthoxylum fagara*)

SALICACEAE—Willow family
coastal plain willow (*Salix caroliniana*)

SAPINDACEAE—Soapberry family
varnish-leaf (*Dodonaea viscosa*)

SAPOTACEAE—Sapodilla family
mastic (*Mastichodendron foetidissimum*)
saffron-plum (*Bumelia celastrina*)
sapodilla (*Manilkara zapota*)
satinleaf (*Chrysophyllum oliviforme*)
wild dilly (*Manilkara bahamensis*)
willow bustic (*Dipholis salicifolia*)

SIMAROUBACEAE—Quassia family
paradise-tree (*Simarouba glauca*)

SOLANACEAE—Nightshade family
canker-berry (*Solanum bahamense*)
Christmas berry (*Lycium carolinianum*)

SURIANACEAE—Bay-cedar family
bay-cedar (*Suriana maritima*)

ULMACEAE—Elm family
Florida trema (*Trema micranthum*)

VERBENACEAE—Verbena family
beauty berry (*Callicarpa americana*)
Florida fiddlewood (*Citharexylem fruticosum*)

ZYGOPHYLLACEAE—Caltrop family
lignum vitae (*Guaiacum sanctum*)

NON-WOODY PLANTS

AGAVACEAE—Agave family
Spanish bayonet (*Yucca aloifolia*)

AIZOACEAE—Carpetweed family
sea purslane (*Sesuvium portulacastrum*)

ARACEACE—Arum family
manatee grass (*Syringodium filiforme*)
water lettuce (*Pistia stratiodes*)

ASTERACEAE—Aster family
coreopsis (*Coreopsis spp.*)
sea ox-eye daisy (*Borrichia frutescens*)

BATACEAE—Saltwort family
saltwort (*Batis maritima*)

BROMELIACEAE—Air plant family
ballmoss (*Tillandsia recurvata*)
cardinal air plant (*Tillandsia fasciculata*)
giant wildpine (*Tillandsia utriculata*)
needle-leaved wildpine (*Tillandsia setacea*)
reddish wildpine (*Tillandsia polystachia*)
reflexed wildpine (*Tillandsia balbisiana*)
Spanish moss (*Tillandsia usneoides*)
twisted air plant (*Tillandsia flexuosa*)

CACTACEAE—Cactus family
prickly-pear (*Opuntia spp.*)

CAMPANULACEAE—Bluebell family
glades lobelia (*Lobelia glandulosa*)

CHENOPODIACEAE—Goosefoot family
glasswort (*Salicornia virginica*)

COMMELINACEAE—Spiderwort family
oyster-plant (*Rhoeo discolor*)*

CRASSULACEAE—Sedum family
kalanchoe (*Kalanchoe spp.*)*

CYPERACEAE—Sedge family

sawgrass (*Cladium jamaicense*)
spike rush (*Eleocharis cellulosa*)

DIOSCOREACEAE—Yam family
air-potato (*Dioscorea bulbifera*)*

DROCERACEAE—Sundew family
round-leaved sundew (*Drocera rotundifolia*)

EMPETRACEAE —Crowberry family
rosemary (*Ceratiola ericoides*)

EUPHORBIACEAE —Spurge family
pineland (or wooly) croton (*Croton linearis*)

GENTIANACEAE—Gentian family
white sabatia (*Sabatia brevifolia*)

HYDROCHARITEAE—Frog's-bit family
hydrilla (*Hydrilla verticillata*)*
turtle grass (*Thalassia testudinum*)

LENTIBULARIACEAE—Bladderwort family
bladderwort (*Utricularia spp.*)

ORCHIDACEAE—Orchid family
butterfly orchid (*Encyclia tampensis*)
cowhorn orchid (*Cyrtopodium punctatum*)
spider orchid (*Brassia caudata*)
worm-vine orchid (*Vanilla barbellata*)
PHYTOLACCACEAE—Pokeweed family
rouge plant (*Rivina humilis*)

POACEAE—Grass family
Florida gamagrass (*Tripsacum floridanum*)
muhly grass (*Muhlenberghia filipes*)
sea oats (*Uniola paniculata*)

POLYGALACEAE—Milkwort family
bog bachelor-button (*Polygala lutea*)

POLYPODIACEAE—Polypodium family
bracken fern (*Pteridium caudatum*)
chain fern (*Woodwardia virginica*)
giant leather fern (*Acrostichum danaeifolium*)
golden polypody fern (*Phlebodium aureum*)
resurrection fern (*Polypodium polypodioides*)
royal fern (*Osmunda regala*)
shoestring fern (*Vittaria lineata*)

strap fern (*Campyloneurum spp.*)
swamp fern (*Blechnum serrulatum*)
sword fern (*Nephrolepis biserrata*)

PONTEDERIACEAE—Pickerelweed family
pickerel-weed (*Pontederia cordata*)
water hyacinth (*Eichhornia crassipes*)

RUBIACEAE—Madder family
small-flowered lily thorn (*Catesbaea parviflora*)

SCHIZACEAE—Curly grass fern family
Old World climbing fern (*Lygodium microphyllum*)*

TYPHACEAE—Cattail family
cattail (*Typha spp.*)

ZOSTERACEAE—Pondweed family
shoal grass (*Halodule wrightii*)

SUGGESTED READING

denotes sources used in preparation of this book.

Ashton, Ray E., Jr., and Patricia Sawyer Ashton. 1981. Handbook of Reptiles and Amphibians of Florida. Part One: The Snakes. Miami: Windward Publishing. 176pp.

Ashton, Ray E., Jr., and Patricia Sawyer Ashton. 1985. Handbook of Reptiles and Amphibians of Florida. Part Two: Lizards, Turtles, and Crocodilians. Miami: Windward Publishing. 191pp.

Ashton, Ray E., Jr., and Patricia Sawyer Ashton. 1988. Handbook of Reptiles and Amphibians of Florida. Part Three: The Amphibians. Miami: Windward Publishing. 191pp.

Bell, C. Ritchie and Bryan J. Taylor. 1982. Florida Wild Flowers and Roadside Plants. Chapel Hill, NC: Laurel Hill Press. 308pp.

Brookfield, Charles M. and Oliver Griswold. 1985. They All Called It Tropical. Miami: Historical Association of Southern Florida. 77pp.*

Carmichael, Pete and Winston Williams. 1991. Florida's Fabulous Reptiles and Amphibians. Tampa, FL: World Publications. 120pp.

Carter, Elizabeth F. 1987. A Guide to the Trails of Florida. Birmingham, AL: Menasha Ridge Press. 129pp.

Cox, W. Eugene. 1989. Everglades: The Continuing Story. Las Vegas, NV: K.C. Publications. 48pp.

Davis, Steven M. and John C. Ogden (eds.). 1994. The Everglades: the Ecosystem and its Restoration. Delray, FL: St. Lucie Press. 826pp.

De Golia, Jack. 1978. Everglades: The Story Behind the Scenery. Las Vegas, NV: K.C. Publications. 64pp.

Deyrup, Mark and Richard Franz (eds.). 1994. Rare and Endangered Biota of Florida, Volume IV. Invertebrates. Gainesville, FL: Univ. Press of Florida. 798pp.

Douglas, Marjory Stoneman. 1988 (rev.). The Everglades: River of Grass. Sarasota, FL: Pineapple Press. 448pp.

FNPMA. 1991. Motorist's Guide to Everglades National Park. Homestead, FL: Florida National Parks and Monuments Association.

FNPMA. 1991. An Activity Guide for Teachers: Everglades National Park (grades 4–6). Homestead, FL: National Parks and Monuments Association.

Gato, Jeanette. 1991. The Monroe County Environmental story. Big Pine Key, FL: Seacamp Association. 368pp.

George, Jean Craighead. 1988. Everglades Wildguide. Homestead, FL: U.S. Dept. of Interior, NPS. Natural History Series, Everglades National Park. 103pp.

Gerberg, Eugene J. and Ross H. Arnett. 1989. Florida Butterflies. Baltimore, MD: Natural Science Publications. 90pp.*

Gilbert, Carter R. (ed.). 1992. Rare and Endangered Biota of Florida, Volume II. Fishes. Gainesville, FL: Univ. Press of Florida. 247pp.

Gingerich, Jerry Lee. 1994. Florida's Fabulous Mammals. Tampa, FL: World Publications. 128pp.

Greenberg, Idaz and Jerry Greenberg. 1977. Guide to Corals and Fishes of Florida, the Bahamas, and the Caribbean. Miami: Seahawk Press. 65pp. Paperback and waterproof editions.

Hoffmeister, John Edward. 1982. Land from the Sea, the Geologic Story of South Florida. Coral Gables, FL: University of Miami Press. 143pp.*

Humphrey, Stephen R. (ed.). 1992. Rare and Endangered Biota of Florida, Volume I. Mammals. Gainesville, FL: Univ. Press of Florida. 392pp.

Kale, Herbert W., II, and David S. Maehr. 1990. Florida's Birds. Sarasota, FL: Pineapple Press. 288pp.*

Kalma, Dennis. 1988. Boat and Canoe Camping in the Everglades Backcountry and Ten Thousand Islands Region. Miami: Florida Flair Books. 64pp.

Kaplan, Eugene H. 1988. A Field Guide to Southeastern and Caribbean Seashores. Boston: Houghton Mifflin. 425 pp.*

Landrum, L. Wayne. 1990. Biscayne, the Story Behind the Scenery. Las Vegas, NV: K.C. Publications. 48pp.

Laughlin, Maureen H., John C. Ogden, William B. Robertson, Jr., Ken Russell, and Roy Wood. 1991. Everglades National Park Bird Checklist. Homestead, FL: Florida National Parks and Monuments Association. 20pp.*

Lazell, James D., Jr. 1989. Wildlife of the Florida Keys. Washington, DC: Island Press. 254pp.*

Lodge, Thomas E. 1994. The Everglades Handbook: Understanding the Ecosystem. Delray, FL: St. Lucie Press. 228pp.

McIver, Stuart. 1989. True Tales of the Everglades. Miami: Florida Flair Books. 64pp.*

Minno, Marc C. and Thomas C. Emmel. 1993. Butterflies of the Florida Keys. Gainesville, FL: Scientific Publishers. 168pp.

Moler, Paul E. (ed.). 1992. Rare and Endangered Biota of Florida, Volume III. Amphibians and Reptiles. Gainesville, FL: Univ. Press of Florida. 291pp.

Morton, Julia F. 1982. Wild Plants for Survival in South Florida. Miami: Fairchild Tropical Garden. 80pp.

Neill, Wilfred T. 1956. Florida's Seminole Indians. St. Petersburg, FL: Great Outdoors Publishing Co. 128pp.

Pranty, Bill. 1996. A Birder's Guide to Florida. Distr. by ABA Sales, P.O. Box 6599, Colorado Springs, CO 80934. 388pp.

Robertson, William B., Jr. 1989 (rev.). Everglades: The Park Story. Homestead, FL: Florida National Parks and Monuments Association. 63pp.*

Rodgers, James A., Herbert W. Kale II, and Henry T. Smith (eds.). 1996. Rare and Endangered Biota of Florida, Volume V. Birds. Gainesville, FL: Univ. Press of Florida. 736pp.

Scurlock, J. Paul. 1987. Native Trees and Shrubs of the Florida Keys. Bethel Park, PA: Laurel Press, Inc. 220pp.

Stevenson, George B. 1992. Trees of the Everglades National Park and the Florida Keys. Homestead, FL: Florida Parks and National Monuments Assoc., Inc. 32pp.*

Stiling, Peter D. 1989. Florida's Butterflies and Other Insects. Sarasota, FL: Pineapple Press. 95pp.*

Stone, Calvin. 1979. Forty Years in the Everglades. Tabor City, NC: W. Horace Carter, Atlantic Publishing Co. 224pp.

Tebeau, Charleton W. 1968. Man in the Everglades. Coral Gables, FL: University of Miami Press. 192pp.*

Tomlinson, P.B. 1980. The Biology of Trees Native to Tropical Florida. Allston, MA: Harvard University Printing Office. 480pp.*

Toops, Connie M. 1988. The Alligator: Monarch of the Marsh. Homestead, FL: Florida National Parks and Monuments Assn. 58pp.

Toops, Connie M. 1989. Everglades. Stillwater, MN: Voyager Press. 96pp.

Toops, Connie and Willard E. Dilley. 1986. Birds of South Florida. Conway, AR: Conway Printing Co. 150pp.

Truesdell, William G. 1985. A Guide to the Wilderness Waterway of Everglades National Park. Coral Gables, FL: University of Miami Press. 64pp.

Voss, Gilbert L. 1988. Coral Reefs of Florida. Sarasota, FL: Pineapple Press. 80pp.*

Will, Lawrence E. 1984. A Dredgeman of Cape Sable. Belle Glade, FL: The Glades Historical Society. 158pp.*

ADDITIONAL SOURCES USED IN PREPARATION OF THIS BOOK
(TECHNICAL OR NOT READILY AVAILABLE)

Artman, L.P., Jr. 1974. The Overseas Railroad. [no publisher listed]. 14pp.

Clarke, Mary Helm. 1949. South Florida Treasure Trails. Tallahassee, FL: Kay Publishing Co. 103pp.

Craighead, Frank C. 1963. Orchids and Other Airplants of the Everglades National Park. Coral Gables, FL: University of Miami Press. 127pp.

Downs, Dorothy. 1982. Miccosukee Arts and Crafts. Miami: Miccosukee Indian Tribe of Florida. 21pp.

Duever, Michael J., John E. Carlson, John F. Meeder, Linda C. Duever, Lance H. Gunderson, Lawrence A. Riopelle, Taylor R. Alexander, Ronald L. Myers, and Daniel P. Spangler. 1986. The Big Cypress National Preserve. Research Report No. 8 of the National Audubon Society, New York. 444pp. (Originally 1979, Resource inventory and analysis of the Big Cypress National Preserve, Univ. of Florida, Gainesville. 455pp.)

Everglades Natural History. March 1953 (Vol. 1, No. 1) to June 1955 (Vol. 3, No. 2). Everglades Natural History Association.

Gleason, Patrick J. (ed.) 1974. Environments of South Florida: Past and Present. Memoir 2: Miami Geological Society. Miami: Miami Geological Society. 452pp.

Griswold, Oliver. 1965. The Florida Keys and the Coral Reef. Miami: The Graywood Press. 143pp.

McGeachy, Beth. 1955. Handbook of Florida Palms. St. Petersburg, FL: Great Outdoors Publishing Co. 62pp.

Meyers, Ronald L. and John J. Ewel (eds.). 1990. 2nd pr 91. Ecosystems of Florida. Orlando, FL: University of Central Florida Press. 763pp.

MMWR. 1989. Seizures temporally associated with DEET insect repellent New York and Connecticut. Morbidity and Mortality Weekly R. 38(39):678-680.

NOAA. 1984. Climatography of the United States No. 20. Climatic summaries for selected sites, 1951–80. National Climatic Data Center, Asheville, NC.

Parks, Pat. 1968. The Railroad that Died at Sea. Brattleboro, VT: The Stephen Greene Press. 44pp.

Stevenson, Henry M. 1976. Vertebrates of Florida (Identification and Distribution). Gainesville, FL: University Presses of Florida. 607pp.

OTHER SOURCES OF INFORMATION

Florida—General

- **Audubon of Florida**
444 Brickell Ave., Suite 850
Miami, FL 33131
(305) 371-6399
www.audubonofflorida.org
- **Canoe Liveries & Outfitters**
www.paddlefl.com or www.
paddling.net/Outfitters/FL
- **DeLorme Mapping Company**
www.delorme.com
*publishes "Florida Atlas &
Gazetteer" (detailed road maps
with guide to outdoor recreation);
available locally*
- **Florida** (official government
site)
www.myflorida.com
- **Florida Department of Natural
Resources**
Division of Recreation and Parks
3900 Commonwealth Blvd., MS 535
Tallahassee, FL 32399-3000
(850) 488-9872
www8.myflorida.com/
communities/learn/stateparks/
index.html
information on state parks
- **Florida Fish and Wildlife Conservation Commission**
620 South Meridian Street
Tallahassee, FL 32399-1600
(850) 921-2736
1-888-FISH-FLORIDA (*buying a
license*)
(561) 625-5122 (*South region*)
www.floridaconservation.org
- **Florida Trail Association, Inc.**
5415 SW 13th St.

Gainesville, FL 32608
(800) 343-1882
www.florida-trail.org/
- **National Park Service**
1849 C Street NW
Washington, D.C. 20240
(202) 208-6843
www.nps.gov
- **The Nature Conservancy**
(Florida Chapter)
222 S. Westmonte Drive, Suite 300
Altamonte Springs, FL 32714
(407) 682-3664
www.tncflorida.org
- **U.S. Fish and Wildlife Service**
1849 C Street NW
Washington, D.C. 20240
(202) 208-4131
www.fws.gov

Florida—South

- **Broward County Parks and
Recreation Division**
950 NW 38th Street
Oakland Park, FL 33309
(954) 357-8100
www.co.broward.fl.us/parks.htm
- **Collier County Department of
Parks and Recreation**
3300 Santa Barbara Blvd.
Naples, FL 34116
(941) 353-0404
http://co.collier.fl.us/
- **The Conservancy of Southwest
Florida**
1450 Merrihue Drive
Naples, FL 34102
(941) 262-0304
www.conservancy.org

• **Corkscrew Land and Water Trust**
2301 McGregor Blvd.
Ft. Myers, FL 33901
(941) 332-7771
www.crewtrust.org

• **Florida Keys National Marine Sanctuary**
P.O. Box 500368
Marathon, FL 33050
(305) 743-2437
www.fknms.nos.noaa.gov/

• **Florida Keys Visitors Bureau**
1-800-FLA-KEYS

• **Florida National Parks and Monuments Association**
10 Parachute Key #51,
Homestead, FL 33034-6735
(305) 247-1216
www.nps.gov/ever/fnpma
publications on south Florida cultural and natural history

• **Friends of the Everglades**
info@everglades.org
(305) 669-0858
www.everglades.org

• **Glades County**
County Courthouse, P.O. Box 10
Moore Haven, FL 33471
(941) 946-0113
www.geocities.com/Heartland/
Prairie/6173/glades.html

• **Greater Homestead-Florida City Chamber of Commerce**
43 North Krome Ave.
Homestead, FL 33030
(305) 247-2332

• **Greater Key West Chamber of Commerce**
402 Wall Street

Key West, FL 33040
(305) 294-2587

• **Hendry County**
County Court House
P.O. Box 1760
La Belle, FL 33935-1760
(863) 675-5217
www.hendryfla.net/

• **Lee County Parks and Recreation**
3410 Palm Beach Blvd.
Ft. Myers, FL 33916
(941) 461-7400
www.lee.fl.us/Parks&Rec

• **Miami-Dade Park and Recreation Department**
275 NW 2nd Street
Miami, FL 33128
(305) 755-7800
www.co.miami-dade.fl.us/
parks/

• **Monroe County**
5100 College Road
Key West, FL 33040
(305) 292-4441
www.co.monroe.fl.us

• **National Audubon Society**
Tavernier Science Center
115 Indian Mound Trail
Tavernier, FL 33070
(305) 852-5092

• **The Nature Conservancy**
Florida Keys Office
(305) 296-3880
www.tncflorida.org/pages/
fl_keys_program.html

• **Palm Beach County Parks and Recreation**
2700 6th Avenue South
Lake Worth, FL 33461
(561) 966-6600

www.co.palm-beach.fl.us/parks/

• **Sierra Club**
http://florida.sierraclub.org/
miami

• **South Florida Water Management District**
3301 Gun Club Road
West Palm Beach, FL 33406
(561) 686-8800
www.sfwmd.gov

• **Tropical Audubon Society**
5530 Sunset Drive
South Miami, FL 33143
(305) 666-5111 (*general information*)
(305) 667-PEEP (*Birding Hotline recording for local sightings*)
www.tropicalaudubon.org

• **Tropical Everglades Visitor Association**
160 US 1
Florida City, FL 33034
(305) 245-9180
(800) 388-9669
www.tropicaleverglades.com/

GLOSSARY

aquifer an underground porous rock formation containing water, especially one that supplies water for wells or springs.

barrier island a low-lying island, usually long and narrow, that parallels the coastal shore and protects the mainland from heavy surf and winds.

bayhead a tree island in the freshwater marsh that may be submerged during the wet season; so named because it usually contains redbay or sweet bay trees.

brackish water that contains some salt and may vary considerably in salinity; usually found where a river meets the ocean.

bromeliad (pronounced "bro-me´-lee-ad") air plant; a plant from the pineapple family that is an epiphyte. Examples are Spanish moss, ballmoss, needle-leaved wildpine, giant wildpine.

coastal prairie areas along the mangrove belt lacking trees and having predominantly succulent-type salt-tolerant plants, such as glasswort and saltwort.

conch (pronounced "conk") a large marine snail common in the shallow waters of south Florida; prized for its food value and decorative shell.

coral a colony of invertebrates bound together by a limestone skeleton that forms the "backbone" of the reef off of south Florida.

cumulonimbus thunderhead; a tall, unstable cloud formation that imparts lightning and rain, common in south Florida in the wet season.

Dade County pine the local name for the variety of slash pine (*Pinus elliotti var. densa*) that grows in Dade County and elsewhere in south Florida; historically very popular for building construction because of its resistance to insect damage and rot.

endangered species a species of plant or animal that has been declared (by a state or federal agency) in danger of becoming extinct if not protected.

endemic originating in a particular locality; indigenous.

epiphyte a plant growing upon or attached to another plant or non-living structure but is not parasitic. Florida has numerous epiphytic bromeliads, orchids, and ferns.

estuary a shallow wetland formed where a river meets an inlet of the sea; among the most productive habitats in the world.

exotic any species of plant or animal that was introduced (intentionally or unintentionally) by humans to an area it did not previously inhabit. Exotic species are undesirable in natural environments because they may outcompete or deplete native species. Examples are melaleuca, Brazilian pepper, domestic cat, common pigeon. Also called invasive and non-native.

hammock a large tree island; an elevated, well-drained tract of land slightly higher than the surrounding wetlands where hardwood trees grow naturally.

herp short for 'herpetofauna,' which means reptiles and amphibians; may refer to either class.

hurricane a cyclone in the Atlantic Ocean having wind speeds of 74 mph or greater.

hydroperiod the length of time in any given year that an area of wetland is inundated by water.

key a small, low-lying island; occasionally used to mean a hammock.

marl mud composed primarily of calcium carbonate, formed chiefly in short-hydroperiod freshwater wetlands; may become solidified.

midden a mound or small hill made by Indians, usually from discarding oyster, clam, or snail shells or bones.

muck organic soil that accumulates under wet conditions; the plant remains are too decomposed to be identified.

native species of plants or animals indigenous to an area.

old growth a forest that has never been logged.

peat organic soil that accumulates under wet conditions and has great water storage capacity; the plant remains can still be identified.

periphyton an assemblage of small plant organisms (mostly algae) attached to surfaces under water or floating; may form a spongy mat insulating the ground from total dehydration during the dry season; vital to the Everglades freshwater marshes.

pineland an area elevated on a ridge, dry most of the year and periodically swept by fires, allowing the establishment of pine trees; also called pine flatwoods.

pneumatophore pencil-like appendage rising from the root of a black mangrove tree; functions as respiratory organ at low tide.

prescribed burn an intentionally set fire on an undeveloped area, planned and controlled by fire ecologists to maintain a healthy habitat.

prop root stilt-like root that supports the trunk of a red mangrove tree.

propagule a seed that begins to germinate while still on the tree.

slough (pronounced "slew") a channel of slow-moving water, slightly deeper than the surrounding freshwater marsh.

solution hole a depression in limestone rock formed by the dissolving action of acidic water, which is created by rainwater mixing with decomposing vegetation.

strand a forest in a slough.

willow head a small cluster of willow trees in a slough; usually has a gator hole associated with it, and the water under the willows is often deeper than the surrounding slough to support the water-loving willows year-round.

xeriscape a landscape or garden with plants that require little water to thrive; especially useful in desert regions and in south Florida where water must be conserved.

INDEX

Illustrations are indicated by boldface. Photos on color pages are indicated by "CP." Checklists are not indexed.

If you enjoyed reading this book, here are some other Pineapple Press titles you might enjoy as well. To request our complete catalog or to place an order, write to Pineapple Press, P.O. Box 3889, Sarasota, Florida 34230, or call 1-800-PINEAPL (746-3275). Or visit our website at www.pineapplepress.com.

Other books in the *Exploring Wild Florida* series:

> *Exploring Wild Central Florida* by Susan D. Jewell. From New Smyrna and Crystal River in the north to Hobe Sound and Punta Gorda in the south, including Lake Okeechobee. ISBN 1-56164-082-4 (pb)

> *Exploring Wild North Florida* by Gil Nelson. From the Suwannee River to the Atlantic shore, and south to include the Ocala National Forest. ISBN 1-56164-091-3 (pb)

> *Exploring Wild Northwest Florida* by Gil Nelson. The Florida Panhandle, from the Perdido River in the west to the Suwannee River in the east. ISBN 1-56164-086-7 (pb)

Common Coastal Birds of Florida and the Caribbean by David W. Nellis. Covering 72 of the most common birds that inhabit the coastal areas of Florida and the islands to the south, this book discusses each bird's own ecological niche, manifested by its nesting, feeding, roosting, and migration habits. Over 250 photographs, mostly by the author, show many features of these birds and their habits never before so fully illustrated. ISBN 1-56164-191-X (hb); ISBN 1-56164-196-0 (pb)

Guide to the Lake Okeechobee Area by Bill and Carol Gregware. The first comprehensive guidebook to this area of the state includes a 110-mile hike/bike tour on top of the Herbert Hoover Dike encircling the lake, part of the Florida National Scenic Trail. ISBN 1-56164-129-4 (pb)

Myakka by Paula Benshoff. Home of the Wild and Scenic Myakka River in Sarasota, Myakka River State Park is a naturalist's dream. Take a detour off the beaten track and enjoy some unique adventures that include watching birds, counting alligators, gazing at stars, identifying flowers and animal tracks, listening to frog calls, and much more. Learn the history of this fragile ecosystem and what Floridians have done to preserve it. ISBN 1-56164-254-1 (pb)

Sea Kayaking in Florida by David Gluckman. This guide to sea kayaking in Florida for novices and experienced paddlers alike includes information on wildlife, camping, and gear; maps of the Big Bend Sea Grasses Saltwater Paddling Trail; tips on kayaking the Everglades; lists of liveries and outfitters; and more. ISBN 1-56164-071-9 (pb)

Sea Kayaking in the Florida Keys by Bruce Wachob. Florida's lower Keys can be experienced in a kayak as in no other way. Including insider information such as directions to remote launch sites, tips for trip planning, and listings of nearby campsites, dining, and lodging, this guide lists thirteen detailed trip descriptions for kayakers of every skill level. ISBN 1-56164-142-1 (pb)

The Springs of Florida by Doug Stamm. Take a guided tour of Florida's fascinating springs in this beautiful book featuring detailed descriptions, maps, and rare underwater photography. Learn how to enjoy these natural wonders while swimming, diving, canoeing, and tubing. ISBN 1-56164-054-9 (hb); 1-56164-048-4 (pb)